WHITNEY GUIDE

20TH CENTURY AMERICAN ARCHITECTURE

200 Key Buildings

WHITNEY GUIDE

20TH CENTURY AMERICAN ARCHITECTURE

200 Key Buildings

SYDNEY LEBLANC

Foreword by Ralph Lerner

WHITNEY LIBRARY OF DESIGN

an imprint of Watson-Guptill Publications/New York

For Michael Gianturco

Senior Editor: Roberto de Alba
Assistant Editor: Sue Shefts Traub
Designer: Jay Anning
Production Manager: Ellen Greene
Front cover photograph © 1992 Norman McGrath

First published in New York in 1993
by Whitney Library of Design
an imprint of Watson-Guptill Publications,
a division of BPI Communications, Inc.,
1515 Broadway, New York, NY 10036

Library of Congress Cataloging-in-Publication Data

LeBlanc, Sydney.
Whitney guide to 20th century American architecture : 200 key buildings / Sydney LeBlanc.
p. cm.
Includes index.
ISBN 0-8230-2174-2
1. Architecture, Modern—20th century—United States.
2. Architecture—United States. I. Whitney Library of Design (New York, N.Y.) II. Title. III. Title: Whitney guide to twentieth century American architecture.
NA712.L4 1993
720'.973'0904—dc20 92-46410
CIP

Manufactured in the United States

First Printing 1993

1 2 3 4 5 6 7 8 / 00 99 98 97 96 95 94 93

CONTENTS

Acknowledgments

Many people have shared my interest in creating a compact guide to America's important twentieth-century buildings, and many have helped in the process. I would like to thank the architects who provided information and photographs of their projects. The owners of these great buildings have also been generous in providing information and photographs; I am thankful for their help, and for their crucial roles in maintaining our preserve of important buildings, often against considerable odds.

I would also like to thank the photographers who made their pictures available for the book. Among them, special thanks are owed to Julius Shulman for sharing his unequaled archive and his immense knowledge of Los Angeles architecture with me; to Houston photographer Richard Payne, for taking time to show me how to look at buildings with a photographer's eye; and to New York photographer Norman McGrath for the stunning photograph of the Guggenheim Museum on the front cover.

The book also benefits from the Foreword by Ralph Lerner, Dean of the School of Architecture at Princeton University, and I thank him for writing about his early architectural travels. I also thank the staff of the School of Architecture library at Princeton University, where I conducted research for the book during my studies there.

The book would not exist without the excellent editors and artists at the Whitney Library of Design. I would like to thank Cornelia Guest, for her crucial role in the project's inception; Roberto de Alba, for his skillful transformation of the book into a lively and useful guide; Sue Shefts Traub, for intelligent editing; and Jay Anning, for the graphic design.

FOREWORD

Like so many young people of my generation, I took an automobile trip around the United States to discover my origins following the upheavals of the late 1960s. I was in the middle of my architectural education at the Cooper Union, and I wanted to see for myself the physical history of the culture in which I intended to work as an architect. I had no particular destination in mind, only a sense that I should see buildings, cities, landscapes, monuments, roads, dams, and bridges alike. Driving west from New York City, I encountered dynamic cities in various states of decay, buildings whose heyday was in the first few decades of this century, little appreciated experiments in building for a "modern" culture between the two world wars, and extraordinary attempts at social progress through a complete reformation of society in the postwar era. My memories are still vivid with the excitement of first seeing the Martin, Robie, and Hollyhock Houses by Frank Lloyd Wright, the IIT campus by Mies van der Rohe, the St. Louis Arch by Eero Saarinen, the Hoover Dam, the Golden Gate Bridge, and the Lovell Beach House by Rudolph Schindler.

Although I was filled with the wide variety of popular images illustrating the value of "hitting the road" that any young American received in the 1950s and 1960s, I also had a personal agenda because of my distrust of the anti-historical ideology of architectural culture at the time. This was still a time when "history" was of little consequence to most architects, and the preservation movement had not yet had much influence. However difficult it was to find what I was looking for, I realize now how meaningful this particular trip was for me as an architect. On my journey I found a country whose architecture should have been completely intact because it had never experienced the ravages of modern warfare, yet was in a state of disappearance simply through neglect.

There were very few comprehensive architectural guidebooks available, particularly for contemporary architecture. Literature relating to architectural, urban, and landscape traditions was spotty, and the very existence and location of buildings was sometimes in question. Fortunately, the last twenty-five years have seen an explosion of writing about architecture, which makes the same journey today quite a bit easier. Sydney LeBlanc, a writer whose own roots are in the traditions of the American South, has accomplished the task of introducing twentieth-century American architecture in this straightforward and engaging guidebook.

Attempting to introduce twentieth-century architecture in the United States in book form, and to a broad audience, raises interesting questions as to how to make the building monuments of this century better understood in their various contexts: chronological, social, topographical, and so on. American architecture in this century came into being through the interplay of regional traditions, influential and idiosyncratic personal styles, local responses to available materials and topographies, and through the influence of architectural images in various national publications. Much of it can only be fully understood in the light of the personal history of architects and their clients. As we approach the end of the century, we can see that the diversity, inventiveness, optimism, and vigor of American architecture makes it, arguably, the most influential national architecture in the world today.

In this book's method we are led to each building as part of a simple chronology, shown a canonical photograph or drawing, and given various other clues suggesting the reasons for its inclusion in the guide. The underlying assumption is that a single visual representation of a building has tremendous significance in its own right, and that architecture may be understood as much through its representation as through the experience gained through a visit. The text extends this theme, requiring each of us to engage the building, its site, its place in the continuum, and the people who made it in a manner activating our own passions as to why this is to be considered within the privileged 200. We never have the full story, only a seduction; sometimes we hear about the site, the architect, the client, or the subsequent influence of a building. The buildings are not organized regionally, but chronologically, stressing larger cultural trends over the more idiosyncratic considerations present within each project. The matter-of-fact nature of a chronology, without any suggestion that history is a seamless chronology, will not prove a hindrance for the traveler, for whom this guidebook will prove a most useful introduction.

RALPH LERNER
Dean of the School of Architecture,
Princeton University

INTRODUCTION

The architectural traveler is an intrepid individual, willing to plan an entire trip to see a special building; to search for half a day to find it; to linger for hours on the doorstep in hopes of getting inside. But the rewards of persistence are self-evident. To understand and enjoy a work of architecture to the fullest, you must see it for yourself.

This book examines 200 important American buildings and provides guidance and information to help you visit them: addresses, phone numbers, days and times the buildings are open or closed, regular tour schedules, and the possibility and mechanics of arranging personal or group tours. The book also provides a compact historical overview of twentieth-century American architecture exemplified by the masterpieces still in existence.

I have selected 200 buildings from among the many thousands that deserve your attention. First, I have included the canonized masterpieces of twentieth-century architecture. These buildings, such as Frank Lloyd Wright's Robie House in Chicago and Ludwig Mies van der Rohe's Seagram Building in New York City, have profoundly affected the course of architectural history. For the remaining selections, the criteria is naturally more subjective and varied. I have tried to strike a balance encompassing diverse locations, building types, and architects, and between early and late representations of styles or careers.

In many cities, local landmarks like New York City's Chrysler Building or Seattle's Space Needle have become beloved civic symbols; they also give travelers a sense of the city shared. On the regional level, buildings like Irving Gill's La Jolla Woman's Club, John Staub's Bayou Bend in Houston, and Addison Mizner's work in Palm Beach so captured popular yearnings that they became the basis of styles that endure to this day. Sometimes, an assemblage of buildings—rather than a single one—attracts our attention. The Art Deco District in Miami Beach and the Usonian community in Mount Pleasant, New York, are good examples.

Foreign architects have produced many of America's outstanding buildings. Besides such historic landmarks as the Farnsworth House by Ludwig Mies van der Rohe and Alvar Aalto's Mount Angel Abbey Library, this book directs you to new work by Renzo Piano, Ricardo Bofill, and Arata Isozaki, among others.

In my selection, I have favored buildings that are accessible or that can be seen from the street, although vegetation or fences sometimes appear to block the view. Some buildings are well preserved and obviously cherished. Others, like Buckminster Fuller's Union Tank Car Dome in Baton Rouge, Louisiana, are rusting away in virtual abandonment under the wary eye of a lone security guard in a pickup truck.

Many of our revered monuments are sadly gone now, but happily others are coming back. Important prototypes like Fuller's Dymaxion House and Albert Frey's Aluminaire House have been dismantled and are now in the process of being reassembled in newly accessible locations.

How to Use This Guide

The main organization of the guidebook is chronological by date of completion (except for a small number of on-going projects, multiple entries, and works in progress). This order is supplemented by two practical cross-references in the back of the book: an alphabetical index of the architects included, and a geographical index, ordered by location. With this triple approach, I hope to make the book more useful and your travels more enjoyable.

Taking advantage of the chronological listing of buildings, you may enjoy browsing through the decades of twentieth-century American architecture. If you are particularly interested in the work of an individual architect or firm, the Index of Architects lists those featured in the book and the locations of their buildings described here. When traveling to a specific city, refer to the Index of Locations to find all the buildings listed under that particular location and its surroundings.

Visitor information is contained in both the boxed heading (the address) and in the final paragraph of each listing: phone number, days and times the building is normally open and closed, the availability and times of regularly scheduled tours, and the possibility and mechanics of arranging special tours. Admission is charged at some buildings; however, I have not attempted to specify prices, which are always subject to change. I advise you to call ahead if admission charges are a concern.

Finally, while most of the buildings included in this guide are accessible all or some of the time, others are resolutely private. Please be mindful of the owners' right to privacy when you visit.

FRANK LLOYD WRIGHT HOME AND STUDIO, 1889-1909

951 Chicago Avenue
at Forest Avenue
Oak Park, Illinois

Frank Lloyd Wright

1

The "funny little house" Frank Lloyd Wright began at age twenty-two with money borrowed from his boss, Louis Sullivan, is a legendary monument and the architectural laboratory of his first golden age. This earliest of Wright's major works shows all his major influences: his love of nature, music, Japanese design, Froebel blocks, and his admiration of Louis Sullivan.

Wright lived here for twenty years, and he built the house and studio in four main stages. Due to constant tinkering, it was really a work in progress, remarkable for the clarity and sophistication of his early ideas. The main house facing Forest Avenue is striking for its sharply pitched roof, brown-stained shingles, and olive trim. Its clear geometry refutes fussy Victorian ornament, and its coloring and cladding follow Wright's deep conviction that architecture should be in harmony with the natural landscape.

Inside, Wright is clearly on the way to the open floor plan, and firmly in control of the grand gesture. For example, the children's playroom features a magnificent barrel-vaulted ceiling that looks ecclesiastical but is said to have been perfect for bouncing balls. The colors have character, especially the earthy red walls and cream ceiling of the master bedroom—all the more beautiful for the evocative murals of Indians on the plains painted by artist Orlando Gianninni. Woodworking is extensive throughout the house and some of Wright's notoriously uncomfortable furniture is also in evidence.

A high point is Wright's famous studio and office, one of his great (and most personal) architectural spaces. The evolving Prairie style can be seen in the central rectangular entry, which is flanked by two octagonal drums. The taller clerestory-windowed structure houses the drafting room, a tiered structure where the eye seems to spiral up toward the light, anticipating by many decades the Guggenheim Museum plan.

The property fell into disrepair after Wright deserted his house and family in 1909. Now in the National Trust for Historic Preservation, it is restored to its 1909 configuration and magically recaptures his spirit as well. The Frank Lloyd Wright Home and Studio Foundation administers the property and offers tours at 11:00 AM, 1:00 PM, and 3:00 PM Monday through Friday and on weekends continuously from 11:00 AM to 4:00 PM. Closed Thanksgiving, Christmas, and New Year's Day. Walking tours of the Prairie School Historic District—the world's greatest concentration of Wright architecture, including more than twenty houses and Unity Temple—take place daily from 10:00 AM to 5:00 PM. For information on tours and special Foundation programs, call (708) 848-1500.

2

One South Calvert Building, 1901

201 East Baltimore Street
Baltimore, Maryland

D.H. Burnham and Company

Only a few Chicago-style skyscrapers were built in the eastern United States, and even fewer are still in existence. One South Calvert—the only structure of its kind in Baltimore—represents the steel-framed "skyscraper" construction method developed in Chicago in the last two decades of the nineteenth century. Its design came from D.H. Burnham and Company, one of Chicago's pioneer skyscraper architects.

Originally the Continental Trust Building, this 16-story structure is clad primarily in stone, but brick and terra-cotta were also used. Besides the steel frame, the Chicago method of skyscraper construction is evidenced in the tall arches at the building's base and in the triple windows placed inside the arches. Ornamentation remains in the classical tradition, with Renaissance Revival pediments over some of the windows; at the top there is a row of columns under a decorated terra-cotta frieze and cornice.

The strength of the building was supremely tested in Baltimore's blistering fire of 1904 when the skyscraper flamed from top to bottom. Its "completely fireproof" interiors burned out entirely in the estimated 2,500-degree blaze, but the structure survived intact, so the fireproofing methods were considered successful on those grounds. In the ensuing restoration, the fire damage was repaired, although the ornamental cornice was not replaced.

Today, the building houses a bank on the ground floor and offices above. During office hours the lobby is accessible, and its marble walls and brass-railed grand staircases are essentially intact.

For general information, call (410) 727-0275.

Metropolitan Museum of Art, 1902 (Central Entrance Pavilion)

**Fifth Avenue at 82nd Street
New York, New York**

Richard Morris Hunt

The bastion of culture that is the Metropolitan Museum of Art in Central Park—an expanse that runs from East 80th to East 84th Street—originated as a colorful Gothic structure designed by Calvert Vaux, erected between 1874 and 1880 and twice expanded unsatisfactorily by other architects. As the collections and influence grew, a larger building with a more cohesive appearance and plan was required. The dean of New York architects, Richard Morris Hunt, received the commission, and although he died before its completion, he knew that this would be his most enduring monument.

Hunt was the first American architect to study at the Ecole des Beaux Arts and his design recalls the grand public monuments of Paris. Hunt's scheme included a massive central entry section with wings enclosing courtyards. Only the main entrance was completed, in 1902, by his son, Richard Howland Hunt. The center still holds, despite repeated expansions since that time. It manages to assert tremendous authority and remains welcoming at the same time because of its broad front stairway and its magnificent arched entry flanked by columns. Medallion portraits of the old masters and personifications of Architecture, Sculpture, Painting, and Music humanize this towering façade.

In 1906, the next wave of expansion was occasioned by a large bequest from Jacob S. Rogers and the prospect of receiving the munificent collection of J. Pierpont Morgan, the museum's president. A new master plan, and the side wings along Fifth Avenue, were designed by McKim, Mead & White.

Contemporary expansions by Kevin Roche and John Dinkeloo in the 1970s and 1980s brought the gridded, reflective glass walls of modern architecture right up against the old classic structure. The light and airy new additions are striking in their own way, but Hunt's main hall has remained one of the truly awe-inspiring spaces in New York City.

The museum is open Tuesday through Thursday, 9:30 AM to 5:15 PM; Friday and Saturday, 9:30 AM to 8:45 PM; Sunday 9:30 AM to 5:15 PM. Closed on Monday, and on Thanksgiving, Christmas, and New Year's Day. Tours take place daily (reservations are required for groups). For tour information, call (212) 570-3711; educational groups call (212) 288-7733.

4

The Flatiron (Fuller) Building, 1903

Broadway at East 22nd Street and Fifth Avenue
New York, New York

D.H. Burnham & Company

The Flatiron Building owes its shape to the triangular slice of land on which it rests, where Broadway cuts a diagonal from East 22nd Street to Fifth Avenue; it owes its name to the common household appliance of the day.

This early New York skyscraper was designed by the famous Chicago architect, Daniel Burnham, a pioneer in the erection of tall buildings and a major force behind the Chicago World's Fair of 1893, which revived a preference for classical buildings at monumental scale.

With the design of the Flatiron Building, Burnham explored the creative possibilities for the skyscraper. Over 20 stories tall, the design employs skyscraper construction—a steel frame encased in masonry—with limestone blocks elaborately ornamented in alternating decorative bands from top to bottom.

In the early 1990s, the building joined in the liveliness of its surrounding Union Square neighborhood when a fashionable boutique clothing store opened on the ground floor. Offices still occupy the space above.

For general information, call (212) 477-0947.

Rhode Island State Capitol, 1903

83 Smith Street
Providence, Rhode Island

McKim, Mead & White

With the ink barely dry on its design, the Rhode Island State Capitol building inspired a wave of statehouse construction across the country. Its 1892 publication in *American Architect* magazine revealed a streamlined version of the United States Capitol building in Washington, a classical white marble monument with symmetrical side wings, a central dome, and rotunda. Four domed tourelles frame the main dome, adding an extra flourish to the overall scheme.

McKim, Mead & White's competition-winning entry pleased the Capitol Commission with its well-organized interior plan and authoritative appearance. Although the design was modified somewhat during construction, the finished building suits its City Beautiful setting atop Smith Hill; a grand, landscaped boulevard provides a ceremonial approach.

The Rhode Island State Capitol is open Monday to Friday 8:30 AM to 5:00 PM. Closed weekends and holidays. Tours are conducted in the mornings only. For information, call (401) 277-2357.

Carson Pirie Scott, 1904

One South State Street
at Madison
Chicago, Illinois

Louis H. Sullivan

A popular turn-of-the-century theme was the need to create a new architecture for the new century. In practice, the advance was more evolutionary than revolutionary. The Carson Pirie Scott store is virtually a freeze-frame of the transition, with one foot firmly planted in the nineteenth century and the other in the twentieth. Designed by Louis Sullivan in 1899 and constructed in two stages culminating in 1904, the building not only spans the two centuries in time but also in style—an extraordinary combination of the traditional and the modern.

Carson Pirie Scott is, in fact, virtually two buildings in one. The bold "Chicago-window" grid of the upper 10 stories is crisply modern. Yet it is superimposed above a two-story classical base embellished with cast-iron panels of wreaths and tendrils (which Sullivan also designed). Sullivan unified the ostensibly competing elements with a curved pavilion of tall colonettes at the corner. For practical purposes, the cornerpiece provides a gracious entry to the store, as well as an off-setting element of vertical energy in an otherwise strongly horizontal composition.

Sullivan's genius at successfully combining multiple stylistic possibilities was matched by his remarkable handling of the new load-bearing steel frame. He was able to free his masonry building from unnecessary mass, which in turn gave him the freedom to design the building in the most modern way.

At the time he designed Carson Pirie Scott, Sullivan was considered to be the master of tall commercial buildings—"skyscrapers" of the times—and the store is considered one of the first great examples of a modern style.

Carson Pirie Scott is a landmark fixture in downtown Chicago, and the store is open during regular retail hours. The store's telephone number is (312) 641-8000. The Chicago Architecture Foundation also includes the store in some of its tours. For information, call the foundation at (312) 922-TOUR.

Darwin D. Martin House, 1904

125 Jewett Parkway
Buffalo, New York

Frank Lloyd Wright

Around the turn of the century, Frank Lloyd Wright found a welcome and devoted patron in Darwin Martin. The president of the Larkin Company, a prosperous mail-order firm, Martin tried Wright out on a small house for his son-in-law in the proposed family compound. Wright's success led Martin to commission a series of homes and offices that advanced Wright's architecture as well as his career. The Larkin Company's administration building, which was built in Buffalo in 1903, famous for its "firsts" of air-conditioning, plate glass windows, and Wright-designed metal furniture, was demolished in 1950. The site is now a parking lot.

Martin's house, the largest of Wright's Prairie Style homes, has fortunately endured, along with two other houses from the original compound. For the tawny brick, two-story main house, Wright majestically restates his simple prairie-home principles: long horizontal lines, interlocking planes, floating rooflines, bands of windows, integral decoration, and harmony with nature. Perhaps because this prairie house is in the city, the gardens take on enormous importance—a pergola extended deep into the property, and the conservatory (and birdhouse) was the size of a small house.

A primary purpose of the prairie house was to "break the box"—to loosen up the confining, cubical room arrangements of Victorian design—and the Martin house has an especially open plan: The large rooms open easily into one another. In the unusually expansive (and expensive) main house, Wright's genius for unified design is much in evidence. Integral with the architecture, Wright designed oak furniture, stained-glass windows, carpets, fabrics, and lighting for the house. In the main ground-floor rooms, a soft golden glow prevailed, with flashes of brilliance from the gold-toned mortar Wright used to cement the Roman bricks.

In 1966, the State University of New York (SUNY) at Buffalo purchased the property: Martin House, the George Barton House (118 Summit Avenue), and the Gardener's Cottage (285 Woodward Avenue). The complex is currently closed and awaiting renovations. For information, call SUNY's School of Architecture at (716) 829-3485.

8

New York Stock Exchange, 1904

11 Wall Street at Broad Street
New York, New York

George B. Post

The New York Stock Exchange building captures a surprising turn-of-the-century contradiction: the longing for the richly ornamented classical architecture of the past in conjunction with the advances of modern technology. Following classical precedents, George Post designed the building as a classical Roman temple façade complete with arches, balustrades, massive columns, and a sculptured pediment filled with mythological figures. But behind the tall columns there is a glass "curtain wall," one of the first in New York City, that floods the cavernous interior trading floor with light.

The frenetic activity of Wall Street trading takes place in one of New York City's great architectural interiors. The exchange is open from 9:15 AM to 4:00 PM, Monday through Friday, except major holidays. Starting at 9:00 AM, the Visitors Center dispenses tickets for free, self-guided tours from the entrance at 20 Broad Street. These tickets go quickly, so plan to get there early in the day. Advance reservations are required for groups of ten or more. For reservations or information, call (212) 656-5168.

SINGER LOFT BUILDING, 1904

561 Broadway
New York, New York

Ernest Flagg

New York's lively Soho district (*so*uth of *Ho*uston Street) offers a high concentration of turn-of-the-century cast-iron buildings and is probably the most intact such neighborhood in the United States. Nevertheless, the entire area was scheduled for demolition in the 1960s to make way for Robert Moses's urban dream of a Lower Manhattan Expressway. Soho is safe now, thanks to the Landmarks Preservation Commission founded in 1973. The neighborhood manages to retain its gritty turn-of-the-century industrial air, even as the old buildings have become occupied with fashionable boutiques and art galleries.

The Singer Loft Building is an especially noteworthy—and beautiful—reminder of the time and the technology. An innovative composition of colored terra-cotta, glass, and steel, the building clearly foretells the coming of the glass curtain wall. Designed by New York architect Ernest Flagg for the Singer Sewing Machine Company, the 12-story L-shaped office and loft tower wraps the corner. The main façade on Broadway rises to a graceful arch below a cornice projecting one floor from the top. Using wrought iron rather than cast iron, Flagg created the delightfully curved balcony railing and tracery framing the great arch. This Broadway façade is echoed by a secondary façade around the corner on Prince Street, where the Singer name is still visible on the transom.

Ernest Flagg designed a number of important New York landmarks, including the venerable Scribners' bookstore (now Brentano's) on Fifth Avenue. Lost now is his 47-story Singer Building and Tower at 149 Broadway, completed in 1908. The prominence of the newer Singer Building overshadowed the earlier and smaller structure in Soho, which came to be called "The Little Singer Building." Today it is the only one, and its loft floors house condominium offices.

With the opening of the Guggenheim Museum's Soho branch, located one-half block up Broadway and across Prince Street, the Singer Loft Building has gained a new visibility thanks to the stream of visitors who make their way to see Arata Isozaki's Guggenheim interiors.

MINNESOTA STATE CAPITOL, 1905

75 Constitution Avenue
St. Paul, Minnesota

Cass Gilbert

The state of Minnesota was only thirty-seven years old when Cass Gilbert received the commission to design its capitol. Gilbert took as his model St. Peter's Basilica in Rome, and particularly Michaelangelo's famous dome for the Vatican. The dome is smaller here, but it is still the building's distinguishing feature, all the more so because of the gold-leaf ball that sits at its top. The gold ornamentation is further carried out in a robust gold-leaf sculpture group over the main entrance that shows a muscular charioteer marshalling four horses and riders, whose arms overflow with Minnesota products; a banner announces "Minnesota."

Up the grand front steps and through the tall archways, visitors enter into a massive rotunda that extends from the first floor to the dome. All four interior floors are lavishly fitted out with the more than twenty varieties of stone used in the halls, stairways, and chambers. Minnesota limestone from Mankato and Kasota is used on the walls throughout. Corridors feature vaulted ceilings decorated with hand-painted arabesques depicting Minnesota's agricultural abundance. Gilbert also commissioned the artwork that decorates the interiors.

The "grand floor" is the second floor, where the Senate, House of Representatives, and Supreme Court chambers are located. The Senate and House Chambers have been restored to their 1905 appearance with skylights, original colors, furnishings, and artwork.

Gilbert supervised construction and decoration of the Capitol. "In the old days," he said, "the architect, the painter, and the sculptor were frequently one and the same man. There is no reason they should not be so now."

While Gilbert was honored for his statehouse design, he is best known for the Woolworth Building in New York City, a then-startling Gothic skyscraper completed in 1913.

The Minnesota State Capitol is accessible from I-94 and I-35E in St. Paul. It is open 8:30 AM to 5:00 PM weekdays; 10:00 AM to 4:00 PM Saturday, and 1:00 to 4:00 PM on Sunday. Free guided tours offered by the Minnesota Historical Society begin on the hour until one hour before closing. The Capitol is closed Easter, Thanksgiving, Christmas, and New Year's Day. For recorded information call (612) 297-3521. Groups of ten or more must reserve two weeks in advance; the number to call for reservations is (612) 296-2881.

FAIRMONT HOTEL, 1906

950 Mason Street
San Francisco, California

Reid Brothers

This huge, white marble hotel fills a city block atop Nob Hill, where it is one of the city's most popular landmarks. Built by the daughter of a Comstock silver king, the original seven-story hotel was beset by disasters. The 1906 earthquake was frightening but not damaging. Shortly before the brand-new hotel opened, a terrible fire almost destroyed it. California's first woman architect, Julia Morgan, restored the structure and completed the interiors. In 1962, Mario Gaidano added a slender 24-story white and gold tower of modern design that offers spectacular views of San Francisco Bay.

The tradition of old-world elegance lives on in the hotel's public rooms, particularly the ornate lobby with its marble walls and columns and grand stairway. There is also a ballroom with clouds painted on the ceiling, and a rooftop garden. The Fairmont Hotel is known to television viewers as the setting of the series "Hotel." And on a historical note, the United Nations Charter was drafted in the hotel's Garden Room.

For visitor information, call (415) 772-5000.

Unity Temple, 1906

875 Lake Street
at Kenilworth Avenue
Oak Park, Illinois

Frank Lloyd Wright

Frank Lloyd Wright's design for Unity Temple, a church and Sunday School for his Unitarian clients, is the world's first modern church. There are no Gothic arches—the lines are straight and bold. Wright rejected the cross-shaped plan so common in church architecture, as well as in his own house designs. Instead he chose a plan based on squares and rectangles, and these elements are interwoven throughout the building. The long, low horizontal lines that had become Wright's residential trademark took a turn for the vertical, and with this change came an interesting new scale and proportion.

Unity Temple's monumental exterior encompasses both the church and the smaller Sunday School beyond, connected by a low entranceway. The building complex is anchored by four massive corner piers, with balconies between them. The walls are solid concrete that were surfaced in pebble aggregate, a new and prophetic breakthrough that helped to change this former "engineering" material into an architectural one. A band of windows is set high into the wall to block out noise from the street and admit to light to the interior.

The interior of Unity Temple is equally monumental. The central auditorium is a massive square with incut corners. There are double galleries on three sides and a pulpit platform on the fourth side with an organ behind it. Sand-finished plaster walls echo the theme of squares and rectangles with their graphic wood trim. The furniture and light fixtures are also by Wright.

Unity Temple offers guided tours on Saturday at noon, 1:00, and 2:00 PM (1:00, 2:00, and 3:00 PM April through October). Sunday tour hours are 1:00, 2:00, and 3:00 PM. For information, call (708) 383-8873.

The Frank Lloyd Wright Home and Studio Foundation, 951 Chicago Avenue in Oak Park, also conducts tours of Unity Temple daily except on Thanksgiving, Christmas, and New Year's Day. For tour information, call (708) 848-1978. For group tour reservations, call (708) 848-0458.

Pierpont Morgan Library, 1907

29-33 East 36th Street
at Madison Avenue
New York, New York

McKim, Mead & White

J. Pierpont Morgan, then the world's richest man and one of the great American collectors, built this library for the rare books and manuscripts that were his passion. The well-traveled, cultivated financier revered Italian Renaissance architecture, which he felt expressed his collection's importance. He could have commissioned anyone, but America's premier neoclassical architects—McKim, Mead & White—happened to be based in the city. For Mr. Morgan, Charles McKim created his masterpiece.

The Morgan Library opened to the public in 1924 and now fills a complex occupying half a city block. Still, "Mr. Morgan's Library" retains the aura of power and privilege—and the bounty of a worldwide collector—in its beautiful period rooms.

As large and opulent as an Italian palazzo, the library portrays the Renaissance idea of integrating all the arts. Architecturally, the Tennessee pink marble structure is classically simple: a broad rectangle with a central, recessed portico entry, accentuated with paired double Ionic columns. Bronze front doors are topped by a sculpted lunette and an angel-borne panel on the cornice. Construction was also classical: The marble blocks are joined by grinding rather than mortar, an ancient Greek technique.

The library contains three splendid main rooms and a rotunda filled with colorful marble surfaces and columns, mosaic panels, and columns of lapis lazuli. The East Room is the main repository for the library's collection of rare books, manuscripts, and drawings. Its walls are lined with three tiers of bookcases made of bronze and inlaid Circassian walnut. Zodiac signs decorate the spandrels; out of sequence, they reflect Morgan's personal reconfiguration of the constellations.

Morgan's private West Room study is artistically and historically fascinating. Here Morgan hosted an extraordinary "fund-raiser" in 1907, hitting up wealthy friends for personal contributions to help the nation avoid impending financial collapse. An artistic highlight is the coffered wooden ceiling from Italy.

In 1991, the old masonry buildings were joined by an elegant new addition, the Garden Court, a glass and steel wave-shaped greenhouse by Voorsanger Associates of New York. The clear vaulted ceiling is supported by a free-standing 55-foot truss tethered by pretensioned cables. Pale-colored materials—Indiana limestone walls, gray and white marble floors, and an elevator clad in panels of pewter—enhance the sense of light and space.

The Morgan Library is open Tuesday through Saturday from 10:30 AM to 5:00 PM; Sunday 1:00 to 5:00 PM; closed Monday and national holidays. Tours are conducted Tuesday and Thursday at 2:30 PM. For information, call (212) 685-0610.

Plaza Hotel, 1907

**Fifth Avenue
at Central Park South
New York, New York**

Henry Janeway Hardenbergh

The grand aristocrat of New York hotels, the Plaza commands its Central Park site as if it were the center of the city. It was certainly designed for the tastes of its fashionable guests—an oversized French chateau that was just like home, only larger.

Henry Janeway Hardenbergh, the Plaza's architect, was known for outstanding residences, including the Dakota Apartments on Central Park West, the city's first luxury apartments.

At the Plaza, Hardenbergh recognized the importance of the corner site; the two main façades would be equally impressive. The building is classically organized, with a distinct base, shaft, and top. The 18-story structure is clad with brick and marble and is capped by a massive cornice and mansard slate roof with gables and dormers and copper cresting. Hardenbergh relieved the massive blockiness of the building by recessing the central sections, and by rounding the corners on the north and south.

When it opened, the hotel had two floors of elegant public rooms with staircases and 800 guest rooms. The Palm Court featured a Tiffany domed glass ceiling, later covered up. A restoration by Lee Harris Pomeroy Architects in New York City revitalized the public and guest areas. The Tiffany ceiling has also been returned to its former glory.

For information, call (212) 759-3000.

UNION STATION, 1907

**Massachusetts Avenue
at North Capitol Street
Washington, D.C.**

D.H. Burnham and Company

Around 1900, "modern" meant railroad, a symbol of progress as well as the most popular travel option. Yet despite the progress of machine technology, and in surprising contrast to the forward architectural thrust of fellow Chicagoans Louis Sullivan and Frank Lloyd Wright, Daniel Burnham looked to the past for his inspiration. In all fairness, he was not alone in this. A veritable frenzy of neoclassical sentiment was sweeping along the east coast, and Burnham embraced it. His railroad gateway to the nation's capital recalls the glories of imperial Greece and Rome, monumental in scale and lavish in ornament.

Union Station fulfilled Burnham's vision of the "noble, dignified classical style." He designed the white marble terminal with a sense of pageantry and procession—the traveler is welcomed by enormous arched porticoes flanked by Ionic columns, surmounted by 25-ton larger-than-life sculptured figures, which represent fire, electricity, agriculture, and mechanics.

The largest structure in the country under a roof at the time it was built, the 97,500-square-foot terminal encompasses three halls: Main, East, and West. The Main Hall is the largest, measuring 220 x 120 feet, enclosed by a 96-foot-high barrel-vaulted and coffered ceiling that admits a flood of natural light through its skylights. The Main Hall is also the most elaborate, with white marble floors decorated with red diamond insets and a gold leaf ceiling. Standing guard from their posts along the ledge of Main Hall mezzanine are thirty-six plaster statues of Roman legionnaires. At its inception, the terminal was a mini-city, complete with hotel, police station, doctor's office, liquor store, swimming pool, Turkish baths, a butcher, a baker, and even a mortuary.

Burnham said, "Make no little plans. They have no magic to stir men's souls." He could not foresee the sad decline of rail travel in the 1950s that almost took his grandiose Union Station down with it. For almost thirty years the building languished in uncertainty. The 1964 landmark designation prevented demolition but failed to inspire any new life or purpose. A 1968 plan for a National Visitor Center failed miserably; opening in 1976, it closed in disgrace after only two years.

The station was finally saved by the Union Station Redevelopment Act of 1981, a public-private effort and massive renovation. Architects Benjamin Thompson & Associates, Inc., architectural preservationists Harry Weese and Associates of Chicago, and others worked to achieve an authentic restoration as well as a viable building. Union Station reopened in 1988.

The station is open twenty-four hours a day. For station information, call (202) 371-9441.

Gamble House, 1908

4 Westmoreland Place
Pasadena, California

Greene & Greene

Gamble House is the ultimate California bungalow. Built for David and Mary Gamble of the Procter & Gamble Company of Cincinnati, it is the standout in a neighborhood so rich with chalet-style Arts and Crafts architecture that the locals call it "Little Switzerland."

The house reveals the many sources Charles S. Greene and his brother, Henry M. Greene, combined in developing this unique California style: elements of the "Shingle Style" homes of the east, Frank Lloyd Wright's "Prairie Style" of the midwest, the Swiss chalet, and Japanese influences. But most of all, the transplanted easterners were inspired by the luxuriousness of nature in their new locale, and by a desire to put tradition behind them.

The Greenes' special skill was creating such a natural-looking house, despite its complicated and highly decorated design. Long and low, Gamble House has deep eaves extending over porches and balconies. Structural timbers were evident, clearly showing how the house was constructed. Large, brown shingles cover the outside walls, and the verandas and sleeping porches feature elaborate stickwork.

Craftsmanship, inside and out, is something to marvel over. The front door, for example, offers a fine piece of Tiffany art glass in the shape of a spreading oak tree. The interior woodworking is legendary, especially the handcrafted, hand-polished teak panels of the entry, living room, and dining room. Even the staircase is a woodwork of art. The Greenes designed the furniture as well.

Gamble House is near the intersection of the 134 and 210 freeways. (Frank Lloyd Wright's La Miniatura is a few blocks away.) Tours are offered Thursday through Sunday from noon until 3:00 PM, except holidays. Reservations for groups of ten must be arranged one month in advance. For information and reservations, call (818) 793-3334.

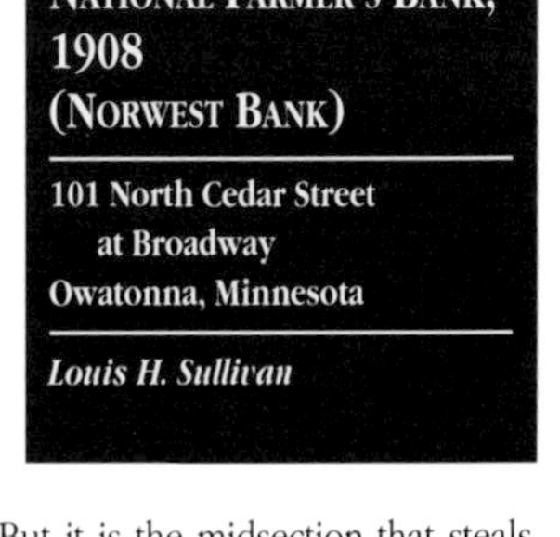

National Farmer's Bank, 1908 (Norwest Bank)

**101 North Cedar Street at Broadway
Owatonna, Minnesota**

Louis H. Sullivan

In the last years of his revolutionary career, his innovative Chicago skyscrapers of the 1890s sadly behind him, Louis Sullivan embarked on a series of bank buildings for tiny midwestern communities. These small but elegant structures are no less admirable than the skyscrapers; in fact the Norwest Bank was honored with its own postage stamp in 1981.

For his skyscrapers, Sullivan had devised a basic division of parts—the base, the midsection, and the top—and this formula also worked for the bank, despite its smaller cube-shaped structure. Here, the base consists of the first floor, which is clad in a beautiful but unornamented red sandstone. But it is the midsection that steals the show. Sullivan's love of ornamentation—and his special ability to combine the decorative with the plain—is evident in the green terra-cotta bands of leaves and acorns outlining the red masonry walls at the front and side of the building. These two main exposures also feature a dramatic center arch inset with windows of brilliant glass mosaic. The top is a simple masonry tier projecting slightly outward.

As a prelude to the richly ornamented interior, Sullivan designed a low main entrance that opens into the enormous central banking room. On the inside, the huge, arched stained-glass windows are detailed with gold leaf, and there are two large murals within the arches. The ornate clock over the vault is the work of Sullivan's partner, George Elmslie, who also assisted in the bank's design and ornamentation.

At the time the bank was built, Sullivan was virtually alone in championing progressive American architecture. He ferociously condemned the rampant neoclassicism brought on by the Chicago World's Fair of 1893, calling it "an appalling calamity." Sullivan predicted that "the damage . . . will last for half a century from its date, if not longer."

The bank suffered its own calamity and failed in 1926, and in 1929 the building was bought by Security State Bank. Later in that eventful financial year, Security was purchased by Northwest Bank Corporation.

Over the years, there have been two major restorations of the remarkable structure: by Harwell Hamilton Harris in 1958 and under the direction of David P. Bowers of Val Michelson & Associates in 1982.

Owatonna is a city of about 20,000 people, located sixty miles south of Minneapolis/St. Paul via Highway 35W. Bank hours are 8:00 AM to 5:30 PM Monday through Friday; 8:00 AM to noon Saturday. For visitor information, call (507) 451-5670.

Robie House, 1909

5757 Woodlawn Avenue
Chicago, Illinois

Frank Lloyd Wright

The evolving architectural genius of Frank Lloyd Wright reached full maturity with his three-dimensional design for Robie House, the largest and most monumental of his early works. Like the "Prairie Style" homes that preceded it, Robie House is long, low, and horizontally oriented. It also reveals a cohesive and streamlined layering that had not been seen before. Wright appears to have been influenced by the developments in modern machine technology, for Robie House resembles the airplane as well as the luxury ocean liner, both of which were objects of great fascination at the time.

Robie House is a Prairie Style house in a city setting, and there is a new tautness that is appropriate to its tight corner lot. Wright's design solution consists of large horizontal slabs, ingeniously stacked to create multiple interior levels, open balconies, and enclosed terraces. The strong horizontal lines of the balcony and the roof are complemented by the exterior bricks, which are also long and thin. Continuous bands of windows alternate with the solid exterior walls of soft, red Roman brick, capped with limestone. The cross-shaped theme of many Wright designs of this period appears in Robie House in the extended overhang of the uppermost story.

As with all of Wright's works, the setting was the key to the design. On the outside, the house acts as a fortress to shield the residents from the traffic of the street, with the entrance hidden away to the right. Inside, Wright achieved privacy by inverting the traditional living arrangement: the living and dining rooms are located on the second floor, with the children's playroom and the billiard rooms below. The interior plan is remarkably long and open, with the living and dining rooms separated by a massive fireplace, the hearth that Wright believed to be the spiritual center of the modern home. The open interior ensures that each major area of the house has access to a porch or balcony, assuring the indoor/outdoor integration that Wright particularly favored.

Robie House is one of the most influential designs in the history of architecture, a demonstration of new ideas that changed the course of architecture and greatly enhanced the place of the architect in the building process.

Robie House is part of the University of Chicago. University guides conduct hour-long tours at noon every day, including weekends, except for Thanksgiving Day and the week from Christmas to New Year's Day. Reservations are required for groups of ten or more. For reservations or information, call (312) 702-8374. Robie House is also a staple of the Chicago Architecture Foundation's tour roster. For CAF schedules, call (312) 922-TOUR.

First Church of Christ, Scientist, 1910

Dwight Way at Bowditch Street
Berkeley, California

Bernard R. Maybeck

First Church of Christ, Scientist is one of two great remaining landmarks of California Arts & Crafts architecture (Gamble House in Pasadena is the other). Like the famous California bungalows of the time, the church is eclectic, romantic, and sympathetic to nature. But it also exhibits a grand sprightliness that is peculiar to its eccentric architect, Bernard Maybeck.

The church appears, pagoda-style, as a series of stepped rooftops with extended rough-hewn gables. Boughs of wisteria drape the ceremonial entrance portico with its freestanding gates, creating an entry that feels open and sheltering at the same time. It leads to a low ceilinged vestibule that gives on to the main church.

While the exterior seems soothing and practically residential, the interior is overwhelming and evocative. The church proper features the simple Greek cross plan, but above that almost anything goes. Colossal wooden beams carved in a Gothic style are mounted on columns and form an "X" across the ceiling. Delicately stenciled in ornamental tracery, these beams seem to float overhead, as walls of factory windows with tiny panes deny the structure's substance. Maybeck, the son of a German immigrant woodcarver, trained at the Beaux-Arts School in Paris. Berkeley's hills are dotted with his California Craftsman bungalows, but the church was his masterpiece. He kept photographs of it by his bedside until the day he died.

Guided tours are conducted the first Sunday of every month at 12:15 PM. Visitors are also welcome at weekly church services on Wednesday at 8:00 PM and Sunday at 11:00 AM. On the third and fifth Sunday of the month (as applicable), an additional evening service is held at 7:30 PM. The building is closed at all other times. Groups of ten or more should make reservations. For information and reservations, call (510) 845-7199.

New York Public Library, 1911 Central Research Library

Fifth Avenue at 42nd Street
New York, New York

Carrère & Hastings

The New York Public Library is an august marble monument surrounded by the friendly buzz and hubbub of an Italian piazza. The broad marble steps facing Fifth Avenue become a terrace, while outdoor cafés on either side provide pleasant, Parisian-style places to eat and linger under the trees. Behind the building, the newly restored and beautifully planted Bryant Park is a breath of fresh air in midtown Manhattan.

A National Historic Landmark, the white Vermont marble palace is among the city's finest Beaux Arts monuments and one of the world's greatest research (noncirculating) libraries. The competition-winning design by Carrère & Hastings won out over their former employers, McKim, Mead & White, although both firms preferred the classic style—and classic materials—for grand public monuments.

In accordance with Beaux Arts ideals, the library's entry is elegant and formal. A pair of "literary lions" carved in stone stand guard on either side of the broad, central stairs. The stairs rise in two tiers to the entrance portico, defined by pairs of fluted columns, high arches, and massive, bronze front doors. It took three sculptors to create the statuary that graces the main façade of this colossal building that stretches two blocks long.

Just inside is Astor Hall, a vast field of marble with high, arched bays on all four sides rising to a segmental vault and a pair of significant marble staircases leading to the upper floors. The overwhelming marble classicism of Astor Hall prepares you properly for the upper two stories, where the circulation spaces of cross-axial plan are all clad with marble and lofty in feeling.

Fortunately, the almost overwhelming formality and monumental nature of the building is enlivened by the pleasant interior light emanating from the two courtyards and by the companionable presence of old wood furniture and trim. And despite the immense size of the building and the collections—housed on eighty-eight miles of shelves—the library functions miraculously well. Librarians pride themselves on being able to retrieve virtually any book in less than ten minutes.

The library's remarkable collection includes the Gutenberg Bible, located in the Rare Books and Manuscripts Room, and Thomas Jefferson's handwritten copy of the Declaration of Independence. Major exhibitions from the library's collection are mounted in Gottesman Exhibition Hall on the first floor, and the Art and Architecture Collection is on three.

The library is open Tuesday and Wednesday from 11:00 AM to 7:30 PM; Thursday through Saturday from 10:00 AM to 6:00 PM, closed Sunday and Monday. Tours are conducted Tuesday through Saturday at 11:00 AM and 2:00 PM and last approximately one hour. Sign up in advance at the Friends of the Library Desk, to the right of the Fifth Avenue entrance. For tour information, call the Volunteer Office at (212) 930-0501.

TALIESIN, 1911-1938

Highway 23
Spring Green, Wisconsin

Frank Lloyd Wright

Frank Lloyd Wright was born just twenty miles from here; he returned to it from Oak Park, Illinois, as a prodigal son in 1911. The land had been in his family for many years, and Wright planned to construct a cottage in the countryside to share with Mamah Borthwick Cheney, his paramour. The cottage expanded into a complex that would be Wright's primary home and studio for the rest of his life.

Twice, in 1914 and in 1925, the house was almost destroyed by fire. The earlier disaster, ignited by a deranged servant, killed Mrs. Cheney and her two children. In rebuilding his beloved Taliesin, Wright used the remaining structure as a base for the new design. Now Taliesin is a 37,000-square-foot self-sufficient complex, arrayed around courtyards and pools. It includes the multi-story main house, guest rooms, Wright's studio and office, a root cellar, a shop area, an ice house, farm buildings, gardens and terraces, and Taliesin dam, a beautiful form of cascading stone.

Wright's "house of the north" (contrasting with Taliesin West, his winter home in Arizona) derives its name from an ancient Welsh word meaning "shining brow"—the brow of the hill. For Wright it was vital that Taliesin become part of the landscape. Taliesin is built of yellow limestone from nearby quarries, laid to resemble natural stratifications. Parts of the main house are separated by function, giving the appearance of clustered pavilions. The multiple rooflines, with their deep overhangs, seem to overlap and provide further unification of the overall design. Stone walls and terraces link the pavilions and outbuildings, courtyards and pools.

A visit inside the main house provides a glimpse of one of Wright's most evocative rooms—the 28 x 36-foot living room that overlooks the valley and water gardens below. Off the living room, a 40-foot walkway cantilevers out into the treetops. Wright's studio is attached to the house by a covered breezeway.

The 600-acre Taliesin estate includes Hillside School (1902), now home to the Frank Lloyd Wright School of Architecture, Midway Farm (1940s), Tan-y-deri House (1906), and Romeo and Juliet Windmill (1897). The landscaped grounds, roads, and dam are vivid reminders of Wright's devotion to nature and its part in the overall architectural composition.

Taliesin is three miles south of Spring Green, Wisconsin, forty-five minutes from Madison. It is owned and operated by the Frank Lloyd Wright Foundation. From mid-June to September, Monday through Saturday at 9:30 AM and 2:30 PM, there is a daily walking tour of the property. The house tours are available from mid-June to September, Thursday through Saturday at 10:30 AM and 12:30 PM. Reservations are required. Hillside Home School is open daily from May through October; tours start at 9:00 AM and continue on the hour until 4:00 PM. For more information and schedule confirmations, call (608) 588-2511.

Grand Central Terminal, 1913

Park Avenue at 42nd Street
New York, New York

Warren & Wetmore

At the time Grand Central Station was conceived and constructed, train travel represented great progress, and a city's train station became a symbol of modernism and a monument to civic pride. Ironically, the architecture of the past was thought to be the most modern expression of the station's importance. As it has turned out, the elaborate Beaux Arts classicism of Grand Central Station befits its dual status as the gateway to America and as a commuter terminal that elevates daily comings and goings into dramatic occasions.

The "new" Grand Central Terminal opened in 1913, the third station to occupy the site. Ten years in construction, the mammoth stone megastructure fills six city blocks above ground, with sixteen city blocks of tracks below grade and elevated streets wrapping the station on the second level. The main 42nd Street façade, with its tall arched windows and massive columns, is crowned by a Mercury clock by Jules Coutan.

Inside, the main lobby and grand concourse offers one of the most glorious enclosed spaces in New York City, and a perfectly positioned marble staircase from which to appreciate the spectacle in its entirety. Architects Warren & Wetmore designed a magnificent interior of stone and marble where light streams in from high semicircular windows on the north and south sides, and through large arched windows on the east and west. The vaulted ceiling presents a celestial scene, a blue dome embellished with the signs of the zodiac, as seen from above.

The engineering is every bit as impressive as the architecture. The station straddles an elaborate two-tier track configuration—the first of its kind—designed by New York Central Railroad's Chief Engineer William J. Wilgus. The stacked tracks were possible because electrification rendered steam engines obsolete; open tracks were no longer required for ventilation. Since the tracks could now be safely enclosed below ground, more land was available for building.

The station's New York City landmark status was endangered when the railroad sought to erect a tower above it. The case went all the way to the Supreme Court, which upheld the constitutionality of landmark law in general and the landmark status of Grand Central in particular. In 1991, however, the status was diminished in another way: Amtrak rerouted its long-distance trains to New York's Pennsylvania Station. Grand Central, the station designed as a gateway to a continent, is now "only" a commuter station, but a very grand one all the same.

The Municipal Art Society conducts one-hour walking tours every Wednesday at 12:30 PM. For information, call MAS at (212) 935-3960. On Friday at 12:30 PM, weather permitting, the Grand Central Partnership offers ninety-minute walking tours of the area, including the Chrysler Building and other nearby landmarks. For information, call (212) 986-9217.

Woolworth Building, 1913

Broadway at Park Place
New York, New York

Cass Gilbert

If Chicago launched the skyscraper, then New York propelled it to new heights. When it opened in 1913, the Woolworth Building ranked as the world's tallest, and as the undisputed trendsetter of the new skyscraper style.

With its breathtaking Gothic spire and medieval details, the Woolworth Building satisfactorily settled the issue of just what a skyscraper should look like. A Gothic cathedral, said Cass Gilbert, provided the proper historical precedent. According to the Beaux-Arts architect, nothing else captured so completely the modern skyscraper's heavenly aspirations. Irreverent New Yorkers quickly christened it the "Cathedral of Commerce."

A symbol of American capitalism at its most robust and powerful, the Woolworth Building's statistics were remarkable at the time: a 792-foot tower; 54 stories of office space for 14,000 workers; a 58th floor observation tower; and a cavernous, vaulted, marble-clad lobby with twenty-nine elevators, two of them express. The building cost $13.5 million, and was paid for in cash.

Even more remarkable today is Gilbert's skillful integration of the skyscraper elements into a unified composition. The 20-story U-shaped base yields gracefully to the rise of the square tower, which steps back twice before reaching the pinnacle, resplendent in all of its spires and gargoyles.

The Woolworth Building was not New York City's first skyscraper, but it was—and still is—one of the most magnificent masterpieces of an ornate, eclectic age. A New York landmark, the building remains F.W. Woolworth's corporate headquarters.

The building is open during regular business hours, so you can walk around the magnificent lobby, but the observation deck is no longer open to the public. Special requests to visit the building should be directed to Woolworth Corporation, Vice President of Public Affairs, 233 Broadway, New York, New York 10279.

La Jolla Woman's Club, 1914

715 Silverado Street
at Draper Avenue
La Jolla, California

Irving Gill

Irving Gill, an early and brilliant prophet of modern architecture in America, retained a love for the Spanish mission tradition of southern California. Through the patronage of Miss Ellen Browning Scripps, a remarkable philanthropist, Gill was commissioned to design the La Jolla Woman's Club; the project cost $40,000 in 1914.

The La Jolla Woman's Club building shows Gill's modern side, as well as his romantic inclination. The white concrete walls are smooth and unornamented and the roof is flat. Large, graceful arches frame the wraparound porch and the leafy columned pergola extends to the street. It is surprising to learn that in this building Gill pioneered tilt-wall construction, pouring concrete onto a huge table tilted fifteen degrees. The forms were lifted into place, with four-inch steel bars providing structural reinforcement. Windows were integrated into the forms.

Inside the main front doors, which are single slabs of hand-polished mahogany on invisible hinges, the interiors are simple but serene. Walls are flush with their casings. Gill used no moldings for pictures, no baseboards or wainscoting that would catch and hold the dust. Light enters through stained-glass windows placed high on the walls and through large windows opening to the gardens.

Gill was born in New York, the son of a contractor. With only a high school education, he was building "modern" structures while his European contemporaries were just formulating theories for them. His acknowledged masterpiece, the Walter Dodge house in Los Angeles, built for a famous patent medicine mogul, was unconscionably demolished in 1970.

Gill's architecture might have been internationally influential—voracious copying of his style gives San Diego its appealing and cohesive appearance—but his career was stunted by the return to full-fledged traditionalism that swept the country from about 1916 to the mid-1930s.

The La Jolla Woman's Club is open Monday through Saturday from 9:00 AM to noon, although it is necessary to make an appointment to visit. For reservations or information, call (619) 454-2354.

L.C. Smith Tower, 1914

Second Avenue at Yesler Way
Seattle, Washington

Gaggin & Gaggin

Even though it was built in 1914, this 42-story skyscraper looks surprisingly modern, with clean lines, large windows, and restrained ornamentation. Its pyramid tower even resembles the pencil-point spires that so often capped skyscrapers built in the 1980s. But the Smith Tower is not a frigid corporate tower; its bronze windows set in solid brass frames give it an overall golden cast. For decades this was the tallest and grandest building west of the Mississippi River, and to this day many Seattle residents consider it a favorite landmark.

Smith Tower's octagonal shape results from its irregular city site, and its design was intentionally dramatic. The original owner, L.C. Smith (as in Smith-Corona), observed the favorable publicity attending the Eiffel Tower's opening in 1889, and he reasoned that superior architecture and engineering would create the same kind of success for his building and his business. It is hard to say that the building alone put Smith-Corona on the map, but Smith Tower certainly has won its place in history as a National Historic Landmark.

Smith went all the way to Syracuse, New York, to hire his architects, Gaggin & Gaggin, who had built nothing taller than a few stories. They designed a building with "no artistic sacrifices," and to the highest technical standards. The interior fireproofing, for example, required 700,000 pounds of metal. The 1,400 doors, 2,000 windows, and 40,000 feet of molding were all hand-painted with eight coats of baked-on enamel resembling mahogany.

In the lobby, Gaggin & Gaggin did not have to utilize faux techniques. Walls are paneled in Alaskan marble and Mexican onyx. Eight copper and brass elevators were installed, and they are still operating today. Every office has windows that open.

An extensive renovation in 1986 brought back the building's authentic luster and restored the small, translucent glass blocks in the sidewalk that illuminate the building from below.

Smith Tower is open during regular business hours. There is a small museum inside with artifacts from Seattle's past. For visitor information, call (206) 622-4004.

Ghiradelli Chocolate Company, 1860-1915 (Ghiradelli Square)

Bounded by Polk, Larkin, Beach, and North Point Streets
San Francisco, California

Various architects

In a miracle of inspired renovation, this four-story, red-brick chocolate factory was combined with neighboring structures to create a spirited multi-level shopping and dining complex with eighty shops and restaurants. San Francisco developer Matson Roth recognized the potential of transforming the vast, loft-style floors of these industrial buildings near Fisherman's Wharf into active, usable commercial space. One new building was added to the mix, and now the entire complex is abuzz with activity throughout the day and night.

Ghiradelli Square originated the "festival marketplace" trend. Open seven days a week, it has become one of the most popular tourist attractions in this most popular American tourist city.

PALACE OF FINE ARTS, 1915

Baker Street at Beach Street
San Francisco, California

Bernard R. Maybeck

At a time when public expositions offered exceptional opportunities for architects to show off, Bernard Maybeck created a magnificently eclectic group of structures for the Panama-Pacific International Exposition of 1915, celebrating the opening of the Panama Canal. The "palace" is a three-part construction: an arc-shaped gallery, a colonnade, and a rotunda. Maybeck's Beaux-Arts training in classical architecture is revealed in the overall design, which he embellished with urns, columns, and statues at monumental scale.

A temporary exhibit never meant to last, the Palace was constructed of plaster of paris mixed with hemp fiber over a wood frame. As it deteriorated, however, it became increasingly dear to the people of San Francisco. In 1959, through the generosity and efforts of Walter S. Johnson, the Palace of Fine Arts was rebuilt in concrete so that this delightful bit of the city's past could be properly preserved.

The Palace of Fine Arts is the only exhibit that remains from the fair; it has been reincarnated into the Exploratorium, a lively museum of science past, present, and future. In 1981, the Palace of Fine Arts was featured on a postage stamp in the series on Architecture.

The Palace of Fine Arts' outdoor structure is always open. The Exploratorium is open Tuesday through Sunday from 10:00 AM until 5:00 PM, Wednesday until 9:00 PM. Closed Monday, except for major holidays. Groups of ten or more should make reservations by calling (415) 561-0308. For general information, call (415) 561-0360.

California Palace of the Legion of Honor, 1916

Lincoln Park
San Francisco, California

George A. Applegarth

A virtual copy of the Legion of Honor Palace in Paris, the San Francisco monument houses an urban art museum focusing on European painting of the sixteenth to eighteenth centuries. A memorial to casualties of World War I, the building announces itself, French style, with a triumphal arch flanked by colonnades and leading to a central courtyard. The museum's core collection, which included a Rodin sculpture, was donated to the city by a French couple, Adolph and Alma de Brettville Spreckels, for whom George Applegarth also designed a French palace replica as their mansion home.

The museum at the California Palace of the Legion of Honor is closed until 1994 for seismic renovations. For information, call (415) 863-3330. Until the museum reopens, the main attraction will be the exterior of the building, with its spectacular park and view of the San Francisco bay.

VIZCAYA, 1916
(THE DEERING ESTATE)

3251 South Miami Avenue
Miami, Florida

Francis Burrall Hoffman

Vizcaya is one of the American great houses, a neoclassical palace overlooking Biscayne Bay. The European past of the last four centuries is conjured up in the architecture—Renaissance, Baroque, and Rococo—and its thirty-four rooms are filled with priceless furnishings from the sixteenth to the eighteenth centuries. The estate's gardens alone are worth the trip.

The estate was constructed as a winter retreat for wealthy industrialist James Deering of International Harvester; he called it Vizcaya, a Basque word meaning "elevated place." Vizcaya evolved into a personal treasure house of European decorative arts. Relics of half a dozen grand European villas are incorporated into its structure, everything from massive doorways to painted ceilings.

The pale pink stucco mansion with its central courtyard was designed by Francis Burrall Hoffman, a New York City architect who left the prominent office of Carrère & Hastings to start his own firm in 1910. The house is surrounded with twenty acres of formal Italian gardens, and an elaborately decorated private casino is included in the complex. Deering's estate captures so perfectly the opulence of wealth before income tax that it was used as the setting for the motion picture *Citizen Kane*. Vizcaya is also said to have inspired its sister in extravagance, Hearst Castle at San Simeon, the home of the real-life Citizen Kane, William Randolph Hearst.

Vizcaya is open to the public every day except Christmas from 9:30 AM to 5:00 PM (the ticket booth closes at 4:30). Special group tours (including foreign language tours) are available by appointment. Reservations are required for groups of twenty or more, and should be made six weeks in advance during the peak months of November through May. For group reservations, call (305) 579-2708. For general information, call (305) 579-2767.

Hallidie Building, 1918

130 Sutter Street
San Francisco, California

Willis Polk

The Hallidie Building is famous for having the first true glass curtain wall in America, but it is fascinating also for its incongruous juxtaposition of trail-blazing technology with remnants from the romantic past, like the delicate, Victorian cast-iron ornamentation that decorates the transparent glass panes.

The grid-paned glass wall is also noteworthy for the way it is mounted. Rather than hanging from the frame, the glass is mounted on projecting brackets three feet in front of it. The glass is so clear that it is virtually invisible and allows the structural frame to show right through. Windows pivot sideways to allow for ventilation and washing. Semicircular wrought-iron fire escapes and diagonal stairs manage to look both practical and whimsical.

Offices (including the San Francisco Chapter of the AIA) fill the eight-story building, which is named for the inventor of the cable car, Andrew S. Hallidie. The office floors have been remodeled many times and little, if any, of the original details have survived.

The Hallidie Building is open during regular business hours. For the best view of the façade, walk across the street to the Galleria shopping complex, where there is a four-story Palladian window overlooking the Building.

For visitor information, call (415) 392-1072.

Woodbury County Courthouse, 1918

620 Douglas at Seventh Street
Sioux City, Iowa

William L. Steel
and Purcell & Elmslie

The Woodbury County Courthouse stands out as a model of progressive architecture at a time when most prominent American designers sought inspiration in the past. This courthouse is no neoclassical fantasy. Its brick walls are broad and the lines are clean. Ornamentation has not been forsaken, but the design is restrained and refined. The larger-than-life statues positioned atop flat, brick columns flanking the entry add just the right accent of monumental elegance and a hint of streamlining.

A great deal of care was given to the building's internal ornamentation. There are brick columns, flat and square like those at the entrance, but here they are capped with vines carved in stone. These columns support a ceiling that is bordered with decorated stone, and in some places the ceiling is given over to the decoration entirely. A large, glass dome set off by terra-cotta ornament illuminates (artificially) the central interior. The original murals are intact.

The trio of architects—William Steel, George Elmslie, and William Purcell—were former associates of Louis Sullivan, whose Chicago firm was instrumental in developing the appearance and technology of the modern skyscraper. It is fitting, then, that they concentrated on the here and now, although most of their colleagues were rummaging around in ancient history.

And now the courthouse has a long history of its own. Its seventy-fifth anniversary occurred in 1993, and to honor this event and to preserve the building, a large-scale restoration by Weatherall Erickson of Des Moines is in progress.

The courthouse is located off I-29 at the Business District exit, north or south. It is open from 8:00 AM to 4:30 PM Monday through Friday. Groups of ten or more should make reservations. For reservations and information, call (712) 279-6539 or 279-6459.

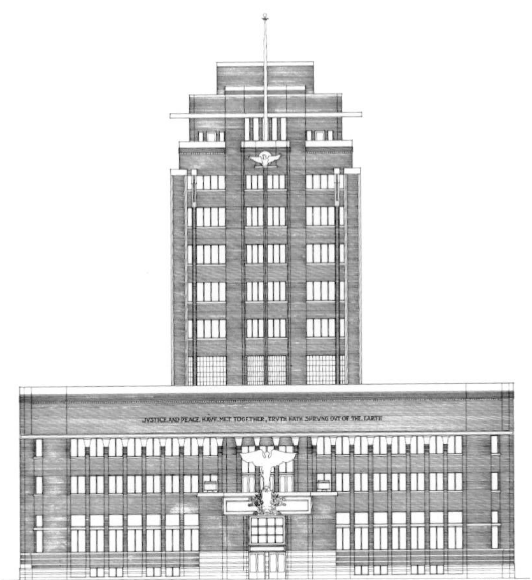

St. Bartholomew's Church, 1919

Park Avenue at East 51st Street
New York, New York

Bertram Grosvenor Goodhue

The Byzantine splendor of St. Bartholomew's Church provides landmark architecture and a cherished garden spot on Park Avenue's last non-commercial site. This picturesque complex is dominated by the church, an elaborately carved and articulated edifice made of salmon-colored brick and Indiana limestone; it is characterized by a flattened dome and a pinnacle that soars to 570 feet. The main entry incorporates a portal designed by McKim, Mead & White in 1902, which served as the entrance to the old St. Bartholomew's Church on Madison Avenue. After Bertram Goodhue's death, a community house was built in a compatible style. Also in the spirit of compatibility, the General Electric tower next door is surfaced in the same warm-colored brick as the Church.

Goodhue's intricate design and lavish ornamentation is a startling contrast to his West Coast work. At the San Diego Exhibition of 1915, he single-handedly revived the Spanish Colonial style still popular today.

In the 1980s, St. Bartholomew's Church ignited a storm of controversy. The church planned to demolish the community house and part of the garden to make way for a large, commercial office tower on the valuable Park Avenue site. The request was denied by New York City's Landmarks Preservation Society, and the church is taking its case to the United States Supreme Court.

The church is open from 8:00 AM to 6:00 PM Monday through Friday. Sunday services take place at 9:00 and 11:00 AM, and tours are given every Sunday following the 11:00 AM service. The number to call for visitor information is (212) 751-1616, extension 212.

Within just a few blocks of the church are a number of twentieth-century architectural monuments, including Grand Central Station, the Pepsi-Cola Building (now Walt Disney headquarters), the Seagram Building, and Lever House.

Barnsdall House, 1921 (Hollyhock House)

4808 Hollywood Boulevard
Los Angeles, California

Frank Lloyd Wright

For Frank Lloyd Wright, the commission for Barnsdall House was the beginning of an idyllic "California Romanza," but for the Chicago oil heiress and art patron Aline Barnsdall, the dream turned out otherwise. Barnsdall's initial request was fairly modest: a home for herself and her young daughter, Sugartop, and a small theater on the property to bring Chicago-style culture to town. With Wright's encouragement, the project mushroomed into a full-blown cultural complex, but only the main residence and two guest cottages were completed.

The two-story main house is situated on top of Olive Hill, contradicting Wright's usual conviction that a building should be of the landscape, not on it. But because the house was to be the center of the 36-acre cultural compound, Wright let it command the hill.

Wright's fascination with ancient Mayan forms is evident. The plain, beige, concrete walls angle slightly inward to imply a subtle pyramid. Cast concrete bands featuring stylized hollyhocks (Barnsdall's favorite flower) provide the ornamentation, both inside and out.

Wright used his favorite cross-shaped plan, which allowed him to juxtapose inside and outside "rooms." To enter the house, you'll walk through an outdoor pergola, and through a low, dark foyer. From here, the enormous living room opens up. Its soft gold walls and pale, watercolor ceiling practically glow. The living room fireplace is virtually mythologized. A reflecting pool is sunk into the floor around it, and a cubist-inspired concrete mural above the mantle depicts Aline Barnsdall's life. Wright also designed much of the furniture, including dining room chairs with the hollyhock motif running up the back.

Aline Barnsdall hated Hollyhock House. The roof leaked, and the cultural complex failed to materialize. After only six years, she donated the property to the city of Los Angeles, which now operates it with the Cultural Affairs Department.

Tours are given Tuesday, Wednesday, and Thursday, hourly from 10:00 AM until 1:00 PM, and on Saturday and Sunday from noon until 3:00 PM. For information, call (213) 662-7272.

Ford Glass Plant, 1922

3001 Miller Road
Dearborn, Michigan

Albert Kahn Associates

A factory building does more than simply shelter an industrial process; the structure serves as an integral part of that process. The Ford Glass Plant is regarded as a classic for its remarkably thorough integration of structural design into a factory process, in this case a process for the manufacture of plate glass for car windows.

Good working light was a primary concern for industrial architects. Rooftop "sawtooth" windows, oriented to the north for all-day illumination, had become a factory design standard. Albert Kahn was among the first architects to abandon this practice, resisting the constriction of north-facing glazing on the placement and alignment of the assembly lines below. To free the hands of the industrial process engineer, Kahn was prepared to design overhead windows facing in every direction, and he routinely did so.

In the Ford Glass Plant, moreover, another major concern was heat—terrific heat—for glass-making requires melting sand in furnaces held at temperatures near 2,500 degrees Fahrenheit. The four smokestacks at the south end mark these furnaces and the beginning of the process line, which extends north through the building. Above the furnaces, in the most intensely heated regions of the building, are the highest roofs. The rising heat was permitted to escape through retractable steel vents 25 feet high. Monitors form roofs extending longitudinally north along the top of the building, placed at heights that help capture and exhaust heat from the glass cooling and processing lines below.

In the era of this building's design, most manufacturers still used multi-story wall-window structures built with reinforced concrete. In the Ford Glass Plant, Kahn used brick only to a height of 14 feet. Above that line, however, he employed only corrugated steel, steel sash, and glass. These materials were sheathed over, rather than abutted between, the building's columns. As a result of this simplification, the cladding process was quick, sure, and inexpensive. Ford was interested in the earliest possible date for production to begin, and rapid cladding proved an excellent way to speed the plant's construction. The Ford Glass Plant became a prototype for much subsequent industrial architecture, and is the lineal ancestor of the little beloved but immensely useful pre-manufactured steel utility buildings that emerged after World War II.

The plant (now considerably altered) is located within Ford's Rouge complex; access is limited and must be pre-approved. To arrange a visit, call (313) 337-3187.

Lincoln Memorial, 1922

The Mall at 23rd Street N.W.
Washington, D.C.

Henry Bacon

The classic ideal of the Greek Doric temple inspired the Lincoln Memorial, one of Washington's most revered public monuments. There is an eternal stillness about this structure, with its perfect proportions, pure white marble, and statue of Abraham Lincoln in profound contemplation, as if for all people and for all time.

Classically minded Henry Bacon designed the 100-foot-tall monument, which rises to approximately nine stories. Following ancient Greek rules for temple construction, Bacon's columns taper toward the top and are slightly convex to correct for visual distortions. Inside the monument, two rows of Ionic columns frame the famous statue of Lincoln by David Chester French, which is considered one of the world's great sculptures.

In some ways, the temple commemorates the Union as much as its hero. The Lincoln Memorial occupies a place of honor at one end of the Mall's reflecting pool, opposite the Washington Monument, and each of its Doric columns represents one of the thirty-six states in the Union at Lincoln's death. When the memorial was completed, there were forty-eight states and their names are inscribed on the parapet above the columns. Murals by Jules Guerin render the freeing of the slaves and the unity of North and South, Lincoln's major achievements.

SCHINDLER HOUSE, 1922

833 North Kings Road
West Hollywood, California

R.M. Schindler

The vision of southern California as a tropical Eden inspired the creation of R.M. Schindler's innovative house and studio, one of the first International Style houses in America. A native of Austria who had apprenticed with Frank Lloyd Wright, Schindler thought it was possible to live outdoors in California year-round, and he devised a brilliant design combining outside "rooms" with the inside ones to take advantage of the warm, sunny climate. A social visionary as well, Schindler joined with a friend, the engineer Clyde Chase, in building a house for both their families to share.

Before long, Schindler learned that he was wrong about the weather—winter finally came, and sometimes it rained. The social experiment also proved unworkable and the friends departed after two years. But the accomplishment of his design remains.

The gray concrete house is just one story with a flat roof, and it is set well back in the landscape of its city lot. The open, pinwheel shape of the plan is a result of the two-family program, which called for a studio and adjacent yard for each couple. The families were to share a common kitchen, an outdoor living room with a fireplace, and a rooftop sleeping porch outfitted with special "sleeping baskets."

Schindler intended the house to be inexpensive (wrong again). For "economy," he and Chase devised an early form of tilt-wall construction by pouring concrete into rectangular forms; the interstices were then filled with glass to create tall, narrow windows. Large, redwood-framed sliding doors, now glass but initially covered in canvas, must have given the house the feeling of a sophisticated tent.

Schindler lived and worked in this house from its completion until his death in 1953. Richard Neutra and his wife shared the house with Schindler in the late 1920s, when it was a center of the Los Angeles avant-garde society. During the 1960s and 1970s, the house became something of a modern ruin. Restoration is in process, and the house is open on Saturday and Sunday from 1:00 to 4:00 PM and by appointment. For information, call (310) 651-1510.

Mrs. G.M. Millard House, 1923

645 Prospect Crescent
Pasadena, California

Frank Lloyd Wright

In the 1920s, Frank Lloyd Wright designed a series of houses in the Los Angeles area that represented a change in direction from his previous residential work.

These new houses, of which the Millard House is the masterpiece, were constructed of an ingenious concrete block cast with geometric patterns. With a single stroke, Wright had invented a new method of construction with built-in decorative possibilities; the pierced concrete blocks introduced an element of openness, light, and airiness to the overall composition. The concrete blocks were cast in molds three or four inches thick, with channels through which steel reinforcing rods were run vertically and horizontally to "knit" the building together on the site. This method came to be known as the "knit block," although the actual process of weaving the blocks together turned out to be more of a nightmare than an improvement.

Besides the differences in construction technique and materials, the Millard house differs radically from the Prairie Houses in its overall orientation. Where the Prairie House was long, low, horizontal, and ground-hugging, the Millard house stands tall and vertical. Compact in plan, the three-story house is vertically organized, with the entrance, living room, guest room, and garage located at the center level, the dining room and kitchen on the floor below, and the master bedroom on the floor above. The two-story living room opens onto a balcony at the front of the house and overlooks the luxurious garden terrace and pool at ground level. The architect's eldest son, Lloyd Wright, supervised the construction and designed both the landscaping and a 1926 studio addition. The compact Millard house is also known as La Miniatura.

The house is a private residence, located just a few blocks from Gamble House.

STORER HOUSE, 1923

8161 Hollywood Boulevard
West Hollywood, California

Frank Lloyd Wright

Rambling up its Hollywood hill, the Storer house shows the results of Frank Lloyd Wright's second experiment with textile block construction and Mayan imagery, which characterized his work in Los Angeles in the early 1920s. Wright's concrete blocks are naturally not ordinary ones, but are custom blocks of plain and patterned designs, some with geometric cutouts to allow the passage of light and air.

Wright's ability to generate excitement and repose simultaneously is seen in this structure. Here he works this magic almost exclusively with the textile blocks, a natural material with a lively pattern. Double-faced, the blocks provide finished surfaces on interior as well as exterior walls.

The block pattern starts at the street, with a 10-foot retaining wall at the foot of the hill that also forms a railing for the terrace on the other side. Behind this wall, the house consists of two wings: a single-story dining and service floor at ground level, and the main entry and two-story living room to the rear of the site. It is this lofty living room, with its Mayan-inspired columns and tall, narrow windows, that constitutes the main façade on the street side; the room opens to a garden court toward the hill.

Wright would soon turn away from the textile block experiment, but at Storer house the construction technique captures Wright's dream of the California Romanza, a house "just haunting enough in a whole so organic as to lose all evidence of how it was made."

The house is a private residence.

AMERICAN RADIATOR BUILDING, 1924

40 West 40th Street, between Fifth and Sixth Avenues
New York, New York

Raymond Hood

When the American Radiator Building was designed, automobile radiators were black boxes often capped with bright header tanks and fittings crafted of polished brass. The building appears to have been inspired by its namesake, as it is black and gold. In fact, Raymond Hood was an industrial designer as well as an architect, and he had designed radiator covers for the company that would commission him to design the building.

There was more to it than this, of course. Hood seems to have chosen black brick to counteract the effect he noticed in light-colored buildings where windows seem to become rows of black rectangles. Hood's black brick was meant to de-emphasize the windows and make the skyscraper appear more monolithic. The effect was quite dramatic when the building was new, but things have changed. Now most of the windows stand out because their shades are defiantly white. The black monolithic effect, so famous in texts, is not much in evidence today.

To break up the rather somber black-on-blackness of the original tower, Hood embellished the top with gold terra-cotta. But this originally splendid effect has also diminished over the years. In 1992, the building looked virtually abandoned. The building is a New York City landmark, so perhaps a revivification is in the works.

The street number above the doors, which is 40, has lost its "0," but the building is easy to identify. The American Radiator Building faces Bryant Park behind the New York Public Library on Fifth Avenue. Within walking distance are two other famous Hood works, Rockefeller Center at Fifth Avenue and 55th Street and the Daily News Building at 42nd Street between Second and First Avenues.

For general information, call the New York Landmarks Preservation Foundation at (212) 983-1197.

Ennis House, 1924

2607 Glendower Avenue
Los Angeles, California

Frank Lloyd Wright

Even from a distance of several miles, the appearance of Ennis House silhouetted against the sky commands attention. A virtual Mayan fortress high on a hill in Griffith Park, overlooking Los Angeles, the house appears to be the master of all it surveys. A favorite location of Hollywood studio executives, the house has starred in many movies, including the infamous *Blade Runner*.

Ennis House is the largest of Frank Lloyd Wright's Los Angeles "knit-block" designs. With these specially constructed concrete blocks, Wright hoped to achieve a simplified construction method as well as an integral ornamentation for his designs. At Ennis House, the 16-inch blocks feature a geometric motif based on the square. Solid blocks form bands of decoration on the long, low garden walls, while open fretwork blocks are used to cover great expanses of the exterior walls.

The geometrically patterned blocks are also used inside the house, where they contribute to the atmosphere of ancient secrets. Changes in ceiling heights and lighting add to the drama. A long, low entrance hall leads to a stairway with a roof abruptly soaring to 22 feet. Wright's art glass windows and doors are beautifully preserved—especially the wisteria mosaic above the living room fireplace.

In 1980, the house was donated by its owner, Augustus Oliver Brown, to the Trust for Preservation of Cultural Heritage. It is open the second Saturday in January, March, May, July, September, and November. Tours are available by reservation only; tickets must be purchased by mail prior to the tour, although occasional exceptions are made, especially for foreign visitors. For tour information, call (213) 660-0607.

Andalucia Apartments, 1926

1471-75 Havenhurst Drive
West Hollywood, California

Arthur and Nina Zwebell

Courtyard housing is a Los Angeles specialty, a civilized response to the balmy climate and mission tradition. One of the earliest, and still among the most charming, examples of courtyard architecture is the Andalucia. This idyllic little compound, built by Arthur Zwebell along with his interior decorator wife, Nina, helped establish the model for the many garden apartments that would be built in Los Angeles and other parts of the country.

The Andalucia is a symmetrical two-story structure that resonates with mission-style features: the plastered, arched entry; a red-tiled roof shading a second-story balcony with hand-turned balustrades; and, in the main courtyard, the Spanish-inspired fountain tiled in a bright and colorful mosaic. As for its courtyard, the Andalucia actually has a series of three, all luxuriously landscaped: an entry court, a central patio with the fountain as centerpiece, and a pool and patio area to the rear.

The Zwebells were not architects and would soon turn their talents to stage-set design, but in the Andalucia they created a magical place that over the years became home to movie stars including Clara Bow and Marlon Brando.

The apartments are privately occupied.

Los Angeles Central Library, 1926

630 West Fifth Street
Los Angeles, California

Bertram Grosvenor Goodhue and Carleton Winslow, Sr.

A beloved Los Angeles landmark, the Central Library is a delightful monument: majestic and dignified, as befits a civic touchstone, but friendly and open to visitors at the same time.

When it was built, the library set new standards for eclecticism. Its blending of Byzantine, Egyptian, Roman, and Art Deco themes in a modern structure was considered quite a breakthrough, and it provided a model for such major civic buildings as the Los Angeles City Hall of 1928 and Goodhue's renowned Nebraska State Capitol. The library design was all the more remarkable considering the architects' recent past. At the San Diego Exposition of 1915, their Spanish Colonial design literally stopped the clock and initiated a national enthusiasm for the mission style. With the library, they were changing architectural directions for the nation once again.

The library's lovely park-like grounds provide a perfect surround for the massive rectangular building, with its chunky central tower that rises to a colorful, tiled pyramid at the top. Variations in the lawn and building design appear on every side, but the most impressive approach displays fascinating sculptured plinths by Lee Laurie that personify the ideals of Science, Art, Statecraft, Philosophy, Letters, and History.

A 1986 fire gutted the library, and Hardy Holzman Pfeiffer is restoring the artful interiors: enormous murals originally painted by Dean Cornwell, depicting the history of California; magnificent stenciled ceilings; and a vaulted central rotunda. The architects will also restore the West Lawn to its pre-parking lot grandeur and reflection-pool elegance. A 300,000-square-foot addition, sympathetic to the original, is scheduled to reopen in 1993. Call (213) 612-3200 for information and schedules.

Lovell Beach House, 1926

13th Street at Beach Walk
Balboa Peninsula
Newport Beach, California

R.M. Schindler

One of the great monuments of modern architecture, Lovell Beach House was the first major International Style house in America. Built for a progressive Los Angeles physician, the house represents R.M. Schindler's breakthrough into the realm of advanced design.

Lovell Beach House displays the pure "machined" characteristics of the International Style: the appearance of weightlessness, white stucco walls, long horizontal lines, and ribbon windows set almost flush with the exterior walls. But on close inspection—for example, the geometric window designs that look a little like Mondrian, and a little like Wright—Schindler's modernism looks both personal and artistic.

The beach house combines grace, lightness, and strength. Schindler brings enormous buoyancy to this fascinating and complex design. The house is lifted above the beach on five concrete cradles that allow light and sand beneath the structure. From near the center of the ground level, a pair of graceful staircases leads up to the main living floor of the two-story house. This main floor is a long, lofty living room open to the ocean, with service rooms to the rear. Upstairs, four bedrooms with sleeping porches are recessed toward the rear of the house.

A private residence, the beach house precedes Dr. Lovell's equally famous residence by Richard Neutra in the Los Feliz section of Los Angeles, which was built a few years later (see page 52).

Bayou Bend, 1927

One Wescott Street
Houston, Texas

John F. Staub

In Houston, a house by John Staub is in the same category as an Addison Mizner house in Palm Beach. It is architecture that succeeds in capturing the dreams, myths, and history of a place so thoroughly that it becomes preferred style—the local classic. The most beloved Staub house, Bayou Bend, is also the most accessible. This gracious southern mansion, with its stunning gardens, is now a museum featuring a premier collection of American furniture, paintings, metals, ceramics, glass, and textiles.

Just five minutes from the downtown skyscrapers, Bayou Bend seems to be in another world entirely. Set within fourteen acres of leafy woods and eight distinctive gardens, the mansion is the centerpiece. John Staub called it "Latin Colonial," a pale-pink stucco house that is classic in design and proportion but festive with cast-iron balconies and trim reminiscent of the New Orleans French Quarter. Staub designed Bayou Bend for a famous Houston philanthropist, Ima Hogg. The only daughter of a former Texas governor, "Miss Ima" was beginning to assemble the collection that would grow to almost 5,000 pieces and prompt her to turn the mansion into a museum. During her long and active life (she died in 1975 at age 93), friendships with Henry Francis DuPont of Winterthur and Joseph Downs, curator of the Metropolitan Museum's American Wing, were among the influences on her selections.

The gardens of Bayou Bend, designed by Ellen Shipman of New York, were carved out of the "dense thicket." Like the collection, the gardens also evolved gradually and today there are eight—White, Butterfly, East, Diana, Clio, Euterpe, Carla, and Topiary—plus the areas of native woods.

Bayou Bend, the museum, opened in 1966 and is owned by the Museum of Fine Arts, comprising the museum's Decorative Arts Wing. The house is closed for renovation through 1993, although the gardens remain open. For reopening information, call (713) 529-8773.

Chicago Tribune Tower, 1927

435 North Michigan Avenue
Chicago, Illinois

Howells and Hood

The skyscraper was born in Chicago, where fascination with tall buildings reached fever pitch in 1922. In that year, the *Chicago Tribune* announced a design competition for the newspaper's new home, symbolizing the power of the press through advanced architecture. The opportunity to design a structure of such high visibility, along with the prospect of a $50,000 prize, drew 260 entries—100 of them from Europe. Architectural critic Paul Goldberger described the competition as "something of a world's fair of skyscraper design."

The winning entry, by John Mead Howells and Raymond Hood, reflected the accepted model for skyscraper design in America—the Gothic cathedral—right up to the circle of buttresses surrounding its crown. It was a lavishly detailed historical design, but a solid and well-portioned one. It triumphed over submissions of the most advanced European modernists, who had yet to build any skyscrapers of their own.

If the American winner was traditional, the European entries presented bold skyscraper innovations. The most highly acclaimed design, a stepped-back tower by Eliel Saarinen of Finland, won second prize, and prompted Saarinen to move to Chicago. Walter Gropius and Adolph Meyer submitted a Bauhaus-style skyscraper, and Adolph Loos' envisioned an 11-story square base surmounted by a gigantic Doric column. The Europeans lost the competition but won the war. Their entries marked the official transition to modern skyscraper design.

Within the last decades of the twentieth century, historical styles regained some measure of respect. The Chicago Tribune Tower has become a venerable landmark in downtown Chicago. Its lobby is open from 8:00 AM to 5:00 PM Monday through Friday. For visitor information, call (312) 222-3232. Also, the building exterior is included in tours conducted by the Chicago Architecture Foundation, 224 South Michigan Avenue, (312) 922-TOUR.

Graumann's Chinese Theatre, 1927 (Mann's Chinese Theatre)

6925 Hollywood Boulevard
Los Angeles, California

Meyer and Holler

A flamboyant picture palace from the grand old days of Hollywood, Mann's Chinese Theatre now draws thousands of tourists each year who are eager to match their handprints and footprints with those of the stars.

The theater was the last one built by showman Sid Graumann, who invented the Hollywood premiere as a public relations event. Graumann's grasp of the spectacular is exhibited in his last movie house, designed by Meyer and Holler. Graumann reputedly imported pillars from a real Chinese temple for the forecourt. But whatever the Chinese theme is lacking in total authenticity, it more than makes up for in sheer audacity.

The entire ensemble clamors for attention. The pagoda-style copper roof on a central tower is the high point, and is flanked by two masonry wings 40-feet tall that extend from the tower to form an elliptical forecourt. The walls facing the street feature full-height pylons on either end of the façade; the pylons are embellished with decorative bands and topped by tall, copper obelisks shooting flames. The walls are green, the doors are Chinese lacquer red.

Most visitors, however, come not for the movies, but to see the signatures—handprints and footprints of the stars—encased in the forecourt's concrete. Local legends credit Douglas Fairbanks and Mary Pickford with starting the tradition by stepping accidentally into the wet cement; others insist it was Norma Talmadge.

Movies are still shown here, and there are neon dragons calling attention to the current marquee. For schedules, call (213) 464-8111.

Los Angeles City Hall, 1928

200 North Spring Street
Los Angeles, California

John C. Austin, John and Donald Parkinson, Albert C. Martin, Sr.

The exuberant spirit of Los Angeles in the 1920s is captured in its symbol of civic pride, City Hall. A consortium of local architects produced this eclectic but memorable design—an Italian-style arched entry and courtyard at the street, a jazzy, stepped-back tower 28 stories tall, and a pyramid topping the roof. Inside, the central rotunda combines the classic marble grandeur of a cathedral with Hollywood "show biz" in more or less peaceful coexistence.

This civic monument became known to millions of Americans in the 1950s, when its image served to identify the setting of the hit television series "Dragnet." But while gaining fame across the country during that decade, City Hall lost some of its prominence at home. A change of building code revoked the former height limitations that had ensured the prominence of City Hall. Now, of course, the 28-story City Hall has been far outstripped in size, but it nevertheless continues to outshine many of its soaring sisters.

Guides conduct tours of the tower and provide a capsule history of Los Angeles. There is an observation deck on the 27th floor for breathtaking views of the sprawling city. For general information, call (213) 485-2121.

Philadelphia Museum of Art, 1928

Benjamin Franklin Parkway at 26th Street
Philadelphia, Pennsylvania

Borie, Trumbauer & Zantzinger

The Philadelphia Museum of Art is called the "Philadelphia Acropolis," and it is in fact one of the largest Greek-temple-style buildings in the world. As a civic event, the museum and the Benjamin Franklin Parkway complement one another in a mixture of City Beautiful planning and Beaux Arts classicism. The stately boulevard provides a properly awesome approach to this obviously important monument. Given the building's size, its classical grandeur, and the art and treasures inside, visiting the museum is a little like visiting Versailles.

The parkway entrance presents the museum's most imposing face: a central portico flanked by symmetrical porticoed wings that form an honor courtyard with a fountain. A wide, ceremonial stairway (famous as the place where the movie hero Rocky "goes the distance") ushers visitors from the street to the courtyard, but the main entrance is on the opposite side, overlooking the Schuylkill River. A walk around the building conveys its full size and the intricacy of such classical detailing as colorful friezes, terra-cotta ornamentation, and griffins on the roof. The building itself is strongly colored the intense natural yellow of its main materials, Mankota and Kasota stone (500,000 tons of it).

The vast museum was built for a city that owned very little art. But the museum's collection of artwork and period rooms now ranks as one of the best in the country. Permanent and temporary exhibits are installed primarily on the two palatial upper floors, E-shaped in plan. The heart of this building is a great, marble stairway flanked with Ionic columns and covered with a barrel-vaulted ceiling. In the dim inner light, this enormous central well, with its marble walls and floors, seems ancient and austere.

The museum's architects—especially Horace Trumbauer—were socially prominent civic boosters. The firm won the museum design by competition, although the design changed radically and frequently in the twenty years between the commission and the completion.

The Philadelphia Museum of Art is open Tuesday to Sunday 10:00 AM to 5:00 PM. Closed Monday and legal holidays. Gallery tours are offered on the hour. For general information, call (215) 763-8100; to hear a recording of daily events, call (215) 787-5488. To arrange special or group tours, call (215) 787-5449.

Worth Avenue, 1928

Via Mizner and Via Parigi
Palm Beach, Florida

Addison Mizner

The rich and seductive tropical style of old Palm Beach is largely the vision of one man, the self-taught Addison Mizner. A well-traveled society architect and bon vivant, Mizner arrived in Florida from his practice in New York. Almost immediately he began transforming this southern jungle land into an elegant winter resort for the wealthy. His clients' dreams, and the architecture of Spain, the French Riviera, and Central America, inspired Mizner's basic formula: light stucco walls in pastel tints, topped with tile roofs and weathered cypress woodwork, and the inevitable coconut tree with its decorative tufted shape and play of light and shade.

The small, upscale shopping enclave off Worth Avenue dates to the early 1920s, when Mizner purchased Joe's Alligator Farm using money from his patron Paris Singer, heir to the sewing machine fortune. Mizner carved out four blocks between the Atlantic Ocean and Lake Worth. The cluster of shops, restaurants, and apartments was built in the same style as Mizner's fabulous villas, with cloistered arcades, Cuban barrel-tile roofs, stucco walls, Venetian arched windows, decorative railings, tiled stairways, and patios with fountains.

Worth Avenue's architecture has remained virtually unchanged. Exclusive boutiques can be found on two shopping levels, connected by steps, bridges, and passageways. Mizner's Mediterranean-style interiors provide instant antiquity via knotty cypress beams, coral keystone, *saultillo* tile floors and stencil painting. If you're "just looking," Mizner's creation of an intimate scale animated by constantly changing details is still a pleasure.

Mizner's office occupied a four-story tower on Worth Avenue. His practice resembled a one-man band: designing; building; manufacturing both clay roof tiles in his own kilns and ironwork with his own blacksmith; and reproducing furniture, which he sold by catalog. Mizner's contribution here is immortalized in the street name, Via Mizner (Via Parigi honors Paris Singer), and in the approximately thirty-six private homes still in Palm Beach. Several more villas incorrectly claim Mizner's cachet, but there is no doubt about the authenticity of Worth Avenue and the Everglades Club that anchors the west end of the avenue.

The Worth Avenue shops are open during regular retail hours. For information, call the Worth Avenue Association at (407) 659-6909.

Arizona Biltmore Hotel, 1929

24th Street and Missouri
Phoenix, Arizona

Albert Chase McArthur

According to the official version of events, Albert Chase McArthur designed the Arizona Biltmore Hotel. But it is the spirit of his collaborator, Frank Lloyd Wright, that pervades it, evidenced in the stretched proportions of the main entry with its oriental roof; the long, low spans of guest room floors; and the unique way the building reverberates with the textures and colors of the desert.

The notion of Frank Lloyd Wright working "incognito and behind the scenes," as he did here, contradicts all evidence of the great architect's ferocious ego. But in 1927, during a particularly low point in his on-again, off-again career, Wright came to Phoenix to assist his former apprentice from Oak Park.

There is no doubt that Wright created the hotel's most visible component: the distinctive combination of plain and patterned, pre-cast concrete blocks. Wright invented the molded block technique for La Miniatura in Hollywood in 1920 (the Millard House, see page 37), and he was taken with the fact that the patterned blocks contained their own "decoration." For the Biltmore, rectangular, gray, steel-reinforced blocks were molded on site from Arizona earth and sand. The decorative blocks feature a bas-relief resembling an abstract palm leaf, and recall ancient Aztec and Mayan motifs. Hollow in the center, the blocks are erected back to back, an ingenious method that provides effective insulation and allows both inner and outer walls to be constructed simultaneously.

Now a landmark hotel and conference center, the Arizona Biltmore is operated by Westin Hotels & Resorts. Since a 1973 fire destroyed the fourth floor and its beautiful copper roof, the hotel has been rebuilt and remodeled six times under the supervision of Taliesin Associates Architects, Wright's successor firm. If anything, the hotel is even more Wrightian than the original. New works based on Wright designs of the period are now installed, such as the lobby's spectacular back-lit geometrical stained-glass mural, *Saguaro Forms and Cactus Flowers*. Copies of Wright's *Biltmore Sprites*, recast from the 1914 original Midway Gardens sculptures, are located on the grounds.

For information, call the Biltmore at (602) 955-6600.

Bullocks Wilshire, 1929 (I. Magnin's Landmark Store)

3050 Wilshire Boulevard
Los Angeles, California

John and Donald Parkman

Greta Garbo bought her trousers in the men's department, Clark Gable ordered paisley wool ski suits, and William Randolph Hearst picked up swimsuits for San Simeon's house guests. While catering to a select clientele, this Art Deco masterpiece also represented retailing at its most radical.

Its suburban location was essentially shocking—people shopped downtown, but automobiles were changing the old ways, and Los Angeles was already a car town. The main entrance faced the parking lot rather than the street, another shocking departure. The forward-thinking owners, John Bullock and P.G. Winnett, envisioned the store as a cluster of individual boutiques. Prominent Los Angeles architects John Parkman and his son Donald first designed the store with a flat roof and multi-windowed façade. Then, Winnett and the younger Parkman discovered Art Deco and Bauhaus designs at the Exposition des Arts Decoratifs in Paris in 1925. This changed everything. Tearing up the original plans, they started over.

In its new incarnation, the store is shaped like an asymmetrical pyramid, stepping up from a five-story base to the ten-story tower, illuminated at night as a beacon to shoppers. Glazed terra-cotta covers much of the exterior, and a thin veneer of black granite surrounds the base. "Zigzag moderne" motifs provide much of the ornament. Copper spandrels embossed in a snowflake pattern border the windows, which rise up the building in vertical rows. Display windows at street level are framed like pictures, with cast brass and bronze overhangs embellished with flowers. Overall, the various metals and sculptural motifs make the building appear luminous.

The extraordinary interiors showed the work of thirteen artists and designers, famous and unheralded. They collaborated with the architects to turn the structural elements into works of art. Copper, nickel, bronze, and brass were combined with masonry, marble, cork, glass, and wood. Woven artworks were commissioned for the walls and floors, including seven carpets by Sonia Delauney.

In March, 1993, the store was closed by its corporate owner, Macy's. For further information, call the Los Angeles Conservancy at (213) 623-2489.

Philip Lovell House, 1929

4616 Dundee Drive
Los Angeles, California

Richard Neutra

It was not until 1932 that the International Style got its name, but outstanding examples of progressive European architecture began to crop up in America in the 1920s. One of the most accomplished of these was the Philip Lovell House, a "health house" designed by Richard Neutra for a Los Angeles physician and health faddist.

A native of Vienna, Neutra worked with Eric Mendelsohn, Otto Wagner, and Adolf Loos before moving to the United States in 1923. After a brief association with Frank Lloyd Wright, Neutra migrated to the West Coast, where Wright had several houses underway.

Here at Lovell House, only the broad, horizontal, cantilevered spans are reminiscent of Wright's work. Otherwise, the "modern" elements prevail: the boxy white modules, the flat walls and roof, the steel frame hung with panels of prefabricated concrete walls, and the standard steel windows. And then there is the architectural purity of the all-white exterior, and the overall sense that the interior volumes are weightlessly enclosed by the exterior elements. In effect, the Lovell House seems about to take off from its landing spot in the Hollywood Hills.

Neutra's breakthrough design of Lovell House became an instant landmark. The house was widely published and highly acclaimed, and it proved that architects and clients in America could be just as progressive as their European counterparts.

The house is a private residence.

Chicago Board of Trade Building, 1930

141 West Jackson Boulevard
Chicago, Illinois

Holabird & Root

A 32-foot-tall aluminum statue of Ceres, the Roman goddess of grain, tops the pyramidal roof of this Chicago landmark. Designed by sculptor John H. Stoors, Ceres is emblematic of what goes on inside: the vigorous daily exchange of contracts on commodities futures, including contracts on grains like corn and wheat. The building is simply a marketplace, but it takes on large symbolic importance. After all, fortunes are made and lost with incredible rapidity in this building's commodity trading "pits."

The Board of Trade building has a landmark-quality location at the end of a city canyon formed by LaSalle Street. Its great vertical windows ascending from the third-floor level reveal the location of the enormous trading room, which is six stories high. The windows are capped, at about the level of the ninth floor, by a monstrous inset clock, flanked and attended by two tall, sculpted figures (representing Risk and Reward, one may freely surmise). The clock marks the passage of the trading day. It also makes a metaphoric nod at the passage of time into the risky, unknowable regions of the future, while inside the traders try to control risk, as of a crop failure, through the artful purchase and sale of grain futures contracts. From the clock upward, the shaft of this skyscraper rises 45 stories to tower over the neighborhood.

The architects, Holabird and Root, took pains to emphasize the vertical. The horizontal lines are carefully understated. The spandrels of the towers, for example, are recessed and discontinuous. The firm, originally formed as Holabird and Roche, has roots in the Chicago architectural tradition that extend back to the late nineteenth century. After a change in partners in 1928, the firm produced an extraordinary series of skyscrapers of the modernistic type, including an addition to the Chicago Board of Trade and the especially notable Palmolive (now Playboy) building.

In the 1930s, the firm was strongly associated with the Art Deco style and the interiors show it. Inside the Board of Trade, at ground level, low corridors lined with shops lead to a lofty three-story lobby, which is regarded as a classic of Art Deco design. Notice the polished glass, nickel, and marble of these interiors, and how beautifully they affect the quality of the light. Then visit the trading room and hearken to the shouting in the pits. The 1982 addition by Helmut Jahn, an 11-story steel-and-glass atrium, is quite a contrast to the original building.

The exchange, including the Visitor's Center, is open from 8:00 AM until 2:00 PM Monday through Friday. For information, call (312) 435-3590. The exchange is featured on Chicago Architecture Foundation tours; for information, call (312) 922-TOUR.

Chrysler Building, 1930

405 Lexington Avenue
New York, New York

William van Alen

For a brief moment, the Chrysler Building won the "world's tallest building" contest going on among skyscraper developers. But the hubcap-studded landmark has endured as one of New York City's most beloved buildings. This Art Deco masterpiece has a liveliness and humor that lifts the spirits, whether viewed from up close, from a distance, or only in photographs (especially the one that shows William van Alen wearing a model of the Chrysler Building as a Halloween costume).

The 77-story Chrysler Building rises 1,048 feet to the top, where most of the action is. Van Alen realized that tall buildings were primarily defined by their pinnacles, and he created an extravaganza of Art Deco detail: five rows of stainless steel arches, diminishing in size toward the top of the building, with each row inset with triangular windows set in a zigzag pattern. A needle-like spire surmounts the entire creation. Curves and zigzags are combined imaginatively, reflecting the Art Deco style of the day as well as Mayan and Egyptian patterns of ancient times. The main shaft of the building receives a fantastic flourish—at each corner van Alen mounted stainless steel gargoyles representing the hood ornament of the 1929 Chrysler automobile. At night, the creation presents a lively show of lights.

The lobby of the Chrysler Building provides some of the best Art Deco detailing in New York City. Rich, red African marble sets the tone for the lobby, where the elevator doors are inlaid with wood and brass in masterful Art Deco patterns.

The Chrysler Building is open during regular business hours and you can walk in and see the spectacular lobby. On Friday at 12:30 PM, weather permitting, the Grand Central Partnership conducts tours of the Grand Central Station area, including the Chrysler Building. Groups meet in front of the Philip Morris Building on 42nd Street and Park Avenue. For information, call (212) 986-9217.

DAILY NEWS BUILDING, 1930

**220 East 42nd Street
at Second Avenue
New York, New York**

Raymond Hood

The remarkable Raymond Hood is famous for taking the Gothic Revival skyscraper to new heights (see the Chicago Tribune Tower of 1927, page 45)—and for helping to define the modern skyscraper's new look. His McGraw-Hill Building (see page 60) was the only American skyscraper in the 1932 International Style exhibition at the Museum of Modern Art in New York City.

With the Daily News Building, Hood captured the soaring quality of the skyscraper in the most modern way—with tall, vertical rows of white brick piers rising crisply toward the sky and culminating in a new, flat top. Although the building reminded many observers of newspapers laid end to end, the appearance resulted from practical considerations. The piers provide the cover for the structural system of steel beams, which alternate with rows of utility conduits to establish the exterior rhythm. New York City's setback requirements played a part in the overall shape, in conjunction with Hood's own shape-making skill.

In these last days before air-conditioning and fluorescent lighting became commonplace, the Daily News Building was built with operable windows. And in fact the windows were a crucial design issue. Hood based the interior modules on windows four-and-a-half-feet wide, the largest size a stenographer could open without assistance. Grappling with New York City zoning rules, Hood also convinced the owner to free up a 25-foot easement on the western lotline so the lower floors could have windows on all four sides.

In rejecting revivalism, Hood did not eliminate tradition altogether. The building's piers, which appear ramrod straight, actually curve slightly inward, like Greek columns. There is also subtle decoration; the spandrels feature a progressive geometric pattern of red and black brick, which enlivens the severity of the white brick piers. A 1960 annex by Harrison & Abramowitz continued Hood's original theme.

The building is open during regular business hours. Be sure to see the giant globe suspended in a cutout of the lobby floor; radiating from the sphere are brass strips set into the terrazzo that show the distance from New York to all the major cities of the world.

Walking tours of the neighborhood are conducted by the Grand Central Partnership, although routes vary and weather can be a factor. Groups meet at 12:30 PM on Friday in front of the Philip Morris Building at 42nd Street and Park Avenue. For information, call (212) 986-9217.

Miami Beach "Art Deco District," 1930-1939

Ocean Drive and Collins Avenue from 5th to 16th Streets
Miami Beach, Florida

Various architects

The renaissance of Miami Beach as a fantasy playground coincides with a renewed appreciation of its unique and colorful architectural heritage. Within the square-mile Architectural Historic District, there are over 650 significant structures, the largest concentration in the country. A light-hearted tropical style incorporating flowers, flamingos, and ocean liners was created by a small number of local architects who often lacked formal training but were wise in the ways of popular appeal.

Miami Beach architecture gained a huge new audience through its starring role as the stylish background of the television series, "Miami Vice." In real life, three different architectural styles can be distinguished, although the design elements are often intertwined.

The "classic" Art Deco buildings (1926–1936) are geometric but elegant, and richly ornamented with tropical themes. Later Art Deco buildings in the streamlined style known as "art moderne" mimicked the machines of motion: planes, trains, cars, and steamships. These are the buildings with rounded walls, eyebrow windows, and futuristic towers; colorful bands of painted racing stripes provide most of the decoration. In the Mediterranean revival buildings, arched windows, clay-tile barrel roofs, stucco walls, wrought iron gates, and courtyards evoke an old world mystique that could be set in Spain, Italy, France, or Morocco.

The Miami Design Preservation League is the primary source for information and activities. On Saturday at 10:30 AM, the League conducts ninety-minute walking tours of the area. The group meets at the League's Welcome Center at 1244 Ocean Drive at Collins Avenue; reservations are not required. In January, the League hosts its big annual event, the Art Deco Weekend Festival. For free-form touring, the League has also published a 192-page paperback entitled *Miami Beach Art Deco Guide*, which you can pick up at the Welcome Center. For information, call (305) 672-2014.

Aluminaire House, 1931

New York Institute of Technology Campus
Carlton Avenue
Central Islip, Long Island, New York

Albert Frey with Lawrence Kocher

Aluminaire House—"A House for Contemporary Life"—first appeared as an exhibit at the Allied Arts and Building Products Exhibition held in New York in 1931. Designed in one week, constructed in ten days, costing 25 cents each cubic foot, this metal-kit prototype was meant to light the way toward progressive, affordable housing.

The first steel and metal house in America, Aluminaire House reflected the fashionable European fascination with machines, together with the American reality of new materials, such as metal and glass, and new technology for using them. Innovations were many. The three-story rectangle was framed with light aluminum beams and sheathed in narrow-ribbed aluminum joined by washers and screws of the same material. All the window frames and doors were framed with steel. The walls were backed with paper-covered insulation board, a composition three inches thick that was said to provide more insulation than 13 inches of masonry.

Of the three interior levels, the only full floor is the middle one, which contains the main living spaces, including a living room two stories tall. The ground level is given over to a porch, a garage, and utility space; the upper floor provides a library, a shower room that cantilevers over the living room below, and a roof terrace covered by its own patch of lawn. With a completeness almost unimaginable on such a short schedule and budget, Aluminaire featured built-in furniture—including inflatable chairs—and ultraviolet lighting for indoor tanning.

Aluminaire House was designed by Albert Frey, a Swiss émigré and crusading modernist who had worked with Le Corbusier and had been in the United States for only one year. His partner, Lawrence Kocher, was an American architect and magazine writer who promoted the progressive spirit of machine-age architecture. The partnership was short-lived; Kocher remained in the east, but in 1934 Frey set up a practice in Palm Springs, California, where he continued to advance his modern ideas.

Only one Aluminaire House was ever built, but it made history as the few American buildings in the 1932 International Style exhibit at New York's Museum of Modern Art. After several rebuildings, Aluminaire House has a new home at the New York Institute of Technology campus on Long Island. Architecture students are reconstructing the metal-kit house. When complete (projected circa 1994), the house will become a museum, open to the public. Aluminaire House archives will be housed there, along with research materials on affordable housing. For information, call (516) 348-3363.

EMPIRE STATE BUILDING, 1931

Fifth Avenue at 34th Street
New York, New York

Shreve, Lamb, and Harmon

The Empire State Building made its debut as the world's tallest building—rising almost a quarter of a mile to 102 stories—and an almost universal symbol of New York City's energy and prominence. It was designed tall to capture the height record, but also to make money, since the building was conceived as a speculative real estate venture.

Workers labored twenty-four hours a day to construct this mammoth tower in just eight months. This feat was possible 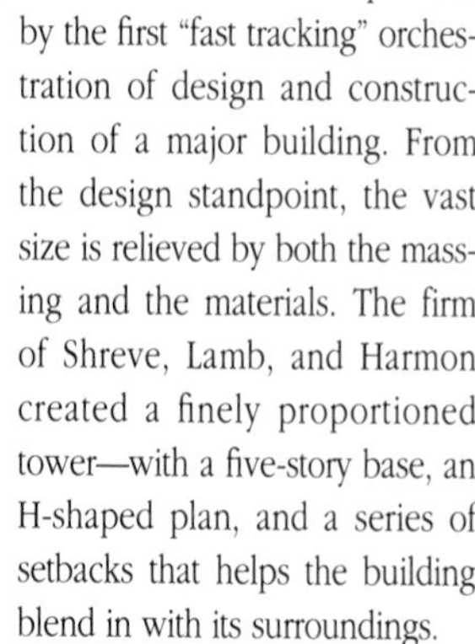 by the first "fast tracking" orchestration of design and construction of a major building. From the design standpoint, the vast size is relieved by both the massing and the materials. The firm of Shreve, Lamb, and Harmon created a finely proportioned tower—with a five-story base, an H-shaped plan, and a series of setbacks that helps the building blend in with its surroundings.

In many ways, the Empire State Building is remarkably reserved. Its monochromatic color scheme—gray Indiana limestone brightened by bands of aluminum and nickel—is extremely low key.

The Empire State Building and its famous observatories on the 86th and 102nd floors are open daily, including weekends and holidays, from 9:30 AM to midnight. Tickets can be purchased until 11:30 PM on the concourse level. Evening views are quite spectacular. For information, call (212) 736-3100.

Kingswood School for Girls, 1931 (Cranbrook Kingswood School)

Cranbrook Academy of Art
1221 Woodward Avenue
Bloomfield Hills, Michigan

Eliel Saarinen

The founding of Cranbrook Academy in 1924 by publisher George G. Booth had the intended effect of providing a rare enclave of artistic instruction, and the fortuitous result of capturing the talents of Eliel Saarinen, the great Finnish architect, who planned to return to his homeland after two years spent teaching at the University of Michigan. Saarinen received the commission to masterplan the campus, to design the buildings and supervise their construction, and to teach architecture as well. It was a commission that was to last for twenty-five years and would produce one of the modern masterpieces of academic architecture and Saarinen's most comprehensive work.

Kingswood School for Girls, with its warm, tan brick, and copper roof, was designed by Saarinen in 1929, constructed in 1930, and completed in 1931. Judging from the overall massing of the school, the ideas of Frank Lloyd Wright were influential: exemplified by the stretched proportion of the main section, with its high horizontal windows tucked beneath a hipped roof and overhanging eaves, as well as by the adjacent wing, which also shows horizontal bands of windows and overhanging eaves. Internally, the changing levels of floors and ceilings and the interior openness are somewhat in the Wrightian style as well. Saarinen, however, imparts his own convictions to all his treatments. Especially noticeable are the telescoping chimneys, a motif that recurs throughout the building.

Over the years, Cranbrook Academy has been a most prominent force in the training of artists and designers, fulfilling Booth's early vision of an institution on the order of the American Academy in Rome. The 125-acre campus is open and you can drive around and see the Girls' School and many other fine Saarinen buildings. The Saarinen-designed art museum is open to the public from 1:00 to 5:00 PM Wednesday through Sunday. Saarinen's own home has also been restored to reflect the way it appeared in 1938, when he last lived there, and it is also open to the public. For information and tour requests, call (313) 645-3142.

McGraw-Hill Building, 1931

330 West 42nd Street
New York, New York

Raymond Hood

When the Museum of Modern Art in New York organized its first exhibition of architecture in 1932, it celebrated those buildings designed in accordance with the principles of the European avant-garde. The term "International Style" was coined to describe these buildings, which were simultaneously lionized and institutionalized by the exhibition. Only one New York skyscraper was deemed worthy of admission into this elite group—the McGraw-Hill Building designed by Raymond Hood, whose work had evolved in the preceding decade from the neo-Gothic Chicago Tribune Tower to the heights of modernism.

"The McGraw-Hill Building comes nearest to achieving aesthetically the expression of the enclosed steel cage," proclaimed the exhibition catalog, intending a compliment. Indeed, the 60-story building's industrial toughness and ribbon windows are all modern, while the color and finishes are more "moderne" or Art Deco, the latest style. Colorful and catchy, the McGraw-Hill Building is clad in a vivid greenish-blue terra-cotta that belies the severity of the structure. The office floors step in three stages, capped by an enormous signboard, creating a shape and an impression that Vincent Skully describes as "proto jukebox."

The McGraw-Hill Company moved to new offices in the 1970s, and now the building is occupied by other tenants. But the McGraw-Hill name, in its original Art Deco style, is still displayed on the main façades.

The building is open during regular business hours.

SUNSET TOWERS, 1931
(ST. JAMES CLUB HOTEL)

8358 Sunset Boulevard
Los Angeles, California

Leland A. Bryant

Sunset Towers was designed by Leland A. Bryant to bring Art Deco elegance from Europe to the United States, and especially to Hollywood's movie star clientele. Errol Flynn, Jean Harlow, Clark Gable, Howard Hughes, and Marilyn Monroe were early residents.

The luxurious apartment house consisted of forty-six apartments on fourteen floors. It was set high up in the Hollywood Hills and offered a spectacular view of the city. When it opened, its size and distinctive Art Deco style were rivaled only by the unprecedented technology employed in its construction. Other buildings have their foundations cast into solid bedrock, but Sunset Towers was built on "rockers" to make it one of the first earthquake-proof buildings in Los Angeles. Its greatest technical distinction, however, was as the first all-electric apartment building in California, and its electric shaving plugs, set beside etched-glass plaques in bathrooms with special moldings, became famous throughout Hollywood.

One of the finest examples of Art Deco architecture in Los Angeles, the building's exterior is pale gray with silver highlights featuring intricate molding. The Los Angeles architect apparently loved machines and movement as much as any European architect of the time, for over the entry he mounted a concrete frieze entitled, "The Age of Travel," depicting U-boats, airplanes, and a zeppelin.

After a long, sad period of neglect, Sunset Towers has been massively renovated as the St. James Club/Los Angeles. Classic Art Deco furnishings were reproduced by Italian craftsmen according to the original specifications, including gondola beds by Emile-Jacques Ruhlmann, ebony desks by Pierre Chareau, and serpentine armchairs by Eileen Gray.

Sunset Towers began its new life as a grand hotel in 1988. For general information, call (213) 654-7100.

Folger Shakespeare Library, 1932

201 East Capitol Street S.E.
Washington, D.C.

Paul Philippe Cret

Paul Philippe Cret was an eclectic architect in the best sense of the word, a French-born, Ecole des Beaux Arts graduate who respected traditional forms but understood that buildings can only be constructed in the present. The Folger Shakespeare Library is wonderfully eclectic too, its stripped-down classic exterior enclosing interiors of Elizabethan grandeur.

The cool, white marble exterior is enlivened by nine bas-reliefs by John Gregory depicting scenes from Shakespeare plays, fluted column-like piers between the tall, narrow, leaded-glass windows, and a frieze of chiseled inscriptions honoring the great playwright. A statue of Puck is prominently placed.

The Folger Library contains an almost unimaginable wealth of material for scholars. The Great Hall and the theater, however, are the main public spaces. A showcase for special exhibitions highlighting the collection, the Great Hall resembles an Elizabethan manor house, with its paneled walls and plastered ceiling impressed with Shakespeare's coat of arms and fleurs-de-lis, and hung with heraldic flags. The theater is meant to suggest an Elizabethan inn courtyard, the setting in which Shakespeare's plays were actually performed at the time he wrote them. Concerts, readings, performances, and other events are held here throughout the year. Outdoors, an Elizabethan garden is filled with herbs and plants from Shakespeare's time.

The Folger Shakespeare Library is open from 10:00 AM to 4:00 PM, Monday to Saturday, and closed on federal holidays. Walk-in tours are given daily at 11:00 AM. Entrance to the museum is free, but admission is charged for ticketed events, such as the plays and concerts. For information about the free exhibits or ticketed events, call (202) 544-7077.

NEBRASKA STATE CAPITOL, 1932

1445 K Street
Lincoln, Nebraska

Bertram Grosvenor Goodhue

The Nebraska State Capitol shows American architecture striving to be modern. This "Tower on the Plains" rises like a Manhattan skyscraper in sleek setbacks from a two-story base. Its overall appearance is smoothly vertical, its ornament subdued, flattened, and geometrical.

These machine-age motifs were blended with the traditional formula for monumental civic architecture. The approach to the building is properly ceremonial, and the plan is symmetrical: a cross within a square forming four interior courtyards. The 400-foot tower culminates in a dome, symbolically ornamented with a 32-foot, 8-ton bronze sculpture, "The Sower," by Lee Lawrie. There was no stinting on tradition when it came to the selection of cladding materials; inside and out, more than forty varieties of marble, granite, slate, and limestone are in evidence.

Homage is paid to local traditions as well. The doors to the Senate are highly carved to represent the "Red Man's Tree of Life." Over on the House side, tooled and inlaid leather-covered doors depict the "White Man's Tree of Life."

Bertram Goodhue was an innovative and influential architect who practiced with Ralph Adams Cram in Boston before opening his own office in New York City in 1914. Originally working in a Gothic Revival style like almost everyone else at the time, he soon progressed from medieval to Mediterranean. Goodhue was working his way into a thoroughly modern architecture when his career was cut short by his early death in 1924.

Free tours are conducted year-round, except for Christmas, New Year's Day, and Thursday and Friday of the Thanksgiving holiday. From Memorial Day to Labor Day, tours are conducted every half hour from 9:00 AM to 4:00 PM; the rest of the year, tours are every hour from 10:00 AM to 4:00 PM. Sunday tours are 1:00 to 4:00 PM. For information or group reservations, call (402) 471-0448.

Philadelphia Savings Fund Society, 1932

12 South 12th Street at Market Street Philadelphia, Pennsylvania

George Howe and William Lescaze

At the time of its construction, the Philadelphia Savings Fund Society Building (PSFS) was the most innovative skyscraper in the world. Its location in Philadelphia comes as something of a surprise, however, given its status as the first skyscraper built to the specifications of the European avant-garde. And in light of the depression of the late 1920s, the wonder is that this icon of modernism was built at all.

The design team consisted of George Howe, a prominent traditional Philadelphia architect-turned-modernist, and a young Swiss architect, William Lescaze. Together they produced a striking new kind of skyscraper, stripped of the historical allusions of the past.

Howe and Lescaze's design solution, often imitated in the intervening years, consisted of a T-shaped tower set on a podium-style base. The success of this arrangement follows from the way it seems to anchor the building visually to the ground while providing a sort of launchpad from which the tower can rise. The strong vertical lines of the skyscraper are balanced by the prominent horizontally banded windows, which wrap the building at its corners. Retail stores occupy the podium base, with the central banking hall on the second level.

In true International Style, the design expresses both the structural frame of the building as well as its volume. The materials are varied, but remain pure and precise: a gray, polished granite base, buff limestone for the banking office façade and for the vertical columns; and gray brick for the spandrels. Ornamentation, a big modernist taboo, is virtually eliminated, unless you count as decoration the enormous PSFS sign that dominates the top of the tower. The architects designed all the furniture, hardware, and fixtures, because the necessary modern elements did not exist.

Howe and Lescaze benefited from having a sympathetic client in James Wilcox, the president of PSFS. The bank still occupies the building, and has respectfully maintained it to preserve its handsome appearance. For information, call (215) 636-6000.

Cincinnati Union Terminal, 1933 (The Museum Center)

1301 Western Avenue
Cincinnati, Ohio

Fellheimer & Wagner with Paul Cret

On one hand, the Cincinnati Union Terminal was a miracle of fortunate timing. The $41 million needed to build it was raised early in 1929; on Wall Street "the window was wide open." After the crash, the easily obtained financing went a long way given deflated construction pricing. The railway station was dedicated in 1933, a wonder of elegance in the pit of the depression.

In the longer view, however, the timing was not so good. The great era of American passenger trains had peaked in 1912, long before the Cincinnati Union Terminal was even designed. So when the terminal opened, its Art Deco façade designed by Paul Cret harked to the future, but the future was already behind it—the station was born a relic.

The building survived because of its own inherent mass and strength—the reinforced concrete semi-dome roof could bounce a wrecking ball. It was too expensive to tear it down.

The interior space is 500,000 square feet, the area of fourteen football fields. The plan conforms to the natural sequence of traffic densities: the maximum space is provided in the vast semi-circular concourse, from which the streams of passengers flowed out, by means of a long covered gallery, to ramps and then to the train platforms. Floor areas diminish in proportion as the foot traffic thinned out toward the train platforms. All this sophisticated space planning lost its logic when the last train left.

In the 1980s, E. Verner Johnson, a Boston architect who specializes in museum design, conceived the terminal anew as a double museum for the Cincinnati Museum of Natural History and the Cincinnati Historical Society. The building—and its surreal and colorful rotunda with the double-life-size murals depicting Cincinnati's history—was spectacularly refurbished in 1986. The vast spaces now house large exhibits (a recreation of the early Cincinnati waterfront, a depiction of the Ice Age replete with gigantic dinosaurs, a free-living bat colony in the building's basement).

Now it has a purpose that can never be made obsolete: history. And the trains (Amtrak) are back, too. Known as the Museum Center, the terminal building is open from 9:00 AM to 8:00 PM. Museum of Natural History hours are 9:00 AM to 5:00 PM Monday through Saturday and holidays (except Christmas and Thanksgiving). For general information, call (513) 287-7000; for museum information, call 287-7020.

RCA Building, 1934 (GE Building)

30 Rockefeller Plaza
New York, New York

Hood & Fouilhoux; Reinhard & Hofmeister; Corbett, Harrison & MacMurray

The RCA/GE Building is the centerpiece of Rockefeller Center, a mini-city located in the heart of midtown Manhattan. This complex of skyscrapers, shops, theaters, and plazas encompasses Radio City Music Hall, the Rainbow Room, an ice rink, and the famous Christmas tree that is lighted the first week in December.

John D. Rockefeller, Jr. envisioned the multi-building complex in 1928, at a time when most builders were thinking in terms of single structures. Mr. Rockefeller hoped to build a home for the Metropolitan Opera Company as part of a larger commercial venture, but the depression intervened. The opera company dropped out, and he was left with three full city blocks to develop.

The RCA/GE Building emerged as a result of the reprogramming, and it is the dominant architectural creation. Clad in gray Indiana limestone, with recessed spandrels of gray metal in a darker tone, the 70-story tower is tall and slender, composed as a slab outlined by a series of slender setbacks. The building had to be designed to fit New York City's restrictive zoning ordinances, but the design team managed to instill great dignity and a sense of repose in the gigantic tower.

The Art Deco bas-reliefs that decorate the exterior are spectacular artworks. Inside the lobby, there is a famous mural, "American Progress," by José Maria Sert.

Perhaps the most influential achievement of Rockefeller Center was not any single building, but the concept that there was strength in numbers—that skyscrapers were no longer to be isolated structures, but part of a larger whole. This fundamental shift of vantage point would change the course of skyscraper development forever.

The building is open during regular business hours. NBC is located here, and you can tour the television studio with tickets purchased in the lobby. Tours are held every fifteen minutes from 9:30 AM to 4:30 PM, Monday to Saturday. For information, call (212) 664-4000.

FALLINGWATER, 1936

Route 381
Bear Run, Pennsylvania

Frank Lloyd Wright

Fallingwater, the most acclaimed of Frank Lloyd Wright's private residences, perfectly dramatizes the architect's conviction that a building should be an integral part of its natural setting. A remarkable interweaving of house and landscape is accomplished with just a few simple elements—native stone, reinforced concrete, glass, and steel—but they are used with a vision and a mastery of technical processes to create Wright's most powerful piece of structural wizardry.

Wright believed that no one else noticed the particular beauty of a site until he built on it, and at Fallingwater, as with many of his designs, he found his inspiration in the setting. At first glance, the boldness of the broad cantilevered beams would seem at odds with the gentle wooded site, but Wright's artistic integration of house and nature is total. Suspended above the waterfall, with the stream flowing alongside its stone side walls, the multi-tiered house is so tied to the rock that it appears to be part of the actual formation.

While the house merges with the rock on one side, it opens out into the landscape on the other. There is a corresponding openness within. Walls are kept to a minimum, and almost every room has a terrace extending it to the outdoors. Continuity of materials, such as stone flooring for both the interiors and terraces, unites indoors and out into a single whole. Wright also designed the furniture and lighting.

Fallingwater was built for J. Edgar Kaufman, a wealthy Pittsburgh merchant. In 1962, the house was donated to the Western Pennsylvania Conservancy, which operates the house and hosts public tours. Today, among Wright's major houses, Fallingwater is the only one with its setting, original furnishings, and artwork still intact.

The house is open Tuesday through Sunday from 10:00 AM to 4:00 PM, with tours every half hour. Closed Christmas, New Year's Day, and Thanksgiving. Advance reservations are required (allow one month for groups of twenty or more). For information call (412) 329-8501.

Fallingwater's rural location is between the towns of Mill Run and Ohio Pyle, about 2½ hours southeast of Pittsburgh.

San Simeon, 1937 (Hearst's Castle)

750 Hearst Castle Road
San Simeon, California

Julia Morgan

In 1919, William Randolph Hearst decided to build a simple bungalow for himself and his movie-star girlfriend, Marion Davies. The site was spectacular—250,000 acres in the Santa Lucia Mountains overlooking the Pacific Ocean—and Hearst was among the world's wealthiest men. Nevertheless, he told Julia Morgan to design something elegant but spartan, something "Jappo-Swisso," whatever that might be.

The exotic fantasy castle shows what happens when a simple idea is attacked with unlimited amounts of time, money, architectural talent, and enthusiasm for empire building. After almost twenty years and $8 million, La Cuesta Encantada ("The Enchanted Hill") had evolved into one of the world's most astonishing private residences, rivaling Versailles in scale and grandeur. In *Citizen Kane,* the motion picture based on Hearst's life, San Simeon becomes the fabled golden mansion, Xanadu.

Everything has a name. La Casa Grande, the main house with its twin towers, commands the high point of the site. Three guest bungalows surround the main house: Casa del Mar, Casa del Monte, and Casa del Sol. For outdoor swimming, there was the monumental 104-foot Neptune Pool of green and white marble, Italian temple façade, and classical colonnade; indoors, guests swam in the mystical blue and gold Murano-tiled Roman Pool.

The architecture is eclectic in the extreme. Spanish Renaissance cathedrals provided the main theme, but Gothic, Classical, and Italian influences abound. An indefatigable collector, Hearst scavenged Europe for treasures to fill the mansion's 100-plus rooms. He thought nothing of dismantling entire suites from Spanish palaces and reconstructing them at San Simeon. The main dining hall, for example, is furnished with 500-year-old choir stalls from Catalonia, seventeenth-century refectory tables, Siennese Palio banners, and a sixteenth-century Flemish tapestry.

Julia Morgan supervised construction of this frustrating project, where completed portions were ripped out and replaced again and again. The first female engineering graduate of the University of California at Berkeley, and the first woman certified at L'Ecole des Beaux Arts in Paris, Morgan was certainly up to the task. Construction probably would have gone on forever, but Hearst finally ran out of money in 1937.

San Simeon is open daily (except Thanksgiving, Christmas, and New Year's Day), with four tours from 8:20 AM to 3:00 PM in winter, later in summer, each lasting almost two hours. For information and reservations, call (800) 444-7275. For foreign language tours, call (805) 927-2084.

WALTER GROPIUS HOUSE, 1938

68 Baker Bridge Road
Lincoln, Massachusetts

Walter Gropius

A dramatic changing of the architectural guard occurred in 1937 when the famous German architect Walter Gropius came to America. The founder of the Bauhaus accepted a position at Harvard's Graduate School of Design, and almost immediately began to revolutionize architecture in this country, starting with his family home in Lincoln. Although Americans had glimpsed modern European architecture in houses designed by Rudolph Schindler and Richard Neutra on the West Coast, Gropius provided a vital "oomph" that turned the tide. Boston became a crucible for the new buildings on the East Coast, described by the writer Ada Louise Huxtable as "the architectural shot heard 'round the world."

The house that Gropius built is modest in scale. On first sight, it appears as a compact white rectangle atop a gentle hill, with its entry projecting forward at an angle in counterpoint to a spiral staircase. Key elements of International Style stand out: the flat roof, the ribbon windows, the second-story roof terrace, the lack of ornamentation, and the impression of volume rather than mass. On the inside, modernist ideals are expressed in the asymmetrical massing, in the open floor plan, and in the use of industrial materials such as steel columns, glass block, and cork floors. Gropius's collaborator, Marcel Breuer, another prominent Bauhaus émigré, built his own house next door and designed much of the furniture in the Gropius House.

Even though the house is precisely designed to form an integrated whole, Gropius permitted himself leeway in this domestication of the International Style. He balanced the Bauhaus influences with local New England traditions—white clapboard walls, which he applied vertically rather than horizontally, brick chimney, screened porch, and fieldstone foundation and retaining walls, and the vine-covered trellis—elements that also served to integrate the house into the surrounding landscape.

Gropius and his family lived for almost three decades in this house, which is now in the care of the Society for the Preservation of New England Antiquities (SPNEA) in Boston. A 1989 restoration proved challenging, because finding mass-produced materials from fifty years past was not always easy, but the house now looks very much as it did during the last decade of Gropius's life.

The SPNEA conducts tours of the house, with its Breuer furniture, family memorabilia, and artwork by Gropius's artist friends, such as Laszlo Moholy-Nagy, Josef Albers, and Henry Moore, among others. The house is open Friday, Saturday, and Sunday afternoons from June 1 to October 15 and on Saturday and Sunday afternoons from November 1 to May 30. For information, call (617) 259-8843.

Marcel Breuer's 1938 residence is located next door, but it is not open to the public.

Ohio Steel Foundry, 1938 (Whemco)

1600 McClain Road
Lima, Ohio

Albert Kahn and Associates

Albert Kahn viewed a factory as a machine, and part of the industrial process, not just the housing for it. He is best remembered for his industrial architecture, a path he embarked on in 1917 at the request of Henry Ford. The auto magnate was searching for a better factory design, one that did not require conventional—meaning painstaking—construction. Ford urged Kahn to develop steel-framed structures with whole walls of glass and lightweight metal that could be quickly and simply built. Kahn's structures became elegant and intelligent prototypes for modern, steel industrial buildings.

Kahn's early work had produced the icons of mass production—the "smokestack industries" and factories still commonly represented as cartoon caricatures. But the Ohio Steel Foundry Roll and Heavy Machine Shop, completed in 1937, suggests how his thinking matured into a spare, fully realized design style. For all the scowling, no-nonsense insistence on utility and function, the foundry turned out to be beautiful. For good working light, it is virtually a glass house.

The raised central section of the roof is a thruway for an overhead mobile crane. Additional glass, canted to the sun, stands on either side of the crane's rails. Interior columns are not there simply to hold up the roof, but also to hold up the crane. Great structural integrity is contributed by trusses under the flat roof. These trusses are kept open, rather than massively webbed, allowing free passage of light and accommodating the need to manipulate and position, with the crane, colossal masses of metal. The tension between great masses and stresses on the one hand, and the high, airy, wide-open feel on the other gives the plant the quality of a well made bridge.

For information, call (419) 222-2111.

Taliesen West, 1938-1959

108th Street
Scottsdale, Arizona

Frank Lloyd Wright

When architects build for themselves, the result often becomes a work in progress. Frank Lloyd Wright designed Taliesin West, his desert home and studio, in 1934, and built it soon after. However, he continued to modify it until he died there in 1959 at the age of 92. This counterweight to his summer home in Spring Green, Wisconsin (also rebuilt several times), superbly shows Wright's genius in marrying site with structure.

"Taliesin West had to be absolutely according to the desert," Wright proclaimed. Its spectacular site, which he selected through a series of overnight campouts, rests on the edge of a plain and the base of McDowell Peak, fifteen miles from Scottsdale. Here, Wright maintained, he "gathered his family and apprentices about him like some Apache chief." The remarkable complex contains living quarters for Wright's family and houses the Frank Lloyd Wright Foundation, the Archives, a School of Architecture, and the Taliesin Fellowship.

Inspired by the "nature masonry" of the surrounding mountains, Wright built Taliesin West with sloping walls of indigenous rock captured in poured concrete—a man-made extravaganza of sublime desert colors in rusty reds, subdued oranges, tawny taupes, and steely gray. Massive redwood beams define the angled roof, which was originally covered with white canvas stretched between the trusses, although the canvas was later replaced with panels of translucent plastic. The buildings are interwoven with terraces, gardens, pools, and pergola in a way that underscores Wright's belief that inside and out should be united always. Wright's stunning collection of oriental art and sculpture also provides a unifying link between the house and the grounds.

Today, Taliesin West is a National Historic Landmark and headquarters of the Frank Lloyd Wright Foundation, which operates the Frank Lloyd Wright School of Architecture and Archives. Taliesin West is also home to Taliesin Associates Architects, Wright's successor firm.

The house is open daily, except New Year's Day, Easter, Thanksgiving, and Christmas. Guided tours of the Kiva Theater, Music Pavilion, Cabaret Cinema, and Wright's private office takes place, weather permitting, from 10:00 AM to 4:00 PM starting on the hour.

The "Behind the Scenes" tour is a three-hour visit, including a slide show and talk by one of Wright's associates. This tour takes place on Thursday mornings, October to May, and also on Tuesday mornings from January to March. Reservations are required.

For recorded tour information, call (602) 860-8810. For reservations and information about special programs, call (602) 860-2700.

Museum of Modern Art, 1939

11 West 53rd Street
New York, New York

Edward Durell Stone and Philip Goodwin

The spiritual and physical home of modern architecture in America, the International Style building of the Museum of Modern Art (MOMA) has disappeared into the expansions and renovations of the past fifty-plus years. Fortunately, the 1939 façade has been preserved, the outdoor sculpture garden is still among the city's most delightful experiences, and the art is not to be missed.

From its original location at New York's upper-crust crossroads of Fifth Avenue at 57th Street, MOMA made its architectural mark by touting European-style modernism in the legendary International Style exhibition of 1932. The message of the show's curators, Philip Johnson and Henry-Russell Hitchcock, was clear. Out with the old, ornate Beaux Arts eclecticism, and in with the new: weightless-looking buildings with white walls, flat roofs, straight lines, and minimal decoration. For its own new home a few years later, MOMA showed the courage of its convictions by erecting the first public International Style building in America.

Designed by European-trained American architect Edward Durell Stone with Philip Goodwin, the museum was small but architecturally avant-garde. Its flat façade was elaborated by a white marble frame, twin bands of windows across the top, and a rounded chrome slab projecting over the entry. A remarkable canopy with saucer-shaped cutouts shelters a glassed-in roof terrace. Viewed in contrast to the classic brownstone buildings on the street, the new building must have looked like something from another planet.

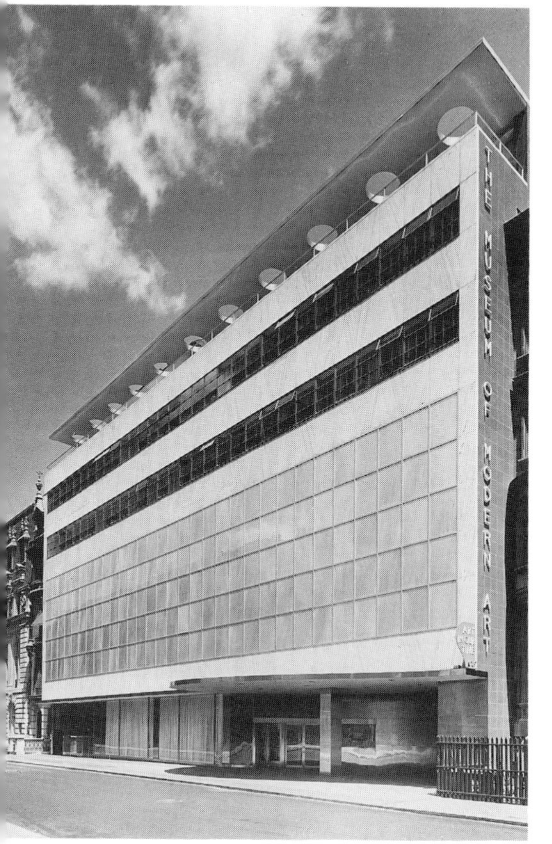

Many changes have occurred over the years. In 1953, MOMA opened the sculpture garden and a new wing designed by Philip Johnson. In 1984, the year of MOMA's most momentous expansion, a 53-story gray-glass residential tower designed by Cesar Pelli was developed on the property to help sustain the museum financially. The old building received a new six-floor wing that doubled gallery space from about 40,000 to 80,000 square feet, and a four-tiered greenhouse addition overlooking the sculpture garden.

The Museum of Modern Art is open every day except Wednesday from 11:00 AM to 6:00 PM, and Thursday evenings until 9:00 PM. For information on tours and exhibits, call (212) 708-9480.

Union Station, 1939

800 North Alameda Street
Los Angeles, California

John and Donald B. Parkinson; J.H. Christie, H.L. Gilman, R.J. Wirth

Union Station captures the Spanish mission influence of southern California, with touches of Streamline Moderne thrown in for good measure. The massive Spanish Colonial Revival façade is enlivened by tall but slender Mexican fan palms that give it a festive and tropical air, which the colorful tilework at the giant arched entry intensifies.

This last great passenger terminal was jointly built by the Southern Pacific, Union Pacific, and Santa Fe Railroads as the major termination for the entire continent. To handle a continent's worth of passengers, the architects designed an enormous main concourse and a lofty waiting room 52-feet high, set with marble floors. In the inside-outside tradition of California architecture, the waiting room is flanked by open courtyards, lush with landscaping.

No longer the continental transportation hub of its early days, Union Station now buzzes mostly with commuters who can daily enjoy the original furnishings, Art Deco signs, and the tropical paradise of the courtyard gardens.

For information about Union Station, call (213) 683-6875. For schedule and ticket information, call (800) USA-RAIL.

Kleinhans Music Hall, 1940
Symphony Circle

Porter North at Pennsylvania Street
Buffalo, New York

Eliel and Eero Saarinen

From his home base at Cranbrook Academy in Bloomfield Hills, Michigan, Eliel Saarinen collaborated with his son, Eero, to design a concert hall that would express orchestral music to the fullest. And when the concert hall was complete, connoisseurs hailed it as the most acoustically perfect music hall in the world. Today, it remains one of the finest concert-going experiences.

Seen from the air, Kleinhans Music Hall is shaped like a cello. These rounded shapes reflect the organization of the interiors: a large 2,938-seat auditorium, the smaller Mary Seaton Room, and the glass-walled lobby that connects them. The main auditorium has a zigzag roof line, which shows the location of the interior stairs and plays against the curves of the outer walls. As designed, the east end of the building was reflected in graceful pools, but these have now been filled in.

For the exterior finishes, the architects selected familiar materials the elder Saarinen had utilized at Cranbrook Academy: golden-hued Wyandotte brick and Mankato stone, which has a pattern resembling zebra wood. On the inside, the Saarinens sought open shapes that would allow sound vibrations to fill the spaces; rounded ceilings and flaring, wood-paneled walls in the larger hall also helped to achieve this goal. Recent investigations show that Charles Eames, a Saarinen associate at Cranbrook who would emerge as one of the most notable architects and furniture designers of the 1950s, was responsible for the furniture in the music hall's administrative offices and dressing rooms.

The collaboration here between Eliel and Eero Saarinen yields an interesting blend of old and new architectural approaches—a freeze-frame catching both the European ideals and devotion to craftsmanship of the elder Saarinen and the expressive curving shapes that would characterize the work of Eero Saarinen on his own.

Kleinhans Music Hall is home to the Buffalo Philharmonic Orchestra, which performs in the main hall; the Buffalo Chamber Music Society holds concerts in the Mary Seaton Room. Tickets for these and other events held at Kleinhans must be obtained from the individual sponsoring organizations. Architectural tourists are welcome, and tours may be arranged by calling Kleinhans Music Hall at (716) 883-3580.

National Gallery of Art, West Building, 1941

Fourth Street
at Constitution Avenue N.W.
Washington, D.C.

John Russell Pope

America's art collection is a relatively new one, but it is contained and celebrated in a pink marble monument that rivals the grand old art palaces of Europe. An extraordinarily generous gift to the nation, the museum owes its existence to Andrew W. Mellon, who donated the $15 million building (in 1941) as well as his exceptional art collection. The respectful design reflects the preference of Mellon and his chosen architect, John Russell Pope, who believed that democratic ideals were best expressed through classical architecture for buildings of such national significance.

While it seems that Pope was oblivious to the outbreak of modern architecture in America, the Beaux-Arts trained designer actually created a very modern building within the classical framework. Here, at monumental scale, Pope's classicism is stripped down to essentials, clean and coherent: an enormous elongated H, with a domed rotunda and columned entry at the center, large halls on either side, and projecting wings with garden courts at both ends. The 522,500 square-foot building is clad in 310,000 cubic feet of Phantasia Rose Tennessee marble; it is one of the largest marble buildings in the world.

Even while working at monumental scale, Pope never lost sight of the art and the people who would view it. He created a progression of spaces from the ceremonial to the personal. Through bronze doors on the Mall, visitors enter the central rotunda, 100 feet across and 103 feet high, set with twenty-four Ionic columns of dark-green vert imperial Italian marble; the walls and entablature are covered in Alabama rockwood limestone, with dark green Vermont marble on the floor. The exhibition galleries feel more like rooms, with decorative treatments designed to suggest the backgrounds used during periods in which the art was executed. The paintings are primarily illuminated with natural daylight, diffused through glass skylights, along with the occasional use of electric lighting.

In 1978, the museum expanded into the East Building, designed by I.M. Pei. The collection has become particularly impressive in nineteenth-century European paintings and Italian Renaissance works, and includes the only Leonardo da Vinci painting found outside of Europe.

The museum is open Monday to Saturday from 10:00 AM to 5:00 PM, on Sunday from noon to 9:00 PM, except Christmas and New Year's Day. West Building tours are conducted Monday to Saturday at 11:00 AM and 3:00 PM, on Sunday at 1:00 and 5:00 PM. For information, call (202) 737-4215.

First Christian Church, 1942

531 Fifth Street
Columbus, Indiana

Eliel Saarinen

Eliel Saarinen, when initially offered the commission to design Columbus' First Christian Church, refused to take on the project. Saarinen had to be convinced that this church was meant to welcome equally the rich and the poor, small children and the elderly. Traditional Gothic and Georgian designs would not work, Saarinen wrote, because "the last drop of expressiveness has been squeezed out of these once so expressive styles." To create the kind of church he had in mind, the Finnish-born architect invented a new, contemporary form—and one of the first contemporary churches in the United States was the result.

Unlike traditional religious buildings, First Christian Church is geometric in design, simple and direct, its grid clearly visible. The sanctuary is housed in the massive rectangular flat-roofed building, with the 166-foot-tall flat-topped bell tower at its side. Built mainly of buff-colored brick and limestone, the church is marked by a large stone cross in the limestone façade.

Serene on the inside, the 144-foot-long sanctuary has a wide center aisle. The outside cross reappears on the inside, on the south wall of the chancel. The chancel area is elevated, and it holds the communion table. A double wooden gateway opens to reveal the baptistery pool. On the west wall hangs a tapestry, "The Sermon on the Mount," designed by Saarinen and his wife, Loja. Saarinen was also joined on the project by his son Eero, who in the early 1960s designed another famous Columbus church, the North Christian Church on Tipton Lane.

A three-story school is connected to the First Christian Church by a two-story bridge set on massive columns. This arrangement forms a lower level arcade flanked by terraces on either side. Charles Eames, who was associated with Saarinen at the Cranbrook Academy in Bloomfield Hills, Michigan, designed the children's furniture.

First Christian Church was the first contemporary building in Columbus, Indiana, a city famed for its architectural wealth. In terms of the number of buildings designed by noted architects, Columbus ranks fourth in the United States after New York City, Chicago, and Los Angeles. The Columbus Visitor's Center hosts tours of more than fifty significant buildings, and the First Christian Church is among the most beloved classics. For tour reservations, call (812) 372-1954. The Visitor's Center is generally open from 9:00 AM to 5:00 PM Monday through Saturday. From April 1 to October 31, the center is also open Sunday from 10:00 AM to 2:00 PM. For complete information, call 1-800-468-6564.

DYMAXION HOUSE, 1947

Henry Ford Museum/Greenfield Village
20900 Oakwood Boulevard
Dearborn, Michigan

R. Buckminster Fuller

Who else but Buckminster Fuller could have given us Dymaxion House? This jaunty little flying saucer with the fin on top seems as unconventional and irrepressible as its illustrious inventor.

But Fuller was perfectly serious. Dymaxion House was his dream house, and the dream was portability—a house designed to be dismantled, packed into a tube, and taken along when the family moved. The structure is circular, because Fuller saw this as the most efficient shape and, therefore, the most economical to build. The tiny 1,075-square-foot house weighed only 6,000 pounds, not much more than some automobiles. Although the house was designed in 1927, it was not produced until after World War II, when a special aluminum alloy developed for aircraft made construction possible.

Only two prototypes were ever built. Fuller intended to mass produce the houses, but he was unable to secure funding. Rumor also has it that the Dymaxion House was leaky and cold.

William L. Graham, and entrepreneur from Wichita, Kansas, bought both Dymaxion prototypes and lived in one of them from 1946 until 1972. The other was never assembled. In 1992, Graham donated the prototypes to the Henry Ford Museum and Greenfield Village in Dearborn, Michigan. The museum is planning to reconstruct Dymaxion House; it is scheduled for completion in early 1995, coinciding with the Buckminster Fuller centennial.

Greenfield Village is open every day, except Thanksgiving and Christmas, from 9:00 AM to 5:00 PM. In winter (January 2 to mid-March), interiors are not accessible. For information about the opening, call (313) 271-1620.

Kaufmann House, 1947

470 West Vista Chino
Palm Springs, California

Richard Neutra

The San Jacinto mountains provide the perfect backdrop for Richard Neutra's most famous desert house. In this relaxed resort environment and near-perfect climate, Neutra pursued his vision of the ideal domestic design. Open and airy, Kaufmann House is defined by a series of floating planes: the pool, the entry canopy, the roof, and the elevated rooftop terrace, with a stout stone chimney serving as the anchor. Great glass walls enclose the house like an invisible shell.

In his equally famous Lovell House in the Hollywood hills, Neutra seemed to delight in changes of level as the house went up the hill. At the Kaufmann house, flatness reigns. The one-story house is composed of straight lines. In plan, a rectangular spine forms the center. A rectangular guest wing extends in one direction, and an L-shaped garage and walkway branch off from the other side, with enclosed gardens being formed in the process. A separate guest cottage stands just north of the main house.

The house is a private residence.

Usonia Homes, 1947–1950

Off Route 120, between Nannahagen Road and Bear Ridge Road
Mount Pleasant, New York

Frank Lloyd Wright, David Henken, and other architects

The small community of Mount Pleasant in Westchester County offers a rare opportunity to see Usonian homes as Frank Lloyd Wright saw them, in a Broadacre City setting of his own design. Some fifty Usonian-style houses show Wright's ideal of unity with variety.

Three of the houses, Friedman House, Serlin House, and Reiseley House, are by Wright, and the others are constructed according to his principles. The homes are clustered on circular one-acre lots, laid out to Wright's 1947 masterplan, and are remarkably unchanged on the whole. The 97-acre community is structured as a cooperative, with residents sharing woodlands, a swimming pool, playgrounds, and a community center, and having a voice in all matters affecting the community. At the time, this arrangement, which seemed truly democratic to Wright, was progressive verging on radical, and to bankers all but unimaginable.

But the world changed drastically between 1940, when Frank Lloyd Wright began planning Usonia Homes with David Henley, and the time the first houses went up in 1947. After World War II, the demand for housing soared and lifestyles became more relaxed and informal. The Usonian house was an ideal and relatively inexpensive solution. Small but spacious, the houses feature open plans and a compact "work center" kitchen at the heart of the house. Patios replace porches, carports replace garages, furniture and ornamentation are built in, and maintenance items were reduced to the minimum.

Starting with Jacobs House in Madison, Wisconsin (1937), Wright devised a kit-of-parts approach to simplify design and construction of the Usonian houses. Chief among these devices are board and batten walls that form both interior and exterior finishes, the 2 x 4-foot planning grid, and concrete floors with in-floor heating. Wright being Wright, standardization did not hinder creativity. In Usonia Homes, with the Friedman House design, Wright continued to explore his circular theme that would culminate in the monumental Guggenheim design.

Usonia Homes is located in Mount Pleasant, an unincorporated area adjacent to Pleasantville, New York, about thirty miles north of Manhattan. The three Wright houses in the Usonia Homes community are Friedman House (1948), Serlin House (1949), altered beyond recognition of the original design, and Reiseley House (1950), still in exceptional condition. All three are private residences. Tours by special arrangement only. For information, call Roland Reiseley, a Board Member of the Frank Lloyd Wright Building Conservancy, at (914) 769-2926.

Baker House, 1948

Massachusetts Institute of Technology
Cambridge, Massachusetts

Alvar Aalto

In the 1940s, the great Finnish architect Alvar Aalto left his homeland to escape the perils of war in Europe. He arrived in the United States to take up a six-year teaching position at the Massachusetts Institute of Technology (MIT), which placed him in close proximity to two giants of European modernism, Walter Gropius and Marcel Breuer, and turned the Boston-Cambridge area into a showplace of new architecture. Aalto's major contribution to architecture in America was Baker House, a dormitory and dining hall for senior-year students overlooking the Charles River.

Baker House breaks out of the box in a dramatic way—a building made into an undulating wave. The design is based on Aalto's theory that the most beautiful scenes are best viewed at an angle. Therefore, no room directly confronts the river view. On the campus side of the building, however, the curves give way to walls that are angular and squared off. The most prominent feature here is an enormous V-shape that results from Aalto's diagonal cantilevering of an outside stairway along one wall, paired with a cantilevered portion of the building on the opposing wall.

The building's interiors show an evolution of Aalto's understanding of how people live in and use a building. Rather than impose the separation of functions that modernism demands—living spaces here, service functions there—Aalto juxtaposes functions. Student rooms take up most of the curvaceous spine, with study rooms, lounges, and lavatories interspersed throughout the building.

In terms of Aalto's career, Baker House marks a new maturity of design, as well as a concern for the timelessness of his buildings. When Baker House opened, many people viewed the sinuous wall of rough dark brick with great alarm. The intervening years, and careful maintenance, have proven Aalto right. Baker House is one of those buildings that only seems to look better with age.

For information, call (617) 253-1000.

Equitable Savings and Loan, 1948 (Far West Federal Bank)

421 S.W. Sixth Avenue
Portland, Oregon

Pietro Belluschi

The new look of America's postwar commercial buildings first appeared in Pietro Belluschi's Equitable Savings and Loan Building in Portland, Oregon. An immediate critical success—in 1948, *Architectural Forum* magazine praised it as "a long overdue crystal and metal tower that catches the lightness of the multi-story cage"—the Equitable Building was soon overshadowed by more prominent structures in larger cities. Nevertheless, its technical and aesthetic accomplishments remain astonishing. It was the first aluminum clad building in America, the first to use double-glazed windows, and the first completely air-conditioned commercial building in the country. At the time it was built, this was the most progressive commercial structure in the world.

A compact "skyscraper" in the International Style, the Equitable Building presents a lively exterior—a shimmering frame of light- and dark-colored aluminum inset with large expanses of luminous, sea-green glass. The pieces are assembled with the precision of fine furniture, and the greatest projection on the façade is confined to seven-eights of an inch. Originally 12 stories, later expanded to 13, the building houses retail shops at street level, where the tall ground floor features a row of brick columns. It was a point of pride that no masonry was used on the upper floors, which indicated a lightness of construction that was greatly admired. To counteract the pristine coolness of the exterior, Belluschi thought the interior should be bright and colorful, and he turned to the artist Alexander Calder for ideas.

Despite its International Style inspiration, Equitable maintained its local connections. Pietro Belluschi was a Portland resident known for his refined residential and church designs. The city was also becoming a center for aluminum production. Belluschi's reputation soon grew to national and international proportions, and he would eventually leave Portland to become Dean of Architecture at the Massachusetts Institute of Technology. In recognition of the building's distinguished status as a prototype of postwar commercial architecture, Equitable (now Far West Federal) received the American Institute of Architects Twenty-Five Year Award in 1982.

The building is open during regular business hours, and you can walk around and see the newly restored public areas. For information, call (503) 323-6423.

CHRIST CHURCH LUTHERAN, 1949

3244 34th Avenue South
Minneapolis, Minnesota

Eliel and Eero Saarinen

In this "honest" church resembling those of his native Scandinavia, Eliel Saarinen utilized the principles of contemporary design in the traditional realm of ecclesiastical architecture. And the impression of solemnity and spirituality became heightened rather than diminished by the new approach.

Starting with an extremely simple basic structure—a steel frame wrapped by walls of light beige brick and stone—Saarinen created a building that responds in a very sophisticated way to variations in sound and light. The church and its 88-foot tower are separated by a glass passage. Natural light from this passage softly illuminates the church interior. There are no parallel walls in the nave, which accounts for the exceptional acoustics.

The church is asymmetrical in plan, and at the same time it is serenely proportioned and balanced. One long wall includes splayed panels of open-jointed brick, which add texture while they help absorb sound. Saarinen used aluminum in new ways. He formed tall, slender crosses (atop the tower and behind the altar) into sleekly evocative sculptures.

This is Eliel Saarinen's last completed work, and a recipient of the American Institute of Architects Twenty-Five Year Award in 1977. Eero Saarinen later added an educational wing to the original church structure.

Visitors are welcome. The church is open from 9:00 AM to 3:00 PM Monday through Thursday, and on Friday until noon. Sunday services are held at 8:15 and 10:45 AM from Labor Day through Memorial Day and at 9:00 AM in the summer. Church members conduct tours of the building upon request. For reservations and information, call (612) 721-6611.

Eames House, 1949 (Case Study House #8)

Chatauque Boulevard,
south of Corona del Mar
Pacific Palisades, California

Charles and Ray Eames

In hopes of sparking design innovations for a war-weary world, *Arts & Architecture* magazine in 1945 sponsored the Case Study House Program on property it purchased for that purpose on the California coast. Charles Eames and his Cranbrook Academy colleague Eero Saarinen were selected to build Case Study House #8, a house and studio. Eames, together with his wife and collaborator, Ray, would live here for the rest of their lives.

Eames actually designed two houses for his site. With the steel framing for his initial plan already delivered to the site, he redesigned the house and studio using the same materials, but in a different way. As finally constructed, the house consists of two rectangular box-like components, a 1,500-square-foot house and a 1,000-square-foot studio, wedged into the side of a hill that is anchored by a concrete retaining wall. An open court lies between them.

Eames sought a house that was light and open, with its structural components clearly visible wherever possible. He set out to meet these objectives using standard interchangeable, off-the-shelf materials and a building block approach. The basic module measures 7½ x 20 feet. Eight of these modules make the house, with five modules comprising the studio. The result is not static, however, for there is great variety within this modular concept. The exterior is clad with stucco, cement, asbestos, and plywood panels, which appear as color blocks of white, blue, red, black, and gray. Three types of glass—transparent, translucent, and wired—are used for the windows.

Inside, Eames contrasted large vertical spaces, such as the 17-foot-high living room, with small and intimate enclosures. A spiral staircase illuminated with a wired-glass skylight leads to the second story. Upstairs, the master bedroom overlooks the two-story living room, but it can be closed for privacy with a sliding screen of translucent glass cloth laminate. Exposed Truscon open-webbed joists and Ferroboard steel decking, painted dark gray, form the ceiling in both the house and studio, a novel use of industrial materials for residential construction at the time.

In 1955, the Eameses documented their love of the house in a film, *House—After Five Years of Living*. In 1978, the Eames House received the American Institute of Architects Twenty-Five Year Award for its "subtle richness of pattern, color, and texture, and a sense of unity of nature which have successfully withstood the test of time."

The house is private and not visible from the street.

Glass House, 1949

New Canaan, Connecticut

Philip Johnson

The see-through house that Philip Johnson designed for himself takes the idea of home and turns it inside out. Walls become windows, and private life is opened up to the outdoors, rather than shielded from it. As a living space, the Glass House works because of its protected wooded setting, and because it is inhabited by only one person. As architecture, the house is almost unequaled in the clarity of its design, apparently willed into existence almost out of thin air.

The Glass House consists of a single room, 32 x 56 feet, which seems to be nothing more than a chimney of dark red brick, arising from a floor of the same material, encased by a cage of steel and a skin of glass. The slenderest detail—a "chair rail" of steel on all sides—provides the tension that visually holds the house together. Opposite walls are identically symmetrical, and each is broken by a door of glass at the center.

The house sits atop a flat rise, surrounded by a wooded valley, and shares the site with a brick-walled guest house and a sculpture garden. To reach the house, there is no direct route. Arriving up the drive to find a solid brick wall, the visitor approaches the house on the diagonal, following first one 45-degree angle path and then another, never confronting the house directly.

Although the Glass House obviously has no rooms in the traditional sense, they are suggested by the placement of the few interior constructions. An entrance hall emerges between the brick cylinder and a low walnut cabinet that contains the kitchen. From here, the natural progression leads to a sitting area defined by a white rug and furnished with a Mies van der Rohe lounge and chairs. The brick cylinder encloses the bathroom facilities, and on its outside wall there is a fireplace. Behind the cylinder there is another walnut storage cabinet, this one protecting the sleeping and writing area located on the north side of the house.

Although Johnson would later turn away from the International Style, the Glass House is almost a pure example of the form. Johnson acknowledges his debt to Mies van der Rohe's Farnsworth House (see page 88), but in the end the house is his own.

Glass House is a private residence.

Johnson Wax Company Research and Development Center, 1949

1525 Howe Street
Racine, Wisconsin

Frank Lloyd Wright

Frank Lloyd Wright was a man in his seventies and still going strong when he designed Johnson Wax, one of the most impressive buildings of his long career. The center consists of the administrative headquarters of 1939 (the famous golf-tee lobby as pictured) and the laboratory tower of 1949. The tower shows Wright at his best, working new wonders with space and light, brick and glass.

The 14-story tower, 40-feet square with rounded corners, rises above a walled courtyard; it is linked to the central administration building by a covered walkway lined with reflecting pools. From outside, the most fascinating feature is the glass tubing that forms glistening wall sections two stories tall, banded in warm red brick. Inside, the laboratory floors are also unique. The labs are segmented into two-story modules: a main floor, which is square, and a mezzanine, which is round. These floors are cantilevered out from a central core containing the elevator, stairs, and mechanical equipment. During the day, the building appears translucent. At night, it glows with an ethereal radiance and the bold shapes of the interior floors are clear.

In designing this building, Wright drew inspiration from two ongoing preoccupations in his pursuit of "organic" architecture—the shape of a tree with its outreaching limbs, and the form of the circle. Before long, this combination was expressed as a spiral, the basis of his design for the Guggenheim Museum in New York City. In these masterpieces of his late career, Wright moved away from external decoration toward something much more like sculpture.

By reservation only, Johnson Wax hosts tours Tuesday through Saturday at 9:45 AM, 11:30 AM, 1:00 PM, and 2:45 PM from March through November. In January and February, tours are at 11:30 AM and 1:00 PM. For reservations and information, call (414) 631-2425. It is best to confirm reservations because corporate activities occasionally necessitate a change in schedule.

V.C. Morris Gift Shop, 1949 (Circle Gallery)

140 Maiden Lane
San Francisco, California

Frank Lloyd Wright

It would be easy to miss the Circle Gallery on Maiden Lane. The street is tiny and can be hard to find, although it is only a few blocks from Union Square. On this street, the gallery stands out because of its simplicity—an almost-blank wall of rust-colored brick with a simple quarter-round entryway outlined in the same brick, surrounding a quarter-round metal front gate. This must be one of the few stores in American history that has no shop windows and no merchandise on display. The building presents a mystery, but it draws you in nevertheless.

And this, of course, is the point. Frank Lloyd Wright was not only practicing architecture, he was seducing the customer. The building exerts a constant pull from the street through the entry and into the selling space. The design practically guides you through the shop by means of a spiral ramp, a precursor of Wright's integral design for the Guggenheim Museum in New York City some twenty years later. So perhaps it is no irony that the current inhabitant is an art gallery.

An interesting feature of Wright's exterior design is the way he used the ordinary brick coursework to give a sharp edge to the façade. At the left edge of the building, Wright has left alternating brick ends exposed, creating a graphic, punched-out line up the side. As was his practice, Wright signed the building with his red ceramic square logo set into the façade.

The telephone number at the Circle Gallery is (415) 989-2100.

TISCHLER HOUSE, 1949

175 Greenfield Avenue
Los Angeles, California

R.M. Schindler

The best-preserved Schindler house in Los Angeles is Tischler House, a multi-level stucco and wood composition distinguished by a series of triangular extensions—slabs, terraces, and trellises—that rise up the hill into which the house is so cozily situated. Schindler's idea of outdoor rooms, lined with trees and scaled to complement the interior, extends the living area out onto the hillside.

For the construction of the tall, narrow house, Schindler worked with an enlarged concrete block, which he offset in alternating bands to form a simple but distinctive pattern. Blue corrugated fiberglass was used for the roof, but conventional materials later replaced the uppermost portions.

The floor plan is as open as the vertical site permits. The main floor of the house is on the second level, accessible by a lofty flight of stairs up the leafy hillside. Inside the front door, Schindler positioned a curved wall of concrete block about 5 feet high that subtly divides the entry from the living room. Its opposite face contains a large fireplace with a beautifully curving metal hood.

The Tischler House owes its design to *Arts and Architecture* magazine, for it was here that Tischler discovered the work of Rudolf Schindler. An artist and silversmith, Tischler's inherent sympathy to Schindler's style is noticeable in the handcrafted hammered silver bowls and tableware he made for the house. These pieces, displayed in the dining area, seem to capture the contemporary spirit of the house, which is now a landmark of the City of Los Angeles.

Tischler House is a private residence.

Farnsworth House, 1950

**RR 2 at Fox River and Milbrook Road
Plano, Illinois**

Ludwig Mies van der Rohe

Mies van der Rohe believed in making architecture by stripping away the nonessentials, which turned out to be practically everything. The Farnsworth House, he said, consists of "practically nothing"—a roof, a floor, four glass walls, eight I-beams, and a terrace. It is essentially a one-room house, about 28 x 77 feet including the porch, but the design effort poured into it was enormous: thousands of hours invested over three years. "This house is much more important than the size or cost would indicate," said Mies. "It is a prototype for all glass buildings."

Although the house was set on 75 acres of meadowland, Mies had no desire to unite the works of man and nature. He preferred to define the difference between them. This detachment is clear in the Farnsworth house: it seems to float on a pedestal four feet above the ground. The white steel frame, glass walls, and white slab of terrace further emphasize the distinction, and the elegant isolation.

The simple glass box, set within the linear white frame, is offset to form a covered porch at one end. There is only one door, on the west side. Inside, Mies used open, clear-span space for the first time. The house has no rooms in the conventional sense. Separate areas for living, eating, and sleeping are suggested by the placement of the few interior structures. A wood-paneled central island contains the kitchen and bath facilities, and these walls, along with a freestanding storage wall, provide the only internal definition. Although the house was not built for air-conditioning, there are only two small, high windows that open.

Dr. Edith Farnsworth, the original owner, failed to appreciate the architectural purity of her new residence, which had cost her dearly. "Something should be done about such architecture as this or there will be no future for architecture. . . . I thought you could animate a predetermined, classic form like this with your presence. I wanted to do something 'meaningful,' and all I got was this glib, false sophistication."

Still, an American private residence by Mies is a very rare thing. After completing the Farnsworth House, Mies turned his attention almost exclusively to the design of such large corporate structures as the Seagram Building in New York City, which seemed much more appropriate for his sleek, detached, and authoritative style.

The house is located about fifty miles southwest of Chicago on the banks of the Fox River. At the time of construction, the house occupied a secluded meadow. Now, the reconstruction of Milbrook Road and a new bridge over the Fox River effectively ended its isolation.

Farnsworth House is a private residence.

United Nations Secretariat, 1950

First Avenue at 42nd Street
New York, New York

Wallace K. Harrison with consulting architects Le Corbusier, Oscar Niemeyer, and Sven Markelius

The United Nations Secretariat holds the honor of being New York's first glass skyscraper. It rises high above the East River, two long walls of blue-green glass flanked by two short walls of warm gray marble. A building this big and this different was bound to cause a stir. Everyone had an opinion. While some critics derided it as "a vast marble frame for two enormous windows," and "a cliff of glass," architects tended to look on it in a more positive light. It is "yummy," said one. Another, misquoting Sam Cooke, said, "It sends me." There was no denying the "U.N. look," which would soon spread across the country.

The United Nations Secretariat's 38 stories, 544 feet tall and 287 feet wide, provide office space for 3,500 diplomats and staff as well as a residence for the Secretary General. The Secretariat is a monument to international cooperation and was itself a cooperative enterprise. Prominent New York City architect Wallace K. Harrison, in association with Max Abramowitz, headed a team of designers from around the world, including Le Corbusier from France and Oscar Niemeyer from Brazil.

The final design owes much to Le Corbusier, but the technology that made possible the curtain walls, the central elevator core, and the air-conditioning was clearly American.

"It was a U.N. job—a collaborative job," remarked Wallace K. Harrison, who gained a reputation for forging consensus and getting results when the chips were down. He was also known for his friends in high places, most notably John D. Rockefeller, Jr., and for his work in designing Rockefeller Center. Although not all his later commissions ended happily, the United Nations Secretariat became quite a symbol of international cooperation. Harrison took professional pride in the fact that modern architecture in the International Style had been used successfully to create a proper building for the international community.

Guided tours are conducted seven days a week from 9:15 AM to 4:45 PM. One-hour English language tours leave every half hour from the Visitor's Center located at First Avenue at 46th Street. For information regarding foreign-language tours, call (212) 963-7539 on the day of the visit. Reservations are required for groups of fifteen or more; call (212) 963-4440 during business hours Monday through Friday. For general information, call (212) 963-7713.

Breuer House, 1951 (Epstein House)

628 West Road
New Canaan, Connecticut

Marcel Breuer

Marcel Breuer is best remembered for his masterpiece, the Whitney Museum, and for his classic furniture designs. Less well known, Breuer's houses also rank as modern classics—especially those the Bauhaus architect built for himself. The house on West Road in New Canaan is the third of Breuer's four homes and is said to have been his favorite. It was the one the Hungarian-born architect lived in for the longest duration, from 1951 until 1976. It shows his conviction that the architect's mission begins with discipline and leads to adventure.

Breuer's first American residential adventure was in Lincoln, Massachusetts, in 1937, the year he came to teach at Harvard with Walter Gropius. The two friends built houses next door to each other, a pair of Bauhaus originals with flat roofs, stark white walls, and catalog materials. Blatantly modern, Breuer's design obscured his novel use of traditional material, such as white clapboard. Breuer's severe Bauhaus style softened somewhat in his next house, a large rectangle cantilevered from a concrete podium that was also clad with wood siding, this time laid on the diagonal.

By the time he built the house in New Canaan, Breuer's interest in local materials had turned to stone. On the street façade, slab walls clad with natural stone co-exist with painted brick and glass to provide most of the visual interest. The entry court is paved with stone, as is the rear terrace; interior floors are bluestone and there is a massive stone fireplace in the living room. Because a large wall of glass opens the house at the rear, the stone is a continuous and natural presence throughout the house.

In plan, the house is U-shaped. Parents and children benefit from having separate wings, which Breuer called a "binuclear" plan, but the public areas of the house are designed to be open. One trend of 1950s houses—shallow windows placed at ceiling height—was pioneered here. Interiors were spartan, in keeping with the Breuers' lifestyle.

In 1981, the house was expanded and remodeled for new owners by Breuer and his long-time collaborator, Herbert Beckhard of New York City. A new children's wing has been connected to the original house, which is still intact and not greatly changed by the addition. If anything, the horizontal emphasis and earthbound quality have been enhanced.

Breuer House is a private residence.

860-880 Lakeshore Drive, 1951

Chicago, Illinois

Ludwig Mies van der Rohe

Mies van der Rohe first envisioned the all-glass skyscraper in the 1920s. A true genius, he designed a structure that could not be built at the time, but some thirty years later the technology was at hand. The long-held dream of the crystalline tower was finally realized in these famous apartment towers, 26 stories of black steel and glass.

Mies described his style of architecture as "skin and bones": evidently nothing more than a steel frame (the bones) with glass inserts (the skin). Streamlined in the extreme, the Lakeshore Drive apartments gain strength in numbers: the two identical towers confront each other at a right angle in a composition of carefully controlled tension. The towers are situated on a travertine base and are elevated two stories above it by columns around the perimeter. At the center of each building, Mies consolidated the elevators and utilities, thereby achieving great freedom in arranging interior living spaces and in designing the outside walls. In a slight elaboration of the skin and bones façade, he added steel "I" mullions, which divide the structural bays. Without this finishing touch to the building, he felt, "It did not look right."

The towers at 860-880 Lakeshore Drive are marvels of precision and refinement, the result of Mies's relentless drive for architectural purity over decades of teaching and practice. The great success of these soaring, flat-roofed glass and steel buildings inspired legions of imitators, changing the face of almost every major city in the world. Unfortunately, very few of the copies hold a candle to the original.

The apartments are private residences, but the Chicago Architecture Foundation includes the towers on their "Architectural Highlights by Bus" tours. For information, call (312) 922-TOUR.

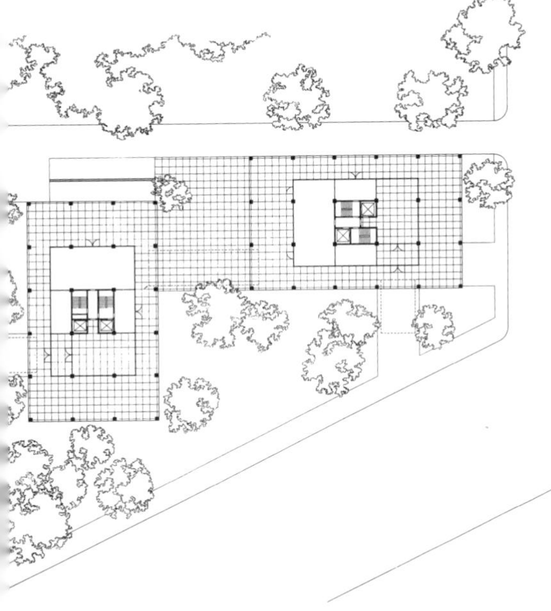

Wayfarer's Chapel, 1951

5755 Palos Verdes Drive South
Rancho Palos Verdes, California

Lloyd Wright

This chapel by the sea is a small but elegant structure built of simple materials: glass walls and gables framed in redwood, with a base and altar of stone. The church was intended to increase our appreciation of nature, and the bounty here is almost overwhelming. Taking advantage of its spectacular setting, the chapel seems to merge with the trees and flowers that surround it, and with the Pacific Ocean at its feet.

The chapel owes its existence to Elizabeth Schellenberg, who lived on the Palos Verdes Peninsula in the late 1920s. She first commissioned Ralph Jester to draw up plans for a church to honor Emmanuel Swedenborg, the Swedish theologian and founder of her religion. The church was delayed first by the depression and later by the war.

When the idea resurfaced, Jester felt his mission-style design was not right for the site; he suggested that Lloyd Wright, Frank Lloyd Wright's eldest son, was the architect for the job. It is evident from the chapel that Lloyd Wright shared his father's view of intermingling of site and structure. Also, Lloyd Wright's training in landscape architecture (he worked for a time with Olmstead and Olmstead on the East Coast) was a valuable contribution to the design. After the chapel's completion in 1951, Wright added the stone tower, colonnade, and visitors center to the original design.

The chapel is open daily. Guided tours are offered on weekends, and groups can be accommodated on other days through reservations at the office from 9:00 AM to 5:00 PM, Monday through Saturday. Sunday services are held at 11:00 AM; all are welcome. For reservations and information, call (213) 377-1650.

Lever House, 1952

390 Park Avenue, between
53rd and 54th Streets
New York, New York

Skidmore, Owings & Merrill

The new look of Lever House revolutionized commercial architecture in New York City with its sleek translucent blue-green glass walls and stainless steel frame. In part, the ground-breaking design resulted from the company's emphasis on cleanliness; for this prominent soap and detergent manufacturer, a clean-looking building was considered essential. Stone and brick become grimy in a city, but glass becomes clean in an instant. To ensure that the building stays that way, a track-mounted gondola system enables two men to wash the entire building in only six days.

In its massing, the Lever House design was as innovative as the materials. The design separates the 24-story building into two strong slabs, a vertical tower rising out of a horizontal base. This broad, podium-type base is raised one floor above ground level and is supported at the perimeter by rows of columns.

At street level, Lever House offers an open plaza with a courtyard garden in the center, an idea that was highly praised for its sensitivity to pedestrians. This scaled-back design also brought a feeling of airiness to the massive canyons of Park Avenue, and new visual interest from the constantly changing reflections on the glass walls.

By today's standards, Lever House would be considered a small office building, less than 290,000 square feet, but its impact was enormous. Besides setting a trend for New York skyscraper design, the design (by SOM partner Gordon Bunshaft) established Skidmore, Owings & Merrill's signature style and position as a premier source of prestigious commercial architecture.

Lever House received the American Institute of Architects Twenty-Five Year Award in 1980, but it soon faced the possibility of destruction so that a larger and presumably more profitable building could be erected on its site. Landmark designation in 1982 halted the threat to this modern masterpiece.

Lever House was built as the Lever Brothers corporate headquarters, and the company continues to occupy it today. The building is open from 9:00 AM to 5:00 PM Monday through Friday, and public exhibitions are often on view in the lobby. For information, call (212) 688-6000.

Yale University Art Gallery Addition, 1953

Yale University
Chapel Street, between York and High Streets
New Haven, Connecticut

Louis I. Kahn

Louis Kahn's art gallery addition was the first modern building at Yale, and the first prominent masterpiece by the architect whom many view as the towering talent of the late twentieth century. At Yale, where he was teaching at the time, Kahn joins a new building to a majestically classic one, maintaining a common sense of scale and grace.

The new gallery is basically a concrete frame warehouse four stories tall. On the garden side, the walls are dark-rimmed glass. A different façade shows its face to the street. Here, a full expanse of beige brick is scored by subtle vertical bands that mark the interior floors. The main entry consists of a sleek, narrow wall of full-height glass. It is set at a right angle to the street, so that this crucial division between the old building and the new one virtually disappears.

As with most of Kahn's buildings, the real excitement lies inside, where space and light are manipulated to powerful effect. The vast concrete floors are deliberately open so that they can be endlessly reconfigured for changing exhibitions by means of movable partitions. This "universal space" is topped by the building's trademark ceiling, an exposed gridwork of concrete tetrahedrons with spotlights mounted within the open struts. In an uncanny way, the rhythmic effect of walking beneath this ceiling enhances the primary purpose of the building: looking at art.

The proverbial late bloomer, Louis Kahn was in his fifth decade when he designed the Yale addition. By the sheer brilliance and power of his architecture, Kahn compensated for a late start. Many Kahn designs were never built, giving his existing buildings almost "untouchable" status. Even the prospect of alteration—as with the Kimbell Art Museum in the 1980s or the Salk Institute in the 1990s—ignites a storm of protest from architects and citizens alike, who demand the preservation of his designs and his intentions.

The Yale Art Gallery is open Tuesday through Saturday from 10:00 AM to 5:00 PM, on Sunday from 2:00 to 5:00 PM, closed Monday, holidays, and the entire month of August in 1993. Introductory tours are conducted twice a week, on Wednesday and Saturday at 1:30 PM. For information about tours and exhibits, call (203) 432-0600.

BACHMAN-WILSON HOUSE, 1954

1423 River Road
Millstone, New Jersey

Frank Lloyd Wright

Frank Lloyd Wright gained fame for his houses and they remained a preoccupation throughout his long and flamboyant career. For wealthy clients, he designed sprawling and highly individualistic structures, such as Fallingwater and Barnsdall House. But the Usonian homes, of which the Bachman-Wilson House is a late example, were meant for average American families.

The name Usonian is Wright's own contrivance, a play on the initials U.S. that expressed his democratic ideals. Usonian homes were small and compact, with flat roofs, open floor plans, and an easy relationship between indoors and out. Not incidentally, these "economical" family homes turned out to cost about twice as much to build as the homes they were intended to replace.

The Bachman-Wilson House is built of undecorated concrete-block. The front is long and flat, with extending eaves. For the entry, Wright employed one of his favorite dramatic devices—a dim, low-ceiling vestibule that ushers visitors into a hall and then into a surprisingly large and light-filled room. This two-story great room, 28 x 35 feet, almost fills the first floor. Its most striking feature is a 10-foot wall of glass and Philippine mahogany that opens to the surrounding forest; four of the panels are doors. Above the glass wall, Wright placed a band of clerestory windows, inset with a repetitive pattern of plywood cutouts, the primary decoration. The radiant-heated concrete floor was originally tinted red.

Wright believed that the hearth was the heart of a home. The Bachman-Wilson House shows how Wright adapted this idea to the Usonian house. It has a core of concrete block, with the kitchen on one side and a fireplace facing the great room on the other. Hallways function as rooms. In the Bachman-Wilson House, the dining room is carved out of such a space. A cantilevered Philippine mahogany balcony wraps the masonry core and forms the hall for the two upstairs bedrooms and the bath. Bedrooms are small, and their ceilings are only 6½-feet high. Balconies of Philippine mahogany are cantilevered off the bedrooms to compensate for their diminutive size.

The house is located about seven miles along River Road, off Highway 544 at Griggstown. The private residence may be accessible on special occasions. For information, write Bachman-Wilson House, 1423 River Road, Millstone, N.J. 08876.

Catalano House, 1954

Catalano Drive
Raleigh, North Carolina

Eduardo Catalano

All his life, the Argentine-born architect Eduardo Catalano has pursued new ways of unifying space and structure. His explorations in the 1950s resulted in a remarkable series of theoretical studies for houses; two were actually built, including the 1956 "House of the Decade," one of the few buildings ever praised by Frank Lloyd Wright.

But it is the house that Catalano built for himself that still captures the imagination. It shows Catalano's ability to be both structurally daring and elegantly simple, and to innovate without sacrificing that elusive quality of being genuine, not contrived.

Catalano's astonishing house seems to be all roof, nothing more than a large glider that has drifted into the forest. And in fact, the roof is the key—a 2¼-inch shell of laminated wood lightly tethered to the earth, supported at only two points. The unusual roof shape, a hyperbolic paraboloid, results from Catalano's explorations into the properties of warped surfaces. Using mathematically pure geometry, he designed the house as a continuous and integral structure.

The membrane roof stretches 87 feet above walls of glass. The connection between the roof and the walls seems effortless, partly due to the thinness of the line between them: just two metal angles join these major structural components. By extending the roofline 12 feet beyond the walls of the small (approximately 1,700 square feet) house, Catalano invokes the all-important sense of shelter, the essence of home.

In architecture, Catalano's hyperbolic paraboloid represents the mathematical optimum: the point where the trough of one curve is simultaneously the peak of another. Catalano's composed shape, which seems architecturally unconventional, is satisfying in part because it is mathematically perfect.

Catalano lived in the Raleigh house for about one year, while teaching at North Carolina State University. In 1956, the Harvard-trained architect began teaching at the Massachusetts Institute of Technology, where he is now Professor Emeritus and maintains a practice in Cambridge.

Catalano's Raleigh house still stands, unnumbered, on a short street bearing his name. It is located just off Ridge Road, visible from the street, but occupied as a private residence.

Fountainbleau Hotel, 1954

4441 Collins Avenue
Miami Beach, Florida

Morris Lapidus

When it opened, the Fountainbleau Hotel was probably the most highly criticized building in America, but now it is one of the most highly praised.

The hotel was the setting for the movie *Goldfinger,* and in fact the Fountainbleau was designed like a movie set, to amaze and to entertain. Built on a curve, the hotel formed a 15-story backdrop for the serpentine swoop of the two-story beachside cabanas (removed in 1979). In between, a formal French parterre garden coexists next to the Olympic-sized swimming pool. "Wonderful nonsense" fills the colorful interior, like the grand lobby staircase to nowhere (now leading to the executive offices) and Lapidus's signature bow-tie pattern inset in the marble lobby floor.

Almost as astonishing as the hotel's ground-breaking design is the fact that it was accomplished for a client who asked for a hotel designed in the French Provincial style. Lapidus soon determined that his client meant *modern* French Provincial, prompting him to come up with a unique answer to his own crazy question, "What kind of chop suey is this?"

The Fountainbleau was the first building Lapidus ever designed. He says he didn't even consider himself an architect when he got the commission, although for twenty years he had created hundreds of trendsetting store designs in New York City. The short-lived shops allowed Lapidus to experiment in ways that would never fly on a building project. This design freedom, and the need to attract paying customers, led Lapidus to an architecture of human nature—an architecture based on what people like and respond to. The stores acted as billboards, drawing shoppers in with Lapidus's constants: curving lines, bright lights, and a sense of occasion. The Fountainbleau was the beneficiary of all he had learned.

Despite his unorthodox designs, Lapidus received a classical architectural education at Columbia University in the 1920s. At school, Europe's emerging modern architecture was mentioned only to be dismissed, a looming danger best avoided. But from Mies van der Rohe, Lapidus encountered the possibilities of opening up space, although Lapidus thought not in straight lines but in curves. For the Fountainbleau, his design began as a series of squiggles.

After all these years, Morris Lapidus need apologize to no one. The Fountainbleau is a much-studied milestone, as is his Eden Roc Hotel, shown here behind the Fountainbleau. And it is still a beautiful building, world famous, far surpassing its more straightforward rivals. It fulfills Lapidus's wish for all his buildings: do anything, but "By God, don't walk by me."

For information, call (305) 538-2000. For tours, ask for Public Relations.

MANUFACTURERS HANOVER TRUST COMPANY BANK, 1954 (CHEMICAL BANK)

Fifth Avenue at 43rd Street
New York, New York

Skidmore, Owings & Merrill

The opening of the Fifth Avenue branch of Manufacturers Hanover Trust Company caused quite a commotion. For the first time, the hallowed symbol of banking security—the vault—was removed from the hidden reaches of the inner sanctum and positioned right out in the front window.

Manufacturers Hanover Trust was also the first glass-walled bank, and only a half inch of plate (and a 30-ton door) separates the vault from the sidewalk. Skidmore, Owings & Merrill radically reversed traditional bank secrecy with invisible walls, bright light, open teller counters, and a polished, stainless steel vault displayed like jewelry in a store window for all passers-by to see.

The bank's five stories include two customer banking floors, offices, and a penthouse for the president. Sheer glass walls are framed by aluminum mullions, and the 22 x 9⅔-foot panes on the second floor held the record as the largest ever installed at the time. To create the maximum impact of all this glass, SOM intensely illuminated the interior of the building so that the glass appeared invisible.

The interiors, for the most part, are cool and professional. One bright spot is a wall-sized sculptural screen of golden steel by Harry Bertoia located in the great banking room on the second floor.

Now a branch of Chemical Bank, the building is open during regular business hours. But you can see the vault in the window as you walk down the street.

For information, call (212) 270-4621.

BAVINGER HOUSE, 1955

730 60th Street
Norman, Oklahoma

Bruce Goff

Outside the mainstream of American architecture, Bruce Goff pursued a career that was mythologically ultra-American—individualistic, innovative, creative, and independent. Bavinger House, a swirling structure set in rugged country, was designed for a sculptor and his family who wanted something different, too.

The Bavingers planned to build the house themselves on a small but beautiful site at the edge of a stream. When cleared, the first level was revealed to be naturally curved, and from this base the shell-like shape of the house emerged. The winding exterior is more than 50 feet tall, 96 feet of continuous wall surface covered with rocks that coils around a steel pole. Cables radiate from this central pole to the spiraling roof, which is covered in copper. Virtually the entire house is suspended from the central mast—the roof, the five principal living areas, an interior stairway, and a suspension bridge that crosses the stream and leads to a garden.

There is no such thing as a room inside; the space evolves upward in a continuous stretch. The five living areas consist of circular pavilions covered in carpet and suspended at various levels from bottom to top. Goff staggered the pavilions to control visibility. For further privacy, the pavilions are draped with netting and opaque curtains, which can be closed or opened.

The Bavinger design is obviously personal, but it is interesting to note that Frank Lloyd Wright's Guggenheim Museum—also based on the spiral shape—was under construction in New York City. But unlike Wright, Goff's largest commissions came toward the end of his enormously productive life. His last work, the beautiful Japanese pavilion of the Los Angeles County Museum of Art, was completed after his death.

The Bavinger House received the American Institute of Architects Twenty-Five Year Award in 1987. It is a private residence, still occupied by the Bavingers, and shielded by trees, except in winter.

Jewish Community Center Bath House ("Trenton Bath House"), 1955

999 Lower Ferry Road
Ewing, New Jersey

Louis I. Kahn

In the off season, the Jewish Community Center Bath House (also referred to as the Trenton Bath House) looks like a tiny compound in an ancient village whose residents long ago moved on. Its four cube-shaped structures with their pyramid roofs sit somewhat forlornly out in an open field. The concrete block cubes cluster around an open-air pavilion in a way that seems tribally protective.

The Bath House is one of Louis Kahn's earliest but most evocative works. It reflects his unique ability to invest ancient forms—the circle, the square, the pyramid, the cross—with new reverence.

Kahn experienced the power of the past while traveling through Italy, Greece, and Egypt in the early 1950s. In visiting ancient sites, he observed that when the architectural details have worn away, only the structure remains. The Bath House design is based on this simple truth. Solid stone-gray walls delineate four large squares, like open columns at each of the corners. Kahn's cross-shaped plan has a circular atrium at the center and a pyramid-shaped roof over each of the hollow columns. The slight space between wall and roof is a masterpiece of dramatic tension. It shows that in Kahn's hands, extreme simplicity can evoke highly complex emotions.

Kahn credited the Trenton Bath House for his earliest insights on organizing space by separating areas that are "served" from areas providing the services, and here it is solved with absolute purity. Services such as restrooms and chlorinating facilities are contained within the "hollow columns" of the walls. These hollow columns, which provide both support and service, also fascinated Kahn as an organizing principle and a source of inspiration. He intended to elaborate these ideas in the community center itself, which unfortunately was never built.

By the early 1990s, the Bath House was in sad shape. Its walls were discolored, its rooftops deteriorating, and its access denied by buckled chain-link fencing. Fortunately, help is finally at hand. In 1992, the Trenton Bath House Foundation was formed to oversee the proper restoration, and to raise the necessary funding. Tarantino Associates of Millstone, New Jersey, has been selected to restore the important structure.

The Bath House is located off Interstate 95, Scotch Road exit, in Ewing, near the New Jersey-Pennsylvania border. Summer swimming programs are available. For information about visiting or contributing, call (609) 883-9550.

Kresge Auditorium, 1955

Massachusetts Institute of Technology
Cambridge, Massachusetts

Eero Saarinen

Kresge Auditorium is a building based on the shape of a sphere. The roof is a three-pointed dome of white, thin-shell concrete, while its interior floor cups upward forming a dome in reverse, a design Eero Saarinen described as "two shell shapes, like a clam." The spherical theme continues with the rounded glass walls and the circular brick podium that surrounds the building.

Rectangular buildings ring the crowded campus site, and Saarinen chose to design in contrast rather than continuity with the surroundings. "We believed that what was required was a contrasting silhouette, a form which started from the ground and went up, carrying the eye around its sweeping shape...at first it seemed strange, but gradually it became the loved one."

Inside, the auditorium houses a small theater on the lower level and a concert hall on the main floor. For acoustical control, Saarinen designed a baffling system he called "floating clouds." The excellent sound quality alone, in Saarinen's view, justified the unusual building shape, which received almost as much negative criticism as praise.

Kresge Auditorium marked a turning point in Saarinen's career. Moving away from strict rectangular buildings of glass and steel, he began to explore a variety of new ideas and forms which were often controversial but always interesting.

For visitor and program information, call Massachusetts Institute of Technology at (617) 253-1000.

S.R. Crown Hall, 1956

Illinois Institute of Technology
State Street, between 34th and 35th Streets
Chicago, Illinois

Ludwig Mies van der Rohe

The long association of the Illinois Institute of Technology (IIT) and Mies van der Rohe resulted in a campus showcase of his architecture, including classrooms, dormitories, laboratories, and a steam-generating plant. In addition, many of the non-Miesian buildings are so faithful to his style that they could easily be mistaken as his work.

Mies came to IIT in 1938 after heading the Bauhaus at Dessau, Germany, which closed in 1933. Two years later, in 1940, he was commissioned to plan a new campus on the south side of Chicago. The long, narrow site was laid out in a rigid order, and the first buildings were equally regimental: two- and three-story structures with black, exposed steel frames, large plate-glass windows, and buff-colored brick.

Crown Hall is considered to be the campus masterpiece. Mies designed it for the College of Architecture, his own department, so this building is the most personal in that respect. As the first all steel and glass structure on campus, it also moved him closer to his ultimate goal of transforming the internal structure into the building's actual form.

A glass-walled pavilion 220 feet long by 120 feet wide, Crown Hall is distinguished and defined by the four massive trusses that straddle the roof. It is clear to even a casual observer that the roof is suspended from the underside of these girders, which are in turn supported by eight exterior steel columns. The roof is cantilevered 20 feet from the outermost columns at the east and west ends, contributing to the "floating planes" effect that Mies began to develop in the Farnsworth House in Plano.

The building entrance, also reminiscent of the Farnsworth House, consists of a floating slab pavilion with wide, shallow steps. This leads into an exhibition space with low, free-standing partitions of finely grained wood. From here, observers enter one of the most majestic spaces in contemporary architecture: a 220 x 120-foot expanse of clear span space, rising 18 feet and filled with light, a feat made possible by the great roof trusses that also contribute so mightily to the outside form.

IIT's Office of Public Relations conducts architectural tours by special arrangement. For information and appointments, call (312) 567-3104. The Chicago Architecture Foundation also includes IIT on its "Architectural Highlights by Bus" tours. For CAF information, call (312) 922-TOUR.

General Motors Technical Center, Administration Building, 1956

6250 Chicago Road
Warren, Michigan

Eero Saarinen

In this wooded, 1000-acre "Industrial Versailles," the automotive giant carries on research and development, engineering, and styling of the cars of tomorrow.

The complex of long, low buildings was designed over a ten-year period by Eero Saarinen in partnership with his father, Eliel, who died in 1950. The Tech Center's splashiest feature is its futuristic stainless steel water tower in a 22-acre pool with Alexander Calder's spectacular "water sculpture," a water wall fountain 155 feet wide and 50 feet high.

Eero tried to design "variety within unity" for the multi-building complex. Unity is established by the five-foot module, horizontal proportions, dark-gray steel frames, green-tinted glass, and green belt surroundings that are common to all. For variety, Saarinen alternated high buildings with low ones, glass walls with brick walls, and buildings seen through trees versus those which open onto the central court. The bright spots include the brilliantly colored glazed ceramic brick of the end walls—blue, red, yellow, and orange—which were fired on site. Dramatic blue-black exhaust stacks placed outside of certain buildings add visual punch.

A number of technical firsts also occurred here: the use of brilliantly colored glazed brick; the prefabricated porcelain sandwich panel that integrates interior and exterior walls; the luminous ceiling with lighting covered by modular plastic pans; and especially the neoprene gasket weather seal to mount windows or metal panels, which soon became a construction standard.

The influence of Mies van der Rohe's rigorous steel and glass method is evident at the Technical Center, but Saarinen soon moved on to experiment with a great diversity of architectural forms that were his alone. His independent career was short but energetic and influential; he was posthumously awarded the American Institute of Architects Gold Medal in 1962.

At this writing, the center is not open to the public. For information, call (313) 986-5715.

Inland Steel Building, 1958

30 West Monroe Street
Chicago, Illinois

Skidmore, Owings & Merrill

Inland Steel's corporate headquarters building is quite a showcase for the company's main product: steel. Structural steel columns, ordinarily positioned inside the glass curtain wall, are here placed prominently on the outside of the long façade of this corner site. Stainless steel panels are used to clad the adjacent service tower, and steel strips are utilized to form the building's window mullions, transoms, and spandrels.

The building's primary technical advances, however, are on the inside. The offices are separated from the service functions by the creation of two adjacent but distinctly different towers. The glass-walled tower houses the corporate offices on nineteen stories, each 10,000 square feet. Elevators, stairs, lavatory facilities, and air-conditioning ductwork are grouped inside the 25-story blank-walled tower. As a result, the office floors are free of structural constraints, thus greatly increasing the possibilities for interior spatial arrangements.

With the Inland Steel building, Skidmore, Owings & Merrill followed the astounding success of their Lever House design in New York City earlier in the decade. During these years, the firm (which had been formed in the 1930s) gained international acclaim for their refined, Mies-inspired steel and glass style, which became a hallmark of corporate wealth and power.

The Inland Steel lobby is open during business hours. The building is included on the Chicago Architecture Foundation's Walking Tours as well as their "Architectural Highlights by Bus." For information, call CAF at (312) 922-TOUR.

Seagram Building, 1958

375 Park Avenue
New York, New York

Ludwig Mies van der Rohe and Philip Johnson

The Seagram Building is an acknowledged masterpiece, and as with buildings of such stature, there are a number of "firsts" associated with it. Seagram is Mies van der Rohe's first building in New York City, the first bronze-colored skyscraper, and the first skyscraper of glass walls from floor to ceiling. Although it was not the first International Style arrival on Park Avenue (Lever House across the street claims this distinction), it is certainly one of the most elegant skyscrapers ever built.

America's honeymoon with International Style buildings is now over, but Seagram's precise design and construction remind us of why the style was captivating in the first place. The design's strength results from its simplicity. The 38-story tower of bronze glass and hand-rubbed bronze mullions and spandrels rises straight up from an elevated granite podium flanked by a pair of reflecting pools with fountains. The soaring quality of the building is achieved by the continuous lines of the bronze mullions, which have been placed outside the glass walls to emphasize the vertical sweep. Because of the delicate way these I-beam mullions create line and shadow, they have been compared to the Ionic columns of classical architecture.

No expense was spared in constructing this building, and the rich materials used outside are continued throughout the interiors, designed by Philip Johnson (including the famous Four Seasons Restaurant). The luxuriousness of the "less is more" architecture at the Seagram Building prompted Henry-Russell Hitchcock to remark after a visit that he had "never seen more of less."

Mies van der Rohe designed the Seagram Building to be a freestanding monument, best to be viewed in pristine isolation. Its success was surely gratifying, but the sheer number of poor imitations came to obscure the contribution of this icon of modernism. In the 1980s, the building itself was compromised by the construction of a new office tower abutting its eastern façade. The Seagram Building received the American Institute of Architects Twenty-Five Year Award in 1984.

Tours of the building are conducted every Tuesday at 3:00 PM except holidays. For information, or for group reservations, call (212) 572-7404.

Union Tank Car Dome, 1958

Brooklawn Road
Baton Rouge, Louisiana

R. Buckminster Fuller

Many architects dream of incorporating experimental technology into their buildings, but Buckminster Fuller made a lifetime career of it. His brainchild, the geodesic dome, is his ingenious solution to the problem of enclosing the maximum amount of space with the minimum amount of material and expense.

The largest geodesic dome ever built is the Union Tank Car Dome, a roundhouse where railroad tank cars are maintained, repaired, and painted. With a volume twenty-three times that of St. Peter's Cathedral in Rome, the dome spans a 384-foot clear span interior and is 120 feet high at its apex.

The igloo-like building consists of 320 interlocking hexagonal steel panels, painted goldenrod, which are braced by steel rods on the exterior, which are painted blue. Three tracks bring railroad cars into the building to a rotating table, which transfers them to one of the fourteen repair bays in the roundhouse. Adjoining the main dome is the painting shed, a half-round extension 200 feet long and 40 feet wide. Inside the central dome, there is a second dome with an open geodesic frame that encompasses the storehouse, offices, and a restaurant. In terms of construction economy, the facility is astounding—only two ounces of steel are used for each cubic foot of enclosed space.

Buckminster Fuller succeeded in proving that we could build more with less. Although Fuller's cheerful counterculture proclamations enthralled the media, his geodesic dome failed to gain widespread acceptance as a building type. But for his real contributions to building technology, Fuller received the American Institute of Architects Gold Medal in 1970.

The Union Tank Car facility has lain fallow for a dozen years. In 1990, Kansas City Southern Railway Company bought it with the expectation of re-opening it. As of 1992, however, the yard remained all but abandoned except for a watchful security guard who may or may not welcome your visit. For information, call the Kansas City Southern yardmaster's office at (504) 379-4241.

Case Study House #22, 1959

1635 Woods Drive
Los Angeles, California

Pierre Koenig

It is a rare architectural photograph that captures not only the essence of a building but also the essence of a generation. Here, photographer Julius Shulman's famous nighttime shot stops the clock to show us the beautiful dream of progressive domestic architecture in the late 1950s.

Pierre Koenig's minimal masterpiece represents the most advanced stage of the Case Study Houses, a post-war program sponsored by *Arts and Architecture* magazine to encourage affordable domestic architecture using the latest materials, techniques, and furnishings.

The one-story house is a study in horizontal planes. It turns a solid wall to the street but opens completely with floor-to-ceiling glass walls in the back to favor the breathtaking view of the city at its feet. Koenig's L-shaped plan features two wings flanking the terrace and pool. The public wing houses the living room, dining room, and kitchen; the private wing contains a master bedroom, children's bedroom, and bath. A central core containing the master bath, dressing room, and service areas connects the two. Surprisingly, the pool abuts the edge of the house in two places, where it is bridged to provide access from the carport to the entry.

In this house, Koenig realizes his ideal of the glass pavilion. His design is also true to the goals of the Case Study program: a simple but refined modular design of standardized materials and an open floor plan with minimal hallways. But Koenig brought the best of nature to this somewhat austere program—the freshness of sunlight for the inside and the tranquility of water for the terrace.

Case Study House #22 is a private residence.

Solomon R. Guggenheim Museum, 1959

1071 Fifth Avenue at 88th Street
New York, New York

Frank Lloyd Wright
Gwathmey Siegel (1992 Museum Addition)

For the man who devoted his life to breaking architecture out of the box, the Guggenheim Museum is the final victory. In this last great work, Frank Lloyd Wright created a giant spiral that rises up from its corner site in ever-increasing circles, culminating in a glass dome 100 feet across at the top. This corkscrew building is hollow at the center; on the inside the spiral becomes a continuous ramp of gallery floors surrounding a light-filled central atrium.

The smooth beige concrete walls are angled outward and correspond to the interior gallery walls, where Wright envisioned the paintings tilted slightly back as on the artist's easel—a romantic notion that has given fits to nearly every museum director who has tried to mount an exhibition. The vantage point for visitors is also unusual. Wright meant for museum-goers to take an elevator to the uppermost floor and walk down. Wright's design presents the exhibition and the architecture as a single entity, and when the art is right the combination can be extremely effective.

The Guggenheim has often been criticized, the standard joke being, "They've got the museum, now they'll just have to build a building to show the pictures." The wish was fulfilled in a 1992 expansion and renovation by Gwathmey Siegel & Associates of New York. A 10-story limestone tower rises discreetly behind the museum, its cool gray stone blocks laid in a subtle "tartan grid" pattern. Four new gallery floors, three of them double height, nearly triple the museum's exhibition space—and provide flat walls. Wright's small rotunda is open to the public for the first time; a new outdoor roof terrace opens onto the trees of Central Park across the street.

Frank Lloyd Wright never lived to see the completion of his final masterpiece, which he designed in the mid-1940s. But he gets the last laugh. The outrage over "landmark tampering" that greeted plans for the annex surely surpassed the original outcry over the flying saucer New Yorkers said had landed in their midst. New York's only building by Frank Lloyd Wright, after all these years, is proudly acclaimed as the museum's own best work of art.

The Guggenheim is open daily, except Thursday and holidays (New Year's Day, Thanksgiving, and Christmas), from 10:00 AM to 8:00 PM. For information, call (212) 423-3500.

Pepsi-Cola World Headquarters, 1959 (Walt Disney Corporation)

500 Park Avenue
New York, New York

Skidmore, Owings & Merrill

This small gem of an office building is a classic in the SOM style of the 1950s. The building stands just 11 stories tall on a tight corner site, a shimmery rectangle of glass and aluminum floating above a one-story base of transparent glass. In contrast to the gargantuan office towers in the International Style, the Pepsi-Cola Building is comprehensible in size and scale, and perhaps this is why its subtle refinements make a stronger impression.

The design consists of minimal materials in perfect proportion. On the office floors, outside walls are single panes of half-inch glass, 9 feet high and 13 feet wide. Wide, sleek aluminum spandrels divide the building horizontally, while slender aluminum mullions against the glass provide vertical definition. The overall transparency of the building is underscored by the placement of steel support beams immediately inside the window walls, where they are clearly visible from the street. Vertical venetian blinds on all windows provide privacy and sun control, and contribute to the building's unified exterior appearance. Building services are unobtrusively grouped within a slim tower of black granite that virtually disappears.

For Skidmore, Owings & Merrill, Pepsi-Cola World Headquarters marked the end of an architectural era—the ultimate perfection of corporate headquarters buildings created in the International Style. By the end of the 1950s, the firm was already moving in new directions. The Pepsi-Cola building changed too, greatly expanded in 1984 to a design by James Stewart Polshek and Partners: a 40-story granite stone tower at its side and a 25-story aluminum and glass structure cantilevered above it. The expansion, which contains both residences and offices, has been praised for respecting the quality and style of the original structure.

The Pepsi-Cola building is now New York headquarters for the Walt Disney Corporation. The building is open during regular business hours.

Malin House ("Chemosphere"), 1960

776 Torreyson Drive
Los Angeles, California

John Lautner

New architectural ideas—and new building techniques—often show up first in small houses, where limited budgets call for innovative solutions. In the late 1950s, when Malin House was designed, "the future" was a source of architectural inspiration, especially themes about outer space. In this context, many people look at Malin House (nicknamed "Chemosphere") and see a hovering spacecraft. But John Lautner designed it as an organic response to an unbuildable site, which can't even be reached by conventional means. To compensate for these problems, the house is mounted on a stout pedestal with steel bracing. The "driveway" is a private funicular (the hill-a-vator) that goes up and down the mountainside, and the carport is located at the base of the pedestal.

"I realized," said the Michigan-born architect John Lautner, "that I could leave the whole natural terrain underneath the house and not disturb the nature at all and just have this house up in the air on one column. The aircraft engineer liked it and I went ahead and did it."

Lautner moved to Los Angeles in 1939 to work with Frank Lloyd Wright and still practices there. He is known for imaginative residential designs. In this case, the 2,200 square-foot house takes the unusual shape of an octagon with a redwood base. On the inside, Lautner divided the house in half, with pie-shaped bedrooms and baths on one side and a single large, open living area on the other. The living area is completely surrounded by sliding glass windows with a magnificent 360-degree view of the San Fernando Valley. The roof is an independent, curved structure that allows for unlimited internal room arrangements, although the original two-bedroom, two-bath design has remained basically unchanged.

Malin House is a private residence.

Guild House, 1961

711 Spring Garden Street
Philadelphia, Pennsylvania

Venturi & Rauch

The architectural community was literally stunned by the first sight of Guild House, a Quaker home for the elderly in Philadelphia. Sitting starkly behind its chain link fence up against the pavement on a gritty edge-of-downtown street, the dark brick six-story building had a storefront façade, a billboard sign, and an outsized anodized bronze television antenna prominently placed on the roof. If the building seemed "ordinary and ugly," well, that was the point.

Guild House was the first pre-postmodern building, a renunciation of almost everything the modern movement had represented for more than forty years. As Venturi explained in his two revolutionary books, *Complexity and Contradictions in Architecture* (Museum of Modern Art, 1977) and *Learning from Las Vegas* (with Denise Scott Brown and Steven Izenour, MIT Press, 1977), architecture is a language with something important to say. This language is complicated and full of contradictions, which cannot be ignored.

So, if Guild House is speaking to us, what is it saying? On the most pedestrian level, it attests to kinship with neighboring inner-city structures. The building's size, setbacks and inelegant windows of different sizes recall public housing blocks. The television antenna was meant to be an ironic commentary on the primary leisure activity of the inhabitants.

On a higher plane, Guild House is classically ordered. The main façade is anchored by a polished marble column centered at the entry, and the façade rises all of a piece to the semicircular lunette window on the top floor. Along the way, there are references to Le Corbusier's Villa Stein in France and Bruno Taut's Horseshoe Housing Development in Berlin, both from the 1920s, to Palladio, to Kahn, and to Frank Furness, the nineteenth-century Philadelphia architect admired by Venturi, who also practices in Philadelphia.

In the years since Guild House, Robert Venturi has evolved from a pop iconoclast to an elder statesman. His firm of Venturi, Rauch & Scott Brown received the American Institute of Architects Firm of the Year Award in 1985. And in 1991, Venturi was awarded the prestigious Pritzker Prize for architecture.

Guild House is still open, but the television antenna has been removed. For general information, call (215) 923-1539.

Dulles International Airport, 1962

Chantilly, Virginia

Eero Saarinen

As the gateway to America's capital city—and the country's first big jet-age airport—Dulles International called for a distinguished national monument, and Eero Saarinen clearly provided one. Surreal by day, ethereal at night, the airport is defined by two massive rows of tapered concrete columns that reach up and out, in tautly controlled tension that gives a beautiful curve to the roof. In a continuous line, the columns pierce the roof and arc up above it. Saarinen likened his design to "a huge, continuous hammock suspended between concrete trees."

To give special significance to the entry, the front façade rises 65 feet, versus 40 feet in back; columns are 40 feet apart on both sides, inset with walls of dark-framed glass.

In designing Dulles Airport, Saarinen continued to push the technological possibilities of molded concrete forms, which he helped pioneer in the Kresge Auditorium and the TWA Terminal in New York. At Dulles, he used light suspension-bridge cables to gird the roof, with concrete roof panels sandwiched between them, which in turn affected the whole design. "The concrete piers are sloped outward to counteract the pull of the cables," he noted. "But we exaggerated and dramatized this outward slope . . . to give the colonnade a dynamic and soaring look as well as a stately and dignified one . . . I think this airport is the best thing I have done."

Saarinen correctly identified Dulles as the masterpiece of his career, which was brief but extremely influential and ended with his untimely death in 1961, before the terminal's completion.

Tours of the terminal are conducted at 10:00 AM on Monday, Wednesday, Thursday, and Friday; there is also a film about the construction. For information and reservations for groups of ten or more, call the Airport Manager's office at (703) 661-2714.

SPACE NEEDLE, 1962

219 Fourth Avenue North
Seattle, Washington

John Graham Associates

The showpiece of Seattle's 1962 World's Fair, Space Needle jubilantly expresses the "Man in Space" theme of a futuristic fair devoted to the wonders of UFOs, the United States space program, Sputnik, and the prospect of men on the moon. Designed, engineered, constructed, and financed by a small group of private investors, Space Needle was also intended to counter Germany's Stuttgart Tower and France's Eiffel Tower. Today it symbolizes Seattle's development as a major metropolitan presence.

Seattle architect John Graham and his team faced a significant challenge in pure conceptual design. No one had ever seen a Space Needle, its form could take any shape, and there was no precedent for its design or construction. John Graham invited concepts from his collaborators, and the ideas ranged from spears with halos to hot air balloon shapes supported by intricate tether designs.

The final design is an elegant steel tripod tower soaring 605 feet into the air, with a high-pinched waist crowned by the flying saucer-like tophouse. Five distinct, layered discs form the tophouse (bottom to top): 1) a revolving restaurant, 2) a mezzanine disk, 3) the observation deck, 4) the mechanical equipment level, and 5) the elevator penthouse. A 50-foot natural gas torch tower topped the penthouse. The underground foundation supporting this fantastic structure weighs as much as the tower itself.

Seattle residents take delight in "dressing up" the Space Needle. It has been a Christmas Tree, a UFO for the UFO Expo, crowned with a crab for Seafood Month, and a birthday cake for its own tenth birthday.

The Space Needle is open daily from 8:00 AM to 1:00 AM daily. Three elevators spirit visitors to the observation deck—in about forty-three seconds—for spectacular views of downtown, Elliott Bay, and Puget Sound. The restaurant is also open to the public. For Space Needle information and reservations, call (206) 443-9800.

TWA Terminal, 1962

John F. Kennedy International Airport
New York, New York

Eero Saarinen

The TWA Terminal is sculpture on a gigantic scale, with its striking resemblance to an eagle just landed. And it is this uncanny image, captured in concrete, that makes the terminal one of the most memorable in the world.

This remarkable structure consists of a vast concrete shell constructed of four enormous barrel vaults canted upward, over rounded glass walls that rise at an outward angle to meet them. The vaulted forms, which are separated by skylights and supported on four Y-shaped columns, create a building that is 50 feet high and 315 feet long, and exceptionally light and airy inside.

Entering this building is like walking into the sculpture promised by the exterior form. Curved and molded shapes are everywhere—the ceiling, stairways, ramps, and counters. The evocation of movement also carries over inside, as you pass through a progression of spaces that are alternately closed and open.

Eero Saarinen considered the fact that some people saw the building as a bird in flight to be coincidental. "That was the last thing we ever thought about," he maintained. His goal, instead, was "to design a building in which the architecture itself would express the drama and specialness and excitement of travel...a place of movement and transition...The shapes were deliberately chosen in order to emphasize an upward-soaring quality of line. We wanted an uplift."

There are no special tours of the terminal, but it is open around the clock. Airport buses connecting the terminals will also give you a view of the exterior.

United States Air Force Academy Chapel, 1962

Colorado Springs, Colorado

Skidmore, Owings & Merrill

The United States Air Force Academy Chapel exerts a powerful spiritual presence as well as a physical one. Its gleaming aluminum wedge-shaped profile dominates flat, rectangular buildings on campus, and holds its own against the Rocky Mountain range in the background.

As a religious symbol, the Chapel is especially remarkable because three distinct congregations—Protestant, Jewish, and Catholic—worship within separate chapels. And each is consistent with the heritage of its faith. This commonality was achieved by combining two ancient religious conventions, the cathedral spire and stained glass, in a new synthesis. The sources are easy to recognize, but their combined power is mysteriously moving.

Viewed from the front entrance, the Chapel's origami-like image suggests hands raised in prayer. From the side, the image changes to reveal a row of seventeen pointed aluminum spires in regimental lock step, a squadron in formation.

The spires consist of 100 tetrahedrons, each 75 feet long. The spaces between the spires are filled with stained-glass strips in twenty-four colors (but no green), shaded from dark to light, which produce vivid interior hues in the daytime and intensely glowing colors at night. The stained-glass windows depict Paul's conversion on the road to Damascus, described by the Chapel's designer, Walter Netsche, as "a strong story, not sweet."

The U.S. Air Force Academy is located at the northern outskirts of Colorado Springs, about sixty miles south of Denver. The Chapel is open Monday through Saturday from 9:00 AM to 5:00 PM and Sunday from 1:00 to 5:00 PM, except for special religious services and holidays. Tours are self-guided, although the Visitor's Center conducts campus tours during the summer. For information, call (719) 472-2555.

Assembly Hall, 1963

University of Illinois
First Street, between Kirby and St. Mary's Roads
Champaign-Urbana, Illinois

Harrison & Abramovitz

The American domed stadium has become a metropolitan set piece. Houston has its Astrodome, New Orleans its Superdome, Cincinnati has one, Pontiac has another, and so on. The ancestor of these ubiquitous mushroom-shaped structures is Assembly Hall at the University of Illinois.

This early domed hall, with its boldly ribbed roof, was conceived in the late 1950s. It was built using concrete post-stressing machinery that had been developed, in that cold war decade, for the construction of Titan ballistic missile silos.

The domed roof, which weighs 4,400 tons, is a clear span structure without any internal columns or supports to block the spectators' views. The load of the roof is borne by a massive compression ring girdling the dome. This ring around the rim of "the oyster" is itself girdled by 614 miles of steel wire. The wire was tensioned up to 130,000 pounds per square inch, and it is the centripetal squeeze of this ring that holds the roof aloft.

The building is architecturally admirable, but its construction was an heroic process of inventing and improvising new tools and techniques. Not least of the problem was thinking through the sequence of construction. For example, the contractor did not fully excavate the structure, which is deeply dished into the earth, until the dome was already finished overhead. In this way, he was able to use shorter, more robust internal supports while the roof was under construction.

The unusual construction process was carefully documented by a faculty member who shot a 35mm photograph from the same spot each day. These slides were discovered after his retirement and compiled into a fascinating slide show. In just forty-five seconds you can watch the dome blossom out of the flat plain in this semi-animated presentation. Ask about it.

In the intervening decades the domed stadium concept has succeeded too well; in Baltimore, for example, the new Oriole Stadium at Camden Yards proclaimed proudly that it was *not* a domed stadium. The University of Illinois Assembly Hall is a reminder that in the beginning, a domed stadium really was a novelty and an intricate, tricky structure to erect. Year in and year out, the roof continues to stay aloft without any visible means of support.

For visitor information, call (217) 333-2923; for information about upcoming events at Assembly Hall, call (217) 333-5000.

Beinecke Rare Book and Manuscript Library, 1963

Yale University
New Haven, Connecticut

Skidmore, Owings & Merrill

With its mission to preserve a valuable cache of rare books and manuscripts, it makes sense that the building housing the Beinecke Library is exceptionally protective—self-contained and almost entirely closed from the outside world. The white marble monument forms the first line of defense. The rare book stacks are further enclosed in bronze glass climate-controlled cages occupying the central core of the library floors; an exhibition gallery surrounds the stacks. The lower level houses reading rooms and offices, as well as an open court enlivened by an Isamu Noguchi sculpture.

The bright white bulk of the library building is lifted above its surrounding pavilion by concrete piers that also frame the gray glass shell of the ground-level entrance. Marble panes, shirred thin to produce a remarkable translucence, are recessed into the overall steel grid. The play of light and shadow transforms the building as the day wears on; at night the interior light produces a continuous glow.

Beinecke Rare Book and Manuscript Library marks a significant transformation in the architectural style of its creators, the architectural firm of Skidmore, Owings & Merrill and Gordon Bunshaft, the library's designer. Turning away from the transparent glass corporate headquarters towers that made them famous in the 1950s, the architects moved on to new kinds of buildings and an increasing diversity of style.

For information, call (203) 432-3771.

Carpenter Center for the Visual Arts, 1963

Harvard University
24 Quincy Street
at Prescott Street
Cambridge, Massachusetts

Le Corbusier (Charles-Edouard Jeanneret)

The legendary Swiss-French architect who called himself Le Corbusier ("the crow") designed only one American building, the Carpenter Center for the Visual Arts at Harvard University. The great modern master was seventy-six years old at the time, and the building became an abridged dictionary of "tricks of the trade" of his long and eventful career. There are the flat roof and walls of the early days, the *brise-soleil* sunshades of the middle years, and the exposed concrete of the late period. Curving processional ramps like those at Carpenter were a constant theme for a man intensely concerned with how people would experience his buildings as they moved in, around, and through them.

The Carpenter Center for the Visual Arts contains classrooms and studio space for students in architecture, painting, and sculpture—and Le Corbusier was accomplished in all three disciplines. The building has been compared to a cubist painting because of the interlocking forms: a square central structure, a rectangular tower, and ramps shaped like guitar picks slotted in at either side. Carpenter Center features a large open space at the center with a skewed square skylight overhead. Studios are located at the perimeter, where light and views are controlled by the spacing of windows in various sizes and by the huge *brise-soleil* sunscreens. It is considered the best constructed of Le Corbusier's buildings.

One of three giants of twentieth-century architecture—along with Frank Lloyd Wright and Mies van der Rohe—Le Corbusier revolutionized architecture again and again. In the 1920s and 1930s, he called for a modern architectural purity of his own devising: weightless-looking white stucco buildings on stilts with smooth walls, flat roofs for terraces, ribbon windows, and no applied decoration. By the 1950s, he was using rough concrete in bulging freeform shapes that seemed ancient and primitive. The last buildings, erected like Carpenter Center in the 1960s, used concrete in a more refined but still powerful way.

The Carpenter Center for the Visual Arts is open Monday through Friday from 9:00 AM to 11:00 PM, Saturday 9:00 AM to 6:00 PM, and Sunday from noon to 10:00 PM, except holidays. Exhibits are mounted in the autumn and spring. For information, call (617) 495-8037.

Yale School of Art and Architecture, 1963

Yale University
Chapel at York Street
New Haven, Connecticut

Paul Rudolph

In the 1960s, Yale University's School of Art and Architecture provoked such extremes of praise and outrage that it was difficult to see how the critics could have been describing the same building. Proponents hailed it for introducing a brilliant new style of modernism, with its massive striated concrete columns and interlocking planes, a building that seemed rugged and sophisticated and like nothing else in America. To the students who used it, the building seemed so imposing and hostile that they tried to burn it to the ground. Now, of course, it is an established monument.

"I want a building to move people," explained Paul Rudolph, who was Dean of the School of Art and Architecture at Yale as well as the architect of record. A Gropius-trained Harvard graduate now practicing in New York City, Rudolph in 1958 designed the school's exterior in a complex asymmetrical series of thick vertical columns, and these masses serve as the organizing principle of the building. The columns are varied in height and juxtaposed against thin, horizontal floor slabs, balcony rails, and walls of tinted glass.

The building is entered from a wide concrete stair that gives onto the second level of an astoundingly complex interior, also raw concrete. There are seven main levels of space for exhibitions, classrooms, and studios, plus a number of partial floors. They are intricately connected and often confounding: in some cases, it is necessary to go upstairs in order to come back down to reach a lower floor. Paul Rudolph has used the pinwheel to describe the internal dynamics of horizontally thrusting wings working against the vertical thrust of the center. Quality of light was clearly a prime consideration, both inside and in the intricate changing play of light and shadow on the columns outside.

For information, call (203) 432-3771.

Huntington Hartford Museum, 1964 (New York City Visitors Center)

2 Columbus Circle
New York, New York

Edward Durell Stone

One of Edward Durell Stone's primary objectives when designing the Huntington Hartford Museum was to make a home for fine art, to present an example that would encourage visitors to bring original artwork into their own homes. The museum's galleries were arranged like landings on a great staircase, and the interiors were finished with rich materials.

The interiors are very different now that the building houses the New York Department of Cultural Affairs and the New York Convention and Visitors Bureau, but the exterior is virtually unchanged. It is an unusually embellished white marble tower on a tiny and constricted site. There are concave curving walls on the two broadest exposures, columns surmounted by large circles around the base, and tall arched windows on the upper floors.

But without a doubt, the building's most notable feature is the grillwork that frames its corners and forms wide bands around the top—the feature that also signs and dates the building as the work of Edward Durell Stone. His use of grillwork at the United States Embassy in New Delhi (1954) set off an architectural fashion in the late 1950s and early 1960s.

When Stone designed the building on Columbus Circle, he was already an experienced and well-known museum designer. Among his credits is the Museum of Modern Art in New York (1937), the first public International Style building in America.

One of Stone's most interesting ideas for the Huntington Hartford Museum was never realized. At the time of construction, Pennsylvania Station was being demolished, and Stone recommended that columns from the grand old Beaux Arts monument be rescued and placed in a circle around the gallery.

The New York City Department of Cultural Affairs office is open from 9:00 AM to 5:00 PM Monday through Friday, closed weekends and holidays. For information, call (212) 841-4100. To contact the New York Convention and Visitors Bureau, call (212) 484-1200.

MARINA CITY, 1964

State Street at the Chicago River
Chicago, Illinois

Bertrand Goldberg

In the early 1960s, the twin towers of Chicago's Marina City administered two shocks to the American system. Most obviously, the tall, rounded cylinders with their petal-shaped balconies astonished viewers accustomed to buildings in rectilinear forms. But the mixture of uses was equally revolutionary: the towers are the focal point of a five-building city within a city where residents can live, work, park, shop, bowl, ice skate, go to the theater, or go boating—a modern urban version of living above the store.

The 60-story twin towers each have 450 apartments on the top forty floors, stacked on top of twenty floors of parking. The apartments radiate out from a central core 35 feet in diameter; since walls angle out to an open horizon, residents experience the sensation of living in boundless space, just barely defined by the curved railings on the semi-circular cantilevered balconies.

Bertrand Goldberg's innovative design results from his explorations of the possibilities of concrete shell construction and a desire to depart from rectilinear shapes. The tubular core houses services and utilities. It also accepts about seventy percent of the weight, while a post and beam cage around the perimeter bears the remainder. The "corn on the cob" towers share the three-acre site with two commercial buildings and a theater of the traditional straight-sided variety.

A native Chicagoan, Goldberg said that a strong wind could "blow the martini right out of your glass" in a traditional tower. For him, the curving forms were not affectations but a source of greater strength and stability in the tall towers—the tallest concrete structures in the world at the time of their construction. Goldberg trained at Harvard and at the Bauhaus in Germany; he is both an architect and an engineer. His inventive use of the concrete shell at Marina City introduced a new phase of modern architecture in America, along with an expanded vision of city living.

For information, call Marina City offices at (312) 661-0046. Also, the Chicago Architecture Foundation includes Marina City on its "Architecture Highlights by Bus" tour; call the foundation at (312) 922-TOUR.

Vanna Venturi House, 1964

8330 Millman Street at Sunrise Lane
Chestnut Hill, Pennsylvania

Robert Venturi

Robert Venturi's house for his mother shows that there's no place like home: it is not an office or a factory, and has no business trying to look like one. Thus, in his first house—and the first postmodern house—he began to overturn decades of modernist doctrine based on the idea of universal space. In returning to a traditional symbolism, Venturi used forms and images that people could recognize. But the "homeyness" is exaggerated and playful. It is, as Paul Goldberger says, "home as a child would draw it."

The house was designed while Venturi was writing *Complexity and Contradiction in Architecture* (Museum of Modern Art, 1977), and it illustrates many of his anti-modern principles: Architecture is a language, full of signs and symbols. Architectural purity is unobtainable in the real world. Contradictions and complexity are inevitable and even welcome.

Although the house is small, it communicates in a big way. The front façade becomes an oversized gable, split in two to reveal the tower and chimney of the upper level. The cheerfully painted stucco walls are ornamented with wood moldings whimsically applied, especially the upside-down smile above the front entry. Windows are asymmetrically placed in the symmetrical front façade. Under a sloping roof, the outside walls are as flat and smooth as in any modernist building. In the rear, the outer wall has been sliced off to create an outdoor porch on the second floor.

Venturi makes an especially pointed criticism of modernism's disdain for the front door. Here, the entrance is marked by a large square opening front and center. Inside, the homelike elements give way to rooms defined by angular walls that contort their dimensions and seem to deny the coziness implied on the outside.

Venturi ushered in a new architecture at a time when people were clearly ready for a change, and for a revival of the human qualities modern buildings ignored. Since then, he and his wife, Denise Scott Brown, have continued to influence architecture with both their ideas and their buildings. They received the American Institute of Architects Firm of the Year Award in 1985, and in 1991, Venturi won the Pritzker Prize for lifetime achievement.

The house is a private residence.

Woodrow Wilson School of Public and International Affairs, 1964

Princeton University
Prospect Avenue
at Washington Road
Princeton, New Jersey

Minoru Yamasaki & Associates

Classical architecture never completely disappears, but it assumes different guises that sometimes provoke a shock of recognition, and sometimes just a shock. The Woodrow Wilson School at Princeton offers a little of each. The bright white temple-like colonnaded structure is startling in contrast to Princeton's mostly stone-gray Gothic campus. But the particular way in which Minoru Yamasaki has interpreted the classical temple—with tall, slender, tapered columns set against dark glass walls—now seems more emblematic of the idealistic 1960s rather than the verities of ancient Greece.

Although the Woodrow Wilson School looks like a two-story structure, there are three floors above ground and one below. The main floor opens to Prospect Street on one side and to a reflecting pool on the other. The lobby is open all the way through, surfaced in cool white marble and furnished with large seating pieces. This floor also contains the library with a double mezzanine, an auditorium, and a dining room. Faculty offices are located on the top floor, and small conference rooms and service areas are located on the lower level.

By the time Yamasaki designed Woodrow Wilson School, the Washington State native had achieved national prominence for his streamlined classic style. His greatest fame would come in the 1970s with the completion of World Trade Center in New York City. These two mega-towers, 110-stories each, have been accused of "scale busting" lower Manhattan. Now, Yamasaki's delicate columns and classical restraint exist in the shadow of a larger and taller new neighbor. For information, call (609) 258-3000.

DANZIGER STUDIO, 1965

7001 Melrose Avenue
at Sycamore Avenue
Hollywood, California

Frank O. Gehry and Associates

Not far from Rudolph Schindler's house of 1922 on Kings Way, one of the first modern homes in America, stands Danziger Studio, an early modern house in the career of Frank Gehry. Schindler's house was astonishing in comparison with the architecture that came before it, but Gehry's early modern house is surprising because of Gehry's own work that came after it. In the intervening years, we have become accustomed to Gehry's architecture at "the edge of absurdity," where anything from chain-link fencing to asphalt kitchen floors is likely to turn up.

Danziger Studio could hardly be simpler, and this is its strength. The artist's studio and residence consists of linked cubes—a pair of offset towers that form a small courtyard. A closed compound of gray painted stucco, the building turns a blank face to both Melrose and Sycamore Avenues; its street-smart walls seem to rise right out of the sidewalk. A one-story wall encloses the courtyard of the main entrance on Melrose; the Sycamore side shows the garage doors and high windows in its otherwise blank façade.

Gehry lightens the interior with large loft-style windows on the private side of the house, and with skylights that beam light into the two-story interiors.

Since Danziger Studio was built, Melrose Avenue has become a "where the action is" kind of street and the blank-walled building is an island of calm. A few blocks away, at 8365 Melrose Avenue, Gehry's Gemini G.E.L. Studios of 1976 show Gehry on the way to something much wilder.

Danziger Studio is a private residence.

Richards Medical Research Building, 1965

University of Pennsylvania
Hamilton Walk
Philadelphia, Pennsylvania

Louis I. Kahn

The design of this modern research facility was inspired by the centuries-old towers Louis Kahn discovered in the northern Italian hill town of San Gimignano in 1951. Kahn's uncanny ability to tap the power of ancient structures for his resonant new forms would before long become legendary. But here, at the brink of his influential career, Kahn was searching for a new order.

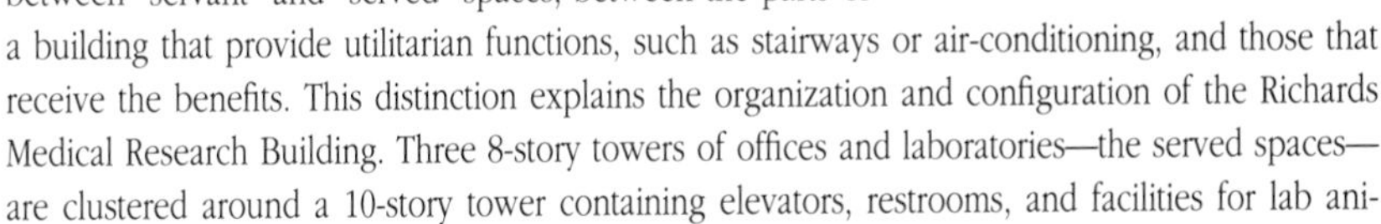

He found his new order in the simple, rational distinction between "servant" and "served" spaces, between the parts of a building that provide utilitarian functions, such as stairways or air-conditioning, and those that receive the benefits. This distinction explains the organization and configuration of the Richards Medical Research Building. Three 8-story towers of offices and laboratories—the served spaces—are clustered around a 10-story tower containing elevators, restrooms, and facilities for lab animals—the servant spaces.

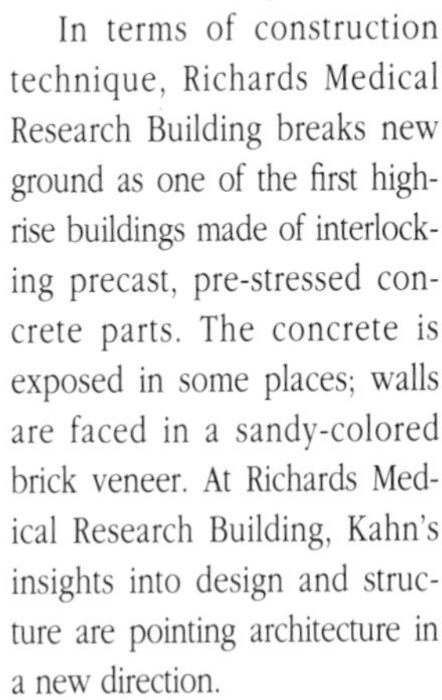

In terms of construction technique, Richards Medical Research Building breaks new ground as one of the first high-rise buildings made of interlocking precast, pre-stressed concrete parts. The concrete is exposed in some places; walls are faced in a sandy-colored brick veneer. At Richards Medical Research Building, Kahn's insights into design and structure are pointing architecture in a new direction.

Louis Kahn taught architecture at the University of Pennsylvania from 1955 until his death in 1974. On campus, the Richards building is part of the University's Medical School complex, and is next door to the nation's first medical college building. For general information, call (215) 898-5000.

Jonas Salk Institute for Biological Studies, 1965

10010 North Torrey Pines Road
La Jolla, California

Louis I. Kahn

All architecture begins with the making of a room, said Louis Kahn, and he saw the street as a room as well, just located outdoors. Somewhere between these ancient ideas of the room and the street lies the great travertine central plaza of the Salk Institute, which opens to the Pacific Ocean and is one of the most spellbinding sights in American architecture.

The Salk Institute is a unique research center conceived by Nobel Laureate and polio vaccine inventor Dr. Jonas Salk as a place where scientists and artists could work together in pursuit of progress, a place where diverse disciplines could find unity. To Salk, the center should be vibrant and alive, the kind of place where you could hang a Picasso.

It is hard to imagine anyone more sympathetic than Louis Kahn for this human but mystical work. Kahn cared deeply about what a building "wanted to be," and he was profoundly in touch with elemental powers that allowed him to bring forth new forms.

Kahn created a masterpiece, with the central garden plaza at the heart of it. Flanking the plaza are two symmetrical laboratory buildings with concrete walls and teak wood insets. Studies for the scientists are contained in separate wings, connected to the main laboratory space with the intention that these new ideas will be "injected" back to the body of the building for further evaluation.

The Salk Institute won the American Institute of Architects Twenty-Five Year Award in 1992. That same year the Institute broke ground for a new building sited in the eucalyptus grove in front of Kahn's masterpiece.

The institute is open Monday through Friday from 8:30 AM to 5:00 PM; on these days, reservation-only tours are conducted at 10:00 AM, 11:00 AM, and noon. For reservations and information, call (619) 453-4100.

Sea Ranch, 1965

Sea Walk
Sea Ranch, California

Moore, Lyndon, Turnbull & Whitaker, Architects

Before Sea Ranch, this stretch of Sonoma County coast about 110 miles north of San Francisco was a remote but spectacular expanse of rocky terrain, fields, and forests above a crashing ocean. The special grandeur of the site evoked strong protective instincts and a sense of responsibility for developing the land without denaturing it.

Charles Moore responded by working with nature rather than against it. His revolutionary design for the first condominiums seems indigenous—it plays to the slope and scale of the surrounding mountains with barnlike shapes, angled rooflines, and unpainted redwood siding. The original condominium complex is a carefully integrated whole harboring ten residences and two courtyards within a composite structure. Individual homes are oriented toward the sun, away from the wind, and to frame exceptional views.

Each home begins as a 24-foot redwood cube—one large room with a tall ceiling—in which a second level is created by mounting a four-poster pavilion against the main wall. Glass bays with window seats, solariums, terraces, decks, and walled gardens elaborate the basic structure and open the homes to the ocean views. To brighten the overwhelming woodiness of the interiors, graphic artist Barbara Stauffacher Solomon painted big, colorful designs on the walls, marking the invention of supergraphics.

Only residents and guests have access to Sea Ranch, a private community now consisting of 2,000 homesites being developed along the sympathetic lines of Charles Moore's original vision. Rentals are available through the Sea Ranch Escape (707-785-2426) and other local agencies. Visitors are welcome at the Sea Ranch Lodge (707-785-2371), a twenty-room inn with swimming pools, tennis courts, and a nine-hole golf course, although the Charles Moore condominiums cannot be seen from this vantage point.

Whitney Museum of American Art, 1966

**975 Madison Avenue
at 75th Street
New York, New York**

Marcel Breuer

The Whitney Museum of American Art—like the Guggenheim Museum a few blocks away—houses its art in a building that is among the greatest works of its collection. And, in fact, landmark quality architecture was an intended goal when the museum's new home in Manhattan's uptown art district was commissioned.

Faced with producing a monumental and memorable building on a tiny corner site, the Bauhaus-trained Marcel Breuer found his solution in a bold but severe design. Starting with a gray granite box, he carved a zigzag profile of broad cantilevered masses that protrude progressively toward the top. The lone exposed side wall on 75th Street is smooth and blank, except for six trapezoidal hooded windows studded randomly about. A single large trapezoid "eye on art" angles out over the main entrance.

Visitors enter the museum by walking through a canopied concrete bridge that spans the sunken sculpture garden and leads into a two-level glass-walled lobby. Above the lobby, there are three gallery floors. The galleries correspond to the exterior cantilevers, and each floor is progressively larger than the one below. Besides the five public levels, there are four floors for administration within the museum's 76,830 square feet of space. A pleasant café on the lower level overlooks the sculpture garden.

When the museum opened it was compared to a private club. The walls were wood-paneled and the floors were covered with parquet, plush carpet, and bluestone. Galleries were furnished with sofas, chairs, desks, and tables of living room quality. Most of these items are gone now. The museum has also retired the modular partition system Breuer designed to work with the precast concrete ceiling.

Since 1981, the Whitney Museum has been in the architectural spotlight pending the planned expansion by Michael Graves. Three design schemes were submitted between 1981 and 1992; not one of these was approved.

The Whitney Museum of American Art is open on Wednesday 11:00 AM to 6:00 PM; Thursday 1:00 to 8:00 PM; Friday through Sunday, 11:00 AM to 6:00 PM; closed Monday. For information about tours and exhibitions, call (212) 570-3641.

Ford Foundation, 1967

320 East 43rd Street
New York, New York

Kevin Roche, John Dinkeloo & Associates

In midtown Manhattan, the most densely developed real estate in America, the Ford Foundation headquarters pioneered the idea of building offices around a lushly planted skylighted garden atrium. Encased in glass braced by rust-colored steel and dramatic overhead trusses, the building's one-third acre semitropical garden with lily pond is one of the city's most spectacular interiors. It is all the more impressive because it visually extends to an adjoining outdoor park.

In 1968, *Architectural Record* hailed the building as "a new kind of urban space." Twelve L-shaped floors of offices overlook the 130-foot atrium, and their floor-to-ceiling sliding glass doors open onto the courtyard. This total openness (only the chairman's office is not on view) is meant to stress the importance of teamwork in reaching the foundation's goals. Architecturally, the open arrangement unifies the building's interiors and blurs the distinction between indoors and out.

The dusky pink granite building has main entrances, and Kevin Roche and John Dinkeloo have created two distinct faces and personalities. The 43rd Street façade is more formal, with a tall *porte cochere* formed by stepping back the first four floors. This relatively blank-walled entrance sets up the surprise of the unseen garden that awaits the visitor. On the 42nd Street side, the garden is strikingly visible through the glass walls, and the entrance leads directly into the garden atrium.

The inner courtyard terraces up one full floor, from 42nd to 43rd Street. This atrium is an indoor public park, and is open from 9:00 AM to 5:00 PM, Monday through Friday. The number to call for more information is (212) 573-5000.

Smith House, 1967

Darien, Connecticut

Richard Meier

The Smith House is meant to be at home in its natural setting, but clearly it doesn't "grow out of the ground" in the manner envisioned by Frank Lloyd Wright. Here the aim is not to mimic the natural characteristics of the landscape, but to receive them. The sun shines more brightly on these pure white-painted wood walls, and pours into the house through its large glass windows. As the day progresses, changing colors of light and the shadow patterns of the trees are played out on its walls. A spectacular view of Long Island Sound is also part of the setting, and the house opens out to it on every level.

The overall composition of the house begins with the site, a gentle hill sloping down to the rocky shore, with the house situated at the highest point. The street façade is flat and reveals little of the interior drama. Beyond the entry façade, the house rotates briskly toward the water view. From the rear elevation, it becomes more clear that the four-level section has prompted the intricate, abstract design. In the vertical stacking, public rooms are separated from private ones, and every resident is allocated an individual private space. Levels and spaces are interlocked—horizontally and vertically—to emphasize the dynamics of moving through light as well as through space.

Smith House is the first in Richard Meier's series of all-white houses, built in the late 1960s and early 1970s. These houses advanced the modernist approach of past avant-gardists, including Richard Neutra and Rudolf Schindler in California, Walter Gropius and Marcel Breuer in the Northeast, and, of course, Le Corbusier in France.

Meier has remained a modernist, and for his body of work he received the Royal Gold Medal and the 1984 Pritzker Architecture Prize.

The house is a private residence and is visible only from Long Island Sound.

Boston City Hall, 1968

One City Hall Square
Boston, Massachusetts

Kallman, McKinnell & Knowles

In tradition-conscious Boston, City Hall is an aggressively modern building of raw concrete rising from a red-brick plaza. The massive, strong-boned structure is exceptionally bold in its vertical lines and in its horizontal planes. But perhaps the building needed to be this determined in order to perform the heavy lifting that was expected of it: providing the spark to ignite renewal of a badly deteriorated part of the old town. Result achieved, City Hall now stands as a focal point for one of the country's most commercially successful downtown shopping centers, Faneuil Hall Marketplace, and a revivified waterfront.

The structure is complicated, with its labyrinth of levels and spaces, but it basically divides into two parts: 1) the red-brick base, which includes the stepped plaza terraces and two below-grade floors that accommodate the sloping site; and 2) the concrete structure of the columns and the upper floors.

The brick terraces are an extension of the city streets, connecting the building to its neighbors, and in fact the plaza levels function like a system of indoors streets. People can move easily through the building, for it is accessible on many levels. Once inside the five-story skylighted lobby, much of the building is clearly visible. Structurally, the building system consists of poured-in-place concrete columns, cores, and trusses. Formwork throughout is left exposed, as is the joining of the precast elements.

Boston City Hall, like Frank Lloyd Wright's Marin County Civic Center, goes beyond the classic architecture that had seemed synonymous with America's public building. For architects Kallman, McKinnell, & Knowles, there is no contradiction in using modern architecture and technology to convey the authority of local government with appropriate dignity.

The building is open Monday through Friday from 8:00 AM to 5:00 PM and occasionally on Saturday. For information, call (617) 635-4000.

Lake Point Tower, 1968

505 North Lakeshore Drive
Chicago, Illinois

Schipporeit-Heinrich Associates

The first skyscraper with an undulating glass wall, Lake Point Tower opened its doors as the tallest reinforced concrete building in the world. Its curved, curtain walls of bronze-tinted glass are set in a framework of bronze anodized aluminum, making it look like a sleek bronze sculpture. The tower is especially striking because of its free-standing location on the Navy Pier promontory, which projects into Lake Michigan. There is the luxury of open space all around.

Apartments at the perimeter have rounded walls and panoramic views. This openness is possible because of the ingenious prism-shaped core, extending the full 645-foot height of the structure. The prism contains elevator shafts, stairwells, corridor supply ducts, and the main electrical distribution systems. It is also designed to withstand all horizontal movements and shear forces—only vertical compression forces are transmitted, through columns, to the caissons.

Lake Point Tower's architects had been students and, later, staff associates of Mies van der Rohe, who had conceived and modeled a similar concept in 1921 in Berlin. It is often remarked that Mies's basic idea was finally realized in Lake Point Tower, but it seems more realistic to view the building as a very largely original use of technology and materials available in the late 1960s.

Because the Lake Point Tower apartments are privately owned, there are no interior tours of the building. However, you can walk into the ground-floor rotunda, which gives a view to the top. A 70-floor restaurant (currently called Cité) is open for lunch and dinner, and for breathtaking views of the city. For building information, call (312) 621-4610. The Chicago Architecture Foundation includes Lake Point Tower on its "Architectural Highlights by Bus" and River Cruise tours; for information, call CAF at (312) 922-TOUR.

Tuskegee Chapel, 1969

Tuskegee Institute
Tuskegee, Alabama

Paul Rudolph

The symbolic religious power of Paul Rudolph's interdenominational chapel at Tuskegee Institute is often compared to Le Corbusier's famous pilgrimage chapel at Ronchamps. With flat, reddish-brick walls arranged in a geometrical spiral—all plans and angles—Rudolph captures the kind of intensity Le Corbusier generated with sensuous concrete curves.

Tuskegee Chapel was originally designed of poured-in-place concrete. Like Ronchamps, the roof of Tuskegee Chapel slopes boldly upward on one side and down on the other, extending to a broad overhang of the entry porch with an outdoor pulpit.

Inside, the tall sheer walls enclose a great asymmetrical room that is mystically—almost magically—illuminated from peripheral skylights in its celestial ceiling. The solid, central part of the ceiling is accordion-shaped, dotted with artificial lights, and appears to float above the congregation like a canopy. Furthermore, this central ceiling curves in two directions, its warped surfaces seemingly on a plane with the incoming light. The roof is formed by open-web steel joists, closely spaced; no two of these joists are parallel.

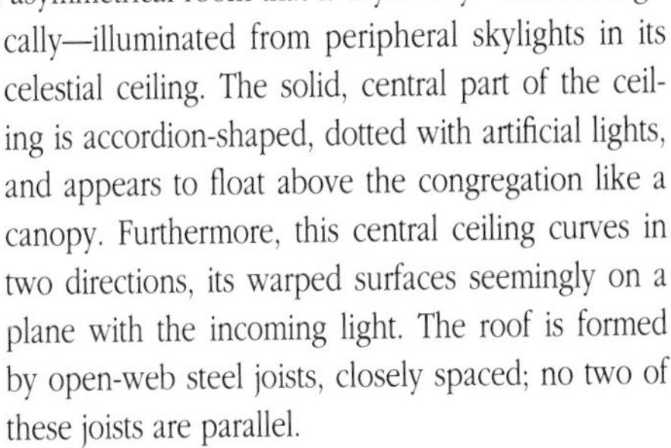

A balcony cantilevers into this main body of the chapel, and the pulpit has its own angled canopy. The famous Tuskegee choir is framed by the angled walls of the chancel, behind the pulpit and facing the congregation. A separate meditation chapel, enclosed by the main spiral form, is lighted by skylights and colored glass windows.

The chapel is open daily from 8:00 AM to 8:00 PM; Sunday services take place at 9:00 AM; and, because the chapel is also designed as a concert hall, musical events are held here as well. For tours and concert schedules, call the Public Information Office at (205) 727-8349.

John Hancock Center, 1970

875 North Michigan Avenue
Chicago, Illinois

Skidmore, Owings & Merrill

The 100-story John Hancock tower is distinguished by prominently displayed diagonal braces, dark glass, and a tapering monolithic appearance. It is vastly famous—one of the buildings that says "Chicago" to most people.

John Hancock Center works visually like a full-sized cutaway model, showing exactly how the designer solved the structural problem of stabilizing such a very tall building against the wind loads and against its own weight. Hiding the diagonal bracing has been traditional, not because of any secret of engineering—it is commonplace—but because it is usually so busy-looking. On a truly enormous building like this one, however, the long and high-reaching diagonal lines have a novel and unexpected grace. They also provide a strong visual reassurance that the building is good and solid, in the same way great bridges are solid.

The rigidity achieved in the John Hancock Center comes from geometry—and geometry weighs nothing. Consider that the structural steel in a typical medium-rise Chicago building weighs about 50 pounds for each square foot of area. Yet in this extreme high-rise, the ratio is only 29.7 pounds of steel per square foot of area, a statistic almost as impressive as the building's height.

The first 41 floors are office and commercial space, with condominiums, an observatory, a restaurant, and broadcast facilities on the upper floors. For these various uses, the external bracing is a great advantage: the absence of internal columns gives tenants nearly complete flexibility in adapting and partitioning their floor spaces for their own use. The altitude, of course, is prodigious. Small planes sometimes fly past the tower's midsection, waving *up* at the people peering down from their windows.

The observation deck on the John Hancock Center is open daily from 9:00 AM to midnight except on major holidays; for information, call (312) 787-3800. For building information, call (312) 751-3680. The building is also featured on Chicago Architecture Foundation tours; for information, call the foundation at (312) 922-TOUR.

Mount Angel Library, 1970

Mount Angel Abbey
East End of College Street
St. Benedict, Oregon

Alvar Aalto

In 1963, the monks of Mount Angel Abbey wrote a heartfelt letter to Alvar Aalto, the Finnish architect renowned for the natural beauty and grace he brought to modern architecture. "We need you," the monks implored. "We have a magnificent monastic site. We don't want to spoil it. . . . Give us a building that will fill our needs in a beautiful and intelligent way." Almost ten years later, the monks' dream was fulfilled, making their library one of only two Alvar Aalto buildings in the United States.

As with most of Aalto's buildings, the Mount Angel Library appears deceptively simple. Entered at the crest of the hill, it looks like a rather plain one-story structure of pale yellow brick. The only ornamentation is an open canopy of redwood, fir and teak, and thin redwood slats screening the windows.

But immediately inside, the building practically explodes with light and space, and the full wonder and complexity of the library's design makes itself clear. At the center is an open well surrounded by two stories and a mezzanine, which ramp down the hill. The rear wall is fan-shaped and overlooks the surrounding view. A curving skylight at the roof floods the library with light by day. At night, Aalto's signature parabolic fixtures provide the illumination.

The main level of the 44,000-square-foot building is an open floor with a low curving wall that echoes the contours of the fan-shaped exterior wall. Besides the entry lobby, this level contains the control desk, the periodical room, and the monastery's treasured rare book collection. Carrels line the outer walls, and the low balcony wall is ringed with a long reading counter outfitted with Aalto-designed lights and stools. The mezzanine and lower floors are primarily given over to stacks positioned like spokes on a wheel. All the furnishings were designed by Aalto down to the door handles. Aalto's way with wood and other natural materials is legendary. His signature slatted wood ceilings appear in the library's control area and auditorium.

The Abbey is forty-five miles south of Portland off Interstate 5's Woodburn exit. Library hours are Monday through Friday, 8:30 AM to 5:00 PM, Monday through Thursday evenings, and on weekends. The library is closed on major holidays and runs on a shorter schedule during the summer. For information and to request guided tours, call (503) 845-3317.

Kimbell Art Museum, 1972

3333 Camp Bowie Boulevard
Fort Worth, Texas

Louis I. Kahn

The architecture of Louis Kahn arises from a mysterious source he called "the realm of the senses," and this is the real territory occupied by his buildings when they have been built. The Kimbell Art Museum, with its fine collection, appeals to more than just our sensual appreciation of sight and space. It reaches all the way to the more mystical associations we invest in buildings, drawing on the collective memory of ancient forms and recognizing how satisfying the forces of rhythm and repetition can be.

At the Kimbell Art Museum, Kahn found his solution in the strong southwestern sun, seeing light as the essence of a museum, the common ground between the viewer and the art. He gave the museum its light, and its form, by resurrecting the vault as his organizing principal and the source of the building's interior luminosity.

The building's apparently simple structure and materials are immediately evident. Kahn laid out six pale-colored concrete vaults side by side: an entrance court, the galleries, a series of garden courts, and a reflecting pool. He created an outside porch by leaving open the two vaults that flank the museum's entrance. The vaults become building blocks: each 100 x 23-foot clear span module has a concrete frame, concrete exterior walls, travertine interior walls, and lead roofs. Even so, this building is much too sophisticated to be considered modular.

A soft, silvery light fills the museum throughout the day. Kahn achieved this luminosity by turning the vaulted roof into what he called a "natural light fixture." He sliced the vault's apex with a full-length skylight and fitted it with a curved, perforated aluminum screen for diffusion. The art can be seen in natural light without suffering damage from the exposure.

The Kimbell Art Museum is the last work completed under Kahn's personal supervision. In the late 1980s, a plan to expand Kahn's design by adding more "modules" was protested so vehemently that the trustees agreed to relent. The museum will remain as Kahn intended.

The museum is open Tuesday to Friday from 10:00 AM to 5:00 PM; Saturday from noon to 8:00 PM; Sunday from noon to 5:00 PM; and closed Monday, New Year's Day, the Fourth of July, Thanksgiving, and Christmas Day. Exhibition tours are Tuesday through Friday and Sunday at 2:00 PM; an introductory walk on Sunday at 3:00 PM; and a special evening tour on Saturday at 6:30 PM. For information and reservations (two weeks in advance for groups), call (817) 332-8687.

Marin County Civic Center, 1972

3051 Civic Center Drive
San Rafael, California

Frank Lloyd Wright

The Marin County Civic Center is Frank Lloyd Wright's testament to democratic government, although he was accused of being a communist for having designed it.

The building was designed in 1958 but not completed until 1972. And like all of Wright's architecture, the setting was the starting point. He saw the beautiful hills north of San Francisco and knew at once that he would span them with three graceful arches.

From this first insight, an amazing complex of buildings evolved in a vast horizontal stretch nearly a quarter of a mile long, tiered with arches, and resembling a Roman aqueduct. This infinite expanse actually consists of two main wings—the Administration Building and the Hall of Justice, with its courts, sheriff's office, and jail. The two wings meet at the dome, a massive and elaborately ornamented structure that houses a library and conference center; a continuous skylight joins the curved roofs of the entire assemblage. Near the dome, mechanical equipment is exotically concealed in a totem-like 217-foot spire.

Using simple materials, Wright has achieved an effect that is fantastic: a composition of tawny pink stucco, a blue plastic-coated roof, bright red and gold window panels, and gold anodized aluminum for the balcony rails, the entrance gate, and the rows of globes that hang from the building's extended eaves. The concrete shell roof is covered with decorative circles, arches, and spheres.

With Marin's long skylighted atrium corridors, Wright unwittingly pioneered an idea that would become a cliché of shopping center design from coast to coast. But here, the skylights work as Wright intended, bringing light and openness to all levels of the interior. Arches open up the exterior walls all around, and balconies provide continuous mobility as outside corridors. Offices have full-height glass walls that expose them to the central atriums, fulfilling Wright's belief that the people's government should be visible and accessible.

The Marin County Civic Center is open from 7:00 AM to 6:00 PM, Monday through Friday and until 8:30 PM on Tuesday. Visitors can wander through the public areas, or arrange for a tour conducted by the Human Resources Department by calling (415) 499-6104.

Phillips Exeter Academy Library, 1972

Exeter, New Hampshire

Louis I. Kahn

One of Louis Kahn's last completed American buildings is the library for Phillips Academy, a private school. On campus, Georgian brick buildings bespeak of tradition; the library manages to coexist peacefully with the older structures while maintaining the clarity and integrity that make a Kahn building special.

Kahn's sympathy with the surroundings affects the exterior, where the walls are brick, flat, rhythmic, and unadorned—a modern complement to the Georgian style. By means of a ground-level arcade, the library confirms its association with the campus by reaching out on all four sides. The entrances can be found at the four corners, sliced off on the diagonal, which Kahn compared to a book with dog-eared pages that tell you where the important parts are located.

On the inside, the almost mystical power of Kahn's architecture is fully exposed in the monumental concrete forms: the curving stairs, the cross-beamed ceiling, and, especially, the mammoth open unframed circles that expose the stacks. The vast interior, almost 90,000 square feet of floor space, is defined by exposed concrete, raw and finished at the same time. It is hard to imagine that anyone but Kahn could have created such a large and open concrete place where the prospect of settling down with a good book still maintains its intimacy.

A dining hall, also designed by Louis Kahn, is adjacent to the library and is faced with the same brick. Its primary features are the large windows in all four dining rooms, and overscaled fireplaces in two of them. The clean lines and towering chimneys of the dining hall complete the strong geometry of Kahn's overall composition.

Throughout most of the year, the library is open Monday through Friday, 7:45 AM to 9:00 PM; Saturday from 9:00 AM to 4:00 PM, and Sunday from 2:00 to 9:00 PM. The library is closed for major holidays; accessibility is also affected by school vacations and other academic schedules, so it is advisable to call first at (603) 772-4311.

TRANSAMERICA BUILDING, 1972

600 Montgomery Street
San Francisco, California

William L. Pereira and Associates

Twenty years ago, professional critics and San Francisco residents alike were convinced that Transamerica's 835-foot pyramid with flippers would permanently devastate the city skyline. But Transamerica has had the opposite effect: its image is now so linked with San Francisco that it often appears on map and guidebook covers for the famous city by the bay.

The Los Angeles firm of William L. Pereira and Associates, known for the space-age restaurant "pods" at the Los Angeles Airport, decided on a pyramid shape, and stuck to it. The base of the building is ringed with huge concrete pillars angled together like tripods in a series of open strutwork pyramids. These strong diagonals point upward, to the bronze-tinted windows set in exposed concrete walls that become increasingly narrow toward the top. And at the top, of course, there is the building's grand gesture, the once-controversial, now-landmark pinnacle.

Transamerica's late-blooming success as a landmark is partly due to the comfort of familiarity, but also to a realization that its design is truly sensible: the pyramid shape admits far more space, air, and light into the area than a bulky box. These considerations add to the vitality of an already bustling scene where three distinctly different neighborhoods come together: the busy financial district, the theme-park bohemian North Beach, and colorful Chinatown. Because San Francisco is a city of hills, arresting views of Transamerica suddenly appear from unexpected vantage points. There are also arresting views *from* Transamerica's 27th-floor observation area. It is open weekdays (except holidays) from 9:00 AM to 4:00 PM. For information, call (415) 983-4000.

World Trade Center, 1972, 1973

Church to West Streets,
Liberty to Vesey Streets
New York, New York

Minoru Yamasaki & Associates

Tourists call these the "Twin Towers," and the *New York Times* architecture critic Paul Goldberger called them ". . . the biggest boxes of all." They are the tallest buildings in New York City and the second tallest in the world. When they were new and raw, however, they were not well received. The per-tower specifications are prodigious: 1,350 feet in altitude, or 110 stories, with 5 million square feet of office space—and these statistics must be multiplied, of course, by two.

In theory, the towers would seem to trivialize the buildings at their feet, which are aged and quite charming. In practice, however, it works out rather well. At the street level, the old neighborhood maintains a sense of human scale and bustle: narrow, noisy, dirty streets with food vendors, smells, and diverse crowds of tourists, brokers, and journalists from the nearby *Wall Street Journal,* while vaguely overhead, receding into the shimmering vertical background, ascend these colossal dual passages to outer space.

Under the towers, there is a second street scene (a cleaned-up version, more like a suburban mall) in the enclosed concourse, which is lined with shops and restaurants, and also provides access to the subways.

The towers, which are owned and operated by the Port Authority of New York and New Jersey, are intriguing for technical reasons. The walls are load bearing. But instead of being conventionally framed in red steel, they are conceived structurally as a mesh cage. The stainless steel clad walls support the building's weight and contribute structural integrity (it successfully withstood a devastating explosion in March 1993). Glass adds no strength, however, and this is why the towers' windows are noticeably narrow.

From the 107th floor observation deck of Two World Trade Center, you can see for fifty miles on a clear day (the super-fast elevator ride takes less than ninety seconds). The deck is open daily from 9:30 AM to 9:30 PM from October through May, and 9:30 AM to 11:30 PM from June through September. Tickets must be purchased on the mezzanine level of Two World Trade Center. For reservations (required for groups of ten or more) and information, call (212) 435-7397.

Federal Reserve Bank of Minneapolis, 1973

250 Marquette
Minneapolis, Minnesota

Gunnar Birkerts and Associates

The old fortress-like bank has been supplanted in recent decades by the open, receptive, and unobstructed look of modern banking facilities. But the new openness sets up a paradox for bank architects. Banks are still expected to provide the absolute security of a bastion—yet they must do it with the wide open feel of a reception center.

In the Federal Reserve Bank of Minneapolis, the problem was solved by splitting the bank's two types of functions into two distinct zones. Activities requiring security were simply buried. Fully sixty percent of the facility's square footage is hidden underground beneath the sloped, landscaped plane of a plaza. Poised above this plaza, suspended in midair between two great vertical towers, is the "airy" part of the bank—its public face—as represented by the administrative and clerical office spaces.

The structure above ground looks like a catenary suspension bridge and works on the same principle. The concrete slab floors of this building are supported by a pair of rigid framed catenaries. The catenary members are hung, sixty feet apart, on either side of the building, and the bank's glass curtain walls are designed to emphasize them visually. Above the curve, the glass is inset into the curve; below the curve, the glass stands forward.

Because the floors are supported in this special fashion, there is no need for columns. The span of the floors is 275 feet, all of it completely clear and uninterrupted. Until this building was built, no one had ever before constructed an office building with such an imposingly long clear span.

On a real bridge, the catenaries are deeply anchored ashore. In this building there are no remote anchors. The tendency for the two towers to topple inward is countered by a pair of 28-foot deep beams that span the top of the building. The load of the floors is thus turned into compression on these beams, which also function as channels to contain the building's mechanical equipment. Nevertheless, an engineering triumph succeeded as a remarkable way to split the personality of a bank into its subterranean and its airy-and-open elements.

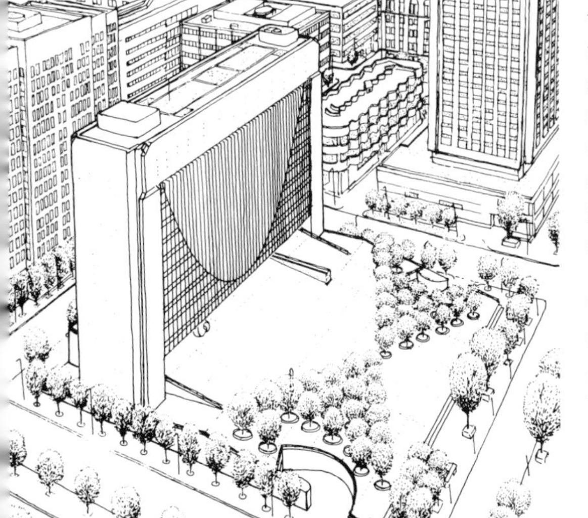

The bank is open from 7:00 AM to 5:30 PM Monday through Friday. For information about guided tours through the building, call (612) 647-4461.

Kresge College, 1973

University of California
at Santa Cruz
Santa Cruz, California

Moore, Lyndon, Turnbull, & Whitaker, Architects

To create a college of dormitories, dining halls, and classrooms, Charles Moore took the idea of an Italian hill town and brought it up-to-date. The white stucco buildings accented in bright primary colors are organized around a 1,000-foot L-shaped "main street" that twists and turns to ensure a progression of interesting views as well as stopping points to encourage chance encounters among the student villagers.

The most noticeable design element is the stage-set cutout wall, which Moore has inserted like screens in layers along the way. Often the walls appear to be freestanding, whether they are broad, flat, and tall to mark a building entrance, or slender columns substituting for balcony railings. The outside stairs are walled in white stucco to match the buildings, which ties them into the overall design while adding a series of bold angles to the broad, flat squares of the cutout walls.

Here, the layering of freestanding elements is cool and spare. This layered effect turns up in many of Charles Moore's designs, and is most gloriously and classically elaborated at the Piazza d'Italia in New Orleans. Moore's designs frequently sum up the spirit of their times and provide the models that will be widely imitated. As Sea Ranch in the 1960s unleashed a decade of timbered townhouses with steeply angled roofs, Kresge College influenced the trend to white stucco construction that was also widely imitated, but not often well, in the 1970s.

For information, call (408) 459-2071.

SEARS TOWER, 1974

Jackson Boulevard, between Franklin Street and Wacker Drive
Chicago, Illinois

Skidmore, Owings & Merrill

The Sears Tower at the time of its construction held the record as the tallest building in the world. Its 110 stories, 1,468 feet tall, are vertically bundled together in nine rectangularly framed tubes. Each tube is 75 feet square, and can be thought of with some accuracy as nine distinct skyscrapers lashed together.

The term that occurs again and again is "Megatube," but not all the component tubes in the bundle rise to the building's full height. Certain tubes terminate at carefully chosen heights to create the visual impression of a naturally occurring crystal, perhaps of calcite or quartz. William Marlin characterized it with a different metaphor: "staggered stacks of catalogs."

Technically, the bundled tube structure handles wind and structural loads without any excess mass. The structural steel weighs just 33 pounds per square foot, which contrasts favorably with the 29-pound-per-square-foot structure of its lean and gracefully cross-braced counterpoint, that other Chicago colossus, the John Hancock Center. Both buildings are virtually airframes compared to conventionally framed Chicago buildings, which require about 50 pounds of steel per square foot to achieve their solidity.

Sears Tower's specification list is a cheerful compendium of gee-whiz statistics. It has 102 high-speed elevators suspended from eight miles of elevator cable; 76,000 tons of structural steel; 17,200 tons of refrigerating equipment; 16,000 bronze-tinted windows; 25 miles of plumbing, 1,500 miles of wiring, and so on. This is a building that has its own zip code.

Sears Tower has recently renovated its 100th-floor Sky Deck and 103rd-floor observatory. There is a new five-minute audio-visual show, as well as exhibits highlighting ten of Chicago's most architecturally significant buildings. The Sky Deck is open daily, from 9:00 AM to 11:00 PM April through September, and from 10:00 AM to 10:00 PM October through March. For more information, call (312) 875-9696.

Best Products Showroom, 1975

Almeda Genoa Shopping Center
Kingspoint at Kleckley Street
Houston, Texas

SITE

In a flat, colorless, and tired part of town, the Best Products Showroom arrived flat, colorless, and a total wreck. Built as a brand new, white brick ruin, the "Indeterminate Façade" appeared to be crumbling all around the merchandise mart it housed. An artfully devised cascade of bricks pours down onto the entrance canopy, a pile of rubble advancing right over shoppers' heads.

The Indeterminate Façade was created by extending the brick veneer arbitrarily beyond the logical edge of the roofline, resulting in the appearance of architecture arrested somewhere between construction and demolition. Like the high concept for a Hollywood movie, the Houston showroom introduced a big idea—build the ruin—which struck a surprisingly responsive chord. Once the initial shock and apocalyptic prophesies subsided, the business and artistic success was undeniable. Best erected seven more "unbuilt" showrooms, and the mail order chain became internationally famous for its fantasy stores in the notoriously downmarket arena of discount merchandising.

SITE is a group of New York artists, and they approached the Best store design as conceptual art at the urban scale. Although the buildings were initially shocking, James Wines has said that this was not their purpose. Rather, their "unfinished" state is meant as a counterpoint to both over-packaging in our consumer economy and to the demand for completeness. Wines describes SITE's design process as "de-architecturisation;" today we would call it deconstruction.

In the 1970s, Best was the nation's largest catalog-showroom merchandiser. The company commissioned SITE to design a series of "unbuilt" showrooms, which are the store with the gouged-out sliding corner entrance in Baltimore, Maryland; the store with "peeling brick" corners in Richmond, Virginia; the abandoned-looking, overgrown façade in Henrico, Virginia; the Ghost Parking Lot in Hamden, Connecticut, and the Inside/Outside Building in Milwaukee, Wisconsin.

After years of success, Best fell on hard times and the collapsing buildings seem eerily prophetic. The crumbling Houston building stands as a deserted monument for the moment—dispossessed by Best and awaiting a new incarnation.

Pacific Design Center, 1975

8687 Melrose Avenue
West Hollywood, California

Cesar Pelli, Gruen Associates

The Pacific Design Center is very big and very blue, prompting its nickname, "The Blue Whale." It is also true that the enormous home furnishings showroom broke the scale of its formerly residential neighborhood, causing the *Los Angeles Times* to describe the building's design as "an attempt to hide a whale in a backyard swimming pool." Nevertheless, since the showroom opened, it has become an architectural landmark and a vast resource for the design community.

Cesar Pelli designed the building (now called the Blue Center) as an enormous six-story extrusion of glass, color, and form. Its blue glass walls rise up to a barrel-vaulted, partially glazed gallery at the top, which helps to streamline the building's massiveness on the outside and gives a sense of destination to the interior. The rear elevation steps back, also alleviating somewhat the enormousness of the building: 750,000 square feet encompassing over 100 million cubic feet of space.

In 1988, the Blue Center was joined by the Green Center showroom, which expanded the giant trade mart complex to 1.2 million square feet.

The Pacific Design Center is open Monday through Friday from 9:00 AM to 5:00 PM, closed weekends and major holidays. Groups may arrange guided tours by calling one week in advance. The center also hosts a schedule of design-oriented programs and exhibitions throughout the year, including their big, annual Westweek show held in March. For information and tours, call (310) 657-0800.

Arcosanti, 1976 (Ongoing)

Interstate 17, Exit 262
Cordes Junction, Arizona

Paolo Soleri

The visionary Italian-born architect Paolo Soleri recognized long ago that suburban sprawl wouldn't always be pretty, that there was a natural limit to unbridled growth. Soleri believes there must be ways for architecture and nature to work in harmony, and he coined the term "arcology" to describe this process, which has become his lifelong search.

In 1976, with the help of students and volunteers, Soleri began building Arcosanti as a prototype arcology for 5,000 people. At this point, it has the air of a busy architectural workshop where life and work are practically inseparable. There are now enough completed buildings to house workshop participants and guests, and to provide for community activities. A number of intriguing structures have been completed, including large, open hangar-like vaults that serve as town squares, the crafts building, a café, a bakery, and a museum.

Soleri, who trained at Taliesin West with Frank Lloyd Wright, divides his time between Arcosanti and Cosanti, a tiny assemblage of hand-built earth-formed concrete buildings he began in the 1960s. Dome House—his innovative 1950s glass and aluminum sphere on track-mounted rotating sections that cooled itself with water jets—is located midway between the two communities (but it is not open to the public).

Cosanti, an Arizona State Historic Site, is located at 6433 Doubletree Ranch Road in Scottsdale. It is open seven days a week from 9:00 AM to 5:00 PM, closed for major holidays. The phone number at Cosanti is (602) 948-6145.

Arcosanti is located about sixty-five miles north of Phoenix, off the intersection of I-17 and Highway 69 (Cordes Junction exit 262). Arcosanti is open seven days a week from 9:00 AM to 5:00 PM, closed Thanksgiving and Christmas. Guided tours for groups of four or more are held every hour on the hour beginning at 10:00 AM. The café and gallery are pleasant places to wait if meeting the quorum causes a delay. Groups of ten or more must make reservations. Arcosanti also has a few inexpensive guest rooms for overnight stays. Workshops include a six-week program and a new one-day workshop as well. For reservations and information, call (602) 632-7135.

John Hancock Tower, 1976

200 Clarendon Street
Boston, Massachusetts

I.M. Pei & Partners

Not too long ago, John Hancock Tower was probably the most ridiculed building in America, a national symbol of architectural trouble. Now it is widely acclaimed as one of the last great skyscrapers of the modern age, a dazzling mirrored parallelogram that is intellectually honest and geometrically pure.

Clearly, this building has had a tumultuous history. But it started in an ordinary way, as a corporate rivalry played out architecturally. In the mid-1960s, one enormous corporation—the John Hancock Mutual Insurance Company—determined to out-build its competitor, Prudential. John Hancock's plan to erect a 60-story, 2-million-square-foot tower on a single block next to Copley Square ignited fierce protest. How could this monolith respect the neighborhood's human-scale architectural treasures: Trinity Church by H.H. Richardson; the Boston Public Library by McKim, Mead & White; and the Copley Plaza Hotel?

A reflective glass skin that would minimize the tremendous mass and reflect the surrounding landmarks on its surface proved to be the start of something much worse. While under construction in 1973, the tower was ravaged by a storm that blew out one-third of the 10,000 windows, each weighing 500 pounds. With plywood filling the gaps, the building became a scandal and a joke: the tallest wooden building in the world.

The building's prominent corporate architects and its designer, Henry Cobb, were able to solve the problems and to emerge with reputations intact. In the final analysis, John Hancock Tower can now be seen as a high water mark of minimalism: a sleek mirrored column with notched sides offering elegant proportions and considerable dignity. Holding a mirror to the landmarks that surround it, John Hancock Tower has finally become one of them.

The John Hancock Tower has a 60th-floor observatory with fantastic views of downtown Boston and with "tours" of downtown architecture from this sky-high location. The observatory is open from 10:00 AM to 10:00 PM seven days a week, except major holidays. For information, call (617) 572-6425.

National Air and Space Museum, 1976

**Independence Avenue, on the Mall between Fourth and Seventh Street S.W.
Washington, D.C.**

Helmuth Obata & Kassabaum

On any given day, as many as 50,000 people will visit the National Air and Space Museum; they will enter, circulate, mill around, stare at great length in wonder, study, shop for souvenirs, attend theaters, and finally exit.

America's most popular museum is a mammoth structure: 685 x 225 feet, with the long dimension facing Independence Avenue. From the Mall, the building looks like a linked series of four distinct buildings, each a 90-foot-tall monolith in pink Tennessee marble, all interconnected by three glass galleries. From the street side, the intervening galleries are accented by huge, visually suspended granite-covered blocks that hang like airborne monuments between the buildings.

The museum building is a wise and thoughtful design. It identifies and solves the real problem of putting airplanes on display, which is to allow visibility from every direction, including above and below. Moreover, planes have complicated shapes that actively resist boxing. No two aircraft are alike in size and configuration—wings, wheels, tails, struts, and engines poke out in every direction.

The sophisticated design solution is the same one kids use for their model planes—they hang them on strong threads from the ceiling. The sky enters the picture thanks to great, glassed-in, display bays. A full panoply of stairs, catwalks, and open mezzanine hallways lets visitors move freely about the place in all three dimensions, to get an excellent look at the exhibits.

The open galleries are framed using pipe trusses, and the airplanes hang on steel cables from these structural devices. The architectural allusion made by these tubular tetrahedrons, longerons, and stringers is precisely that of an aircraft fuselage. It visually demonstrates the real-world problems that confront aeronautical and aerospace engineers: the static and dynamic stresses the airplane must bear, and the need to add structural strength without adding weight. As a building design element, these truss tubes may not be much of a metaphor for the human spirit taking flight, but they are a perfectly elegant metaphor for the engineering ideas that got us off the ground.

The Air and Space Museum is open daily from 10:00 AM to 5:30 PM. Closed Christmas Day. For information, call (202) 357-2700.

Pennzoil Place, 1976

700 Milam Street
Houston, Texas

Philip Johnson & John Burgee

The twin bronze-black towers of Pennzoil Place almost touch. More than the buildings themselves, the ten-foot sliver of sky between them is riveting. Now you see it, and then you don't. The drama is best experienced by car as you curve around downtown on the elevated freeway—a processional view Philip Johnson calls "automobilistic."

In terms of commercial architecture, the striking appearance of Pennzoil Place helped launch a trend for designer buildings. In place of the predictable glass box, Johnson and Burgee introduced two identical towers shaped like trapezoids—a square with a triangle appended to it. Instead of the traditional flat roofs, the tops of these buildings are sliced off on the diagonal. There is considerable "wasted" space in the pointy corners of every floor. These buildings defied all traditional real estate expectations, yet 1.2 million square feet leased like hotcakes.

Pennzoil's spectacular atrium-entry also caught on. Here, the street level space between the two towers is enclosed within a triangular sloping glass roof to form a glass courtyard eight stories at its apex, with shops and restaurants in the court.

For eight years Pennzoil Place virtually defined the Houston skyline. But in 1984 the vast Republic Bank Tower went up across the street and stole some of the thunder, despite the fact that the new bank's architects—Philip Johnson and John Burgee—were presumably most sympathetic to the uniqueness of Pennzoil Place.

For general information, call (713) 224-5930.

Yale Center for British Art, 1977

Yale University
1080 Chapel Street
at High Street
New Haven, Connecticut

Louis I. Kahn

The Yale Center for British Art was Louis Kahn's final commission. And in one of modern architecture's most striking coincidences, it is located across the street from the Yale Art Gallery, the first major work of Kahn's career.

At the Yale Center for British Art, Kahn's life-long determination to simplify is evident inside and out. The grid-like exterior consists of a four-story concrete frame filled with panels of dark glass and pewter-toned stainless steel; on the interior, the concrete grid is inset with oak panels. A recessed corner cutout at Chapel and High Streets marks the entry, and it propels visitors into a glorious interior court that rises full height, naturally illuminated by a clear glass roof. Skylights on the roof diffuse natural light throughout the top floor galleries and the second interior courtyard of the library.

Kahn respected all parts of a building, and perhaps for this reason the vertical stainless steel shafts of the mechanical systems occupy an exposed position right in the middle of it. Also a central feature is the cylindrical stairway, with walls of concrete and floors of travertine. Interior colors and materials—travertine marble, white oak, undyed wool carpeting, and natural linen wall coverings—provide a subtle background in which the works of art become paramount.

Kahn expected the pewter-paneled museum to "look like a moth on a cloudy day and on a sunny day like a butterfly." Sadly, he died before its completion. Kahn's former associates, Anthony Pellechia and Marshall Meyers, assumed the tricky task of figuring out the final details of what Kahn would have wanted. They surely succeeded; and almost mystically, the reflection of Kahn's first great building can be seen in the dark glass panes of his concluding one.

Paul Mellon donated the building and the core collection. Today, the Center houses the most comprehensive body of English paintings, prints, drawings, rare books, and sculpture outside Great Britain.

The center is open Tuesday through Saturday from 10:00 AM to 5:00 PM and Sunday from noon to 5:00 PM; closed Monday and major holidays. Scheduled gallery tours take place Thursday and Saturday at 11:00 AM; one Saturday every month, an architectural tour is also conducted at 11:00 AM. For information, call (203) 432-2800 or 432-2850. For tours, call (203) 432-2858.

BASS HOUSE, 1978

Fort Worth, Texas

Paul Rudolph

In Paul Rudolph's complex and powerful design for the Bass House are echoes of two of modern architecture's most important residences. There are the tantalizing overlapping cantilevers reminiscent of Fallingwater (see page 67), and the elevated, translucent quality of the Farnsworth House (see page 88). But more importantly, the house is a continuation of Rudolph's own concerns: the interactions of vertical and horizontal thrusts, and how strongly opposing forces can be brought into balance to achieve serenity.

Rudolph's landmark Art and Architecture building at Yale University (see page 119) uses a pinwheel concept to contain these forces, which are solidly grounded in vertical towers of massive striated concrete. At the Bass House, commissioned in the early 1970s, the pinwheel recurs as an organizing principle: there is a central courtyard and the cantilevers extend outward on all sides. The balance this time is a delicate one. A series of light-looking horizontal layers amount to something incredibly strong.

Bass House is built up in three dimensions, layer upon layer, with white enameled, wide-flange structural steel, aluminum sheathing, glass, and white porcelain. The overall structure basically consists of three main levels, which Rudolph subdivides into twelve floor levels, fourteen ceiling heights, and a small penthouse. At the core of the house is a fireplace that rises exposed through all levels, with the two-story living room, the upper study, the library, and the stairs arrayed around it.

The intricately layered structure has accomplished Rudolph's primary goal of space-making, by which he means the whole space, inside and out. The house becomes a series of interlocking volumes that creates both bright spaces and dark ones, high and low spaces, and exhilarating progressions in, around, and through them.

Integral to the design are the outdoor spaces: terraces on many levels, the central courtyard, a swimming pool, and an auto court. The spatial dynamics, inside and out, would not be complete without the superb collection of contemporary artwork and the evocative gardens designed by Robert Zion, Russell Page, and Anne Bass.

The house is a private residence.

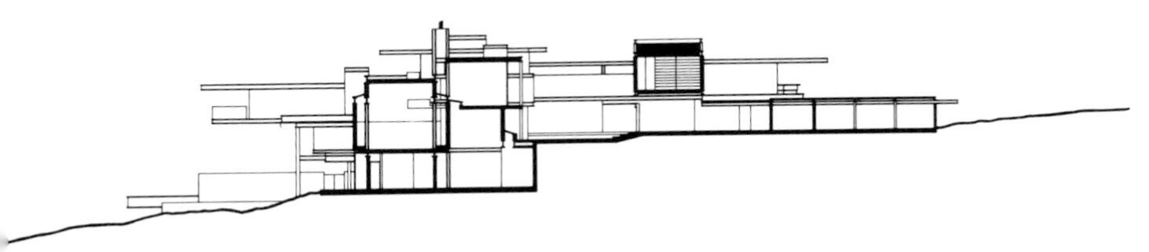

Frank Gehry House, 1978

1002 22nd Street
at Washington Avenue
Santa Monica, California

Frank O. Gehry

The shock of the new was nowhere more startling than in Frank Gehry's house in Santa Monica. Starting with a traditional Dutch cottage in a conventional Los Angeles neighborhood, Gehry literally tore the house apart. When the pieces came together again, the traditional façade vanished behind a new one: a jagged asymmetrical wall of corrugated metal, and panels of raw plywood topped by a cyclone fence. Some of the original studs remained exposed, and the kitchen was paved with asphalt. This was startlingly novel architecture, but it worked, and Gehry's reputation as a major design innovator was secured.

Gehry's architectural bravura launched a fascination for reconfiguring standard industrial materials in abstract combinations, although Gehry resisted the trend's designation of "deconstruction." Reacting against the blank modern buildings of the International Style, Gehry chose to move forward with a new and personal vision, rather than to recreate the styles of the more distant past. The Toronto-born architect received the Pritzker Prize in 1989 in honor of his success in bringing art back to architecture. He also showed that serious architecture can also be fun.

The house is a private residence.

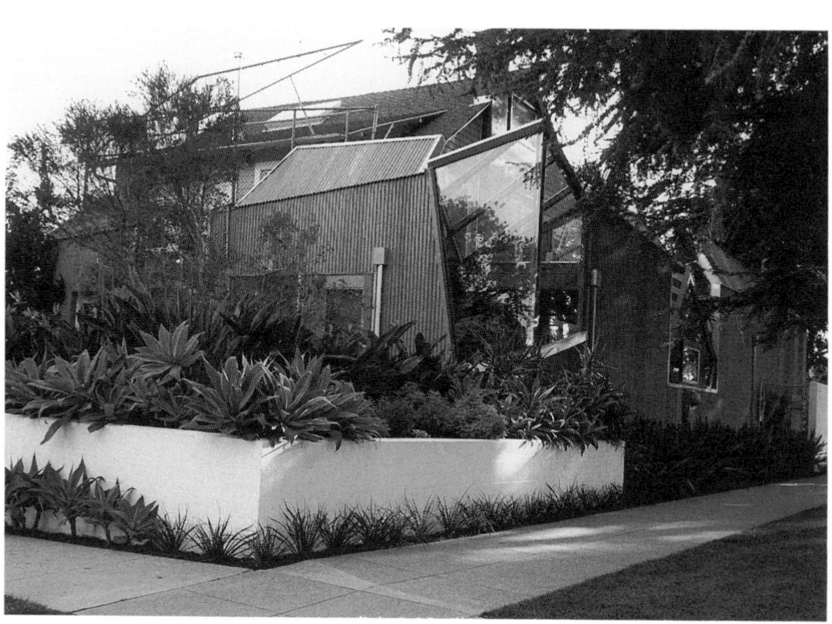

NATIONAL GALLERY OF ART, EAST BUILDING, 1978

Pennsylvania Avenue at Constitution Avenue and Fourth Street
Washington, D.C.

I.M. Pei & Partners

In contrast to the neoclassical columns and statues of official Washington monuments—including the original National Gallery of Art by John Russell Pope across the street—I.M. Pei's East Building is a study in elegant simplicity. Its dusky-pink marble walls are taut, flat, and smooth, ornamented solely by the razor-sharp precision of the design and construction. But it is also a lively and convivial place that wants to attract large audiences to its constantly changing exhibits.

At the heart of the East Building's apparent simplicity is the triangle, a complicated shape that requires intricate design skill to carry off at large scale. And the East Building is more than just a single building; it is a complex of almost 300,000 square feet that includes an underground connection to the old museum. Pei has used the triangle scheme to organize the major functions. The largest triangle houses the seven-level museum; beside it a study center for scholars occupies a smaller triangle. They are linked by yet another triangle, a skylighted court with an immense, red Calder mobile suspended from the center of this 60-foot-high space. Because the main entrance is purposefully low and compressed, this spectacular light-filled court seems to explode into view. Not just a visual surprise, this central courtyard serves as a primary conduit to the museum galleries by means of elevated walkways and a grand staircase.

For all the differences between the old neoclassical museum and the new contemporary one, there are also similarities. Both buildings exist because of the unparalleled generosity of the Mellon family. In sympathy with the old museum, I.M. Pei decided to clad the new building with marble from the same Tennessee quarry.

I.M. Pei studied under Walter Gropius at Harvard University, and the modern architectural principles he learned there have stayed with him throughout his career. But unlike many modern architects, Pei is sensitive to surroundings. The East Building is precisely aligned with Pope's National Gallery building, and their entrances face each other across Fourth Street.

The museum is open Monday to Saturday from 10:00 AM to 5:00 PM, Sunday from noon to 9:00 PM, closed Christmas and New Year's Day. Tours of the East Building are conducted Monday to Saturday at 1:00 PM and Sunday at 2:30 PM. For information, call (202) 737-4215.

Piazza d'Italia, 1979

300 Block of Poydras Street
New Orleans, Louisiana

Charles Moore with August Perez and Associates and Ron Filson

Its brilliant colors are somewhat faded now, but the Piazza d'Italia remains one of Post Modernism's most visible and impressive icons. The Piazza celebrates New Orleans's Italian community, and the style is right in tune with its setting. New Orleans, that most European of American cities, has long been devoted to the ideals that in the 1970s would be called "postmodern"—a lively historical tradition, an affection for color, a love of humor, and a tolerance for theatrical mischief.

The Piazza d'Italia is an open-air stage set, with a triumphal arch as a centerpiece and a series of curved, freestanding walls in the classical Italian orders arrayed before it. Punched-out walls with columns (some of stainless steel) straddle the fountain, which cuts a wide swath as it cascades down various steps and levels. From a high vantage point, the plaza is revealed to be a big bull's-eye of concentric brick paving, and the fountain is a map of Italy, the waters recreating the Po, the Tiber, and the Arno. At night, the plaza is illuminated with neon.

Charles Moore's respected work as an "art" architect and force for change has elevated him to the top of his profession; in 1991, he received the American Institute of Architects Gold Medal, the equivalent of a lifetime achievement award. Now at the University of Texas School of Architecture in Austin, Moore has always been known for his ability to delight while keeping high standards. "We try to make it happy," he has said of his architecture. At the Piazza d'Italia, Moore provides the humor, thankfully free of the in-joke quality that make later Post Modern efforts so tiresome. In good fun, the architect's face is cast into fountains spouting water jets, added by Moore's associate architects on the project to honor his contribution.

Also an honor to Charles Moore, the architecture here still looks fresh, although the "city that care forgot" has unfortunately forgotten to take care of this Post Modern masterpiece.

Because it is an outdoor pavilion, the Piazza is always open.

The Atheneum, 1980

North and Arthur Streets
New Harmony, Indiana

Richard Meier & Associates

There are now approximately 900 residents of New Harmony, Indiana (the same number present at the utopian community's creation in 1814), but this small population has generated a fascinating and innovative history. New Harmony claims the first kindergarten, the first vocational school, the first free public school system, and the first free library in the country. This history is preserved and displayed with exhibits and films here in the New Harmony visitors center, itself a prime tourist attraction.

The Atheneum's gleaming, hyper-white modernism—its sharp angles, undulating curves, bold ramps, and striking stairs—present quite a contrast to the surroundings: quiet, green cornfields on the banks of the Wabash River. The prominence of ramps and stairs on the outside alerts viewers to the importance of procession, from outside to inside, and within the interior as well. You can move through the porcelain-clad building via the central spiral stair or the taut ramp system. Either way, exhibits of New Harmony's past are intercut with views of its present—the landscape framed by carefully positioned windows. Because the internal ramp rotates five degrees off the main grid, spaces seem to compress and expand as you move through the intricately layered structure. The final destination of this elaborate journey is the rooftop observation terrace overlooking the town; the exposed exterior stairs make an appropriately dramatic exit from this lofty perch.

The building's largest space, the auditorium, is impressive and austere. White walls, a charcoal carpet, an aluminum slatted ceiling, and wooden pews call to mind the themes of modernism, Alvar Aalto, and Shaker design.

Richard Meier's sophisticated modern architecture has been uniquely influential, both in this country and internationally. Meier's career has consistently explored the limits of modern architecture, and the Atheneum marks a transition from the early houses (which were white) to more commercial commissions, like the High Museum in Atlanta (also white).

The Atheneum is open daily from 9:00 AM to 5:00 PM. Individuals and small groups are welcome during these hours; arrangements for large groups should be made in advance by calling (812) 682-4488.

Garden Grove Community Church, 1980 (Crystal Cathedral)

12141 Lewis Street
Garden Grove, California

Philip Johnson & John Burgee

A few blocks from Disneyland, the glittering silver geometry of Garden Grove Community Church (known as the Crystal Cathedral) appears on the flat Orange County landscape. From certain angles, this all-glass mirrored structure might be mistaken for an early-1980s suburban office building. But there is a giant cross atop the tower next door that begins to reveal the religious context.

Inside, the architecture takes over completely. Churchgoers are dazzled by special effects, particularly the giant bright white honeycomb of a ceiling that admits subdued light, which seems to be emitted from some great beyond. This effect is achieved by a structural network of painted steel tubes that brace opposing planes of the glass ceiling to its full height. Stunning effects thus result from the unusual plan, an elongated four-point star 415 feet long and 207 feet wide, and from the angled roof that rises to 128 feet at its apex.

Designed for television minister Reverend Robert M. Schuller of drive-in church fame, the Crystal Cathedral ministers to a large congregation. The church proper seats almost 3,000 congregants in pews on the main floor and in triangular balconies; during services, glass doors 90-feet high swing open to accommodate the drive-in participants.

Church tours are conducted Monday through Saturday every half hour from 9:00 AM to 3:30 PM; Sunday services take place at 9:00 and 11:00 AM, and at 6:30 PM. For information, call (213) 971-4000.

THORNCROWN CHAPEL, 1980

**Highway 62 West
Eureka Springs, Arkansas**

E. Fay Jones

This tiny chapel in the Ozark woods makes up in grandeur what it lacks in size. With a stunning virtue of simplicity, Fay Jones has used just a few materials—which could be carried up the hillside site by two workmen—to create an abstract nondenominational church as impressive and timeless as a Gothic cathedral. In 1991, the results of an American Institute of Architects survey of its national membership overwhelmingly named this travelers' chapel as the best American building since 1980. It is one of those very few structures that appeals to both the public and to the architectural profession.

The little chapel is just 24 feet wide, 60 feet long, and 48 feet high. And while it is tucked into a wooded site, its composition is almost totally revealed, and completely focused. Its most arresting feature is the cross-braced ceiling, with timbers sequentially layered to create an open framework pattern of rhythmic repetition that carries the eye the whole length of the chapel. Everything serves to enhance, or not detract from, this dramatic effect: the chapel walls are glass and wood, the floors and side-wall supports are fieldstone. Nature provides the ornamentation. And the lighting seems supernatural.

In fact, Jones has described the chapel as being "aligned with nature." This naturalistic approach, and the geometric, handcrafted woodwork of the chapel, calls to mind the work of Frank Lloyd Wright, with whom Jones apprenticed at Taliesin in Spring Green, Wisconsin, in 1953. Later that year, Jones established his practice in Fayetteville and began a thirty-five-year teaching career at his alma mater, the University of Arkansas. Jones's residential designs employ many of the same natural themes found in Thorncrown, and with the publication of the chapel his early work found a wider audience to admire them. For his lifetime achievements, Jones was awarded the American Institute of Architects Gold Medal in 1990.

The chapel is located one mile west of Eureka Springs on Highway 62 West, and its hours are seasonal: April to October, 9:00 AM to 6:00 PM; November, 9:00 AM to 5:00 PM; March and December, 11:00 AM to 4:00 PM; closed January and February. Nondenominational Sunday services also vary according to the season. In 1989, the Jones-designed Worship Center was completed at Thorncrown. For information on tours and times, call (501) 253-7401.

M.D. Anderson Hall, 1981

Rice University School of Architecture
Houston, Texas

James Stirling, Michael Wilford and Associates

James Stirling won the Pritzker Prize in 1981. Anderson Hall, the London architect's first American project, opened later that year, and the spotlight naturally turned to it. How had Stirling applied his forthright, imaginative, mostly high-tech approach to the renovation and expansion of a 1940s building on a campus with an emphasis on context?

The simple answer is that Stirling and Wilford took a contextual approach to the outside and a modern approach to the interiors, using the building's public spaces as a connection. Adopting the "Rice style," a somewhat Mediterranean mix of banded terra-cotta brick with limestone trim, red tile roofs, and arched arcades, the architects make it difficult to tell where the old building stops and the new one begins. But there are clues to the work of Stirling and Wilford: the gabled west façade with a tall recessed arch, an offset round window high inside the arch, a column in the middle of the entrance, and two conical skylights rising from the roof.

A pleasant courtyard is formed by the extension of the new Anderson Hall wing, and an arched arcade makes a fine transition from the campus to the building. The two main entrances are topped by the conical skylights. Inside, the galleries, jury room, studios, and offices seem cool, white-walled, and primarily functional.

Stirling died in 1992 at the age of 66, still enjoying the enormous renown that came to him for his Neue Staatsgalerie in Stuttgart, Germany, of 1984, considered to be one of the most important new museum designs in the world. There will be, then, only a handful of buildings in America designed by James Stirling: Anderson Hall at Rice University; the Arthur M. Sackler Museum at Harvard University (see page 175), completed in 1985; and the Performing Arts Center at Cornell University, which opened in 1989. For visitor information, call (713) 527-8101.

Columbus City Hall, 1981

123 Washington Street
Columbus, Indiana

Skidmore, Owings & Merrill

Columbus takes great pride in its architecture, and for good reason. This small town of about 30,000 people is home to more than fifty architecturally noteworthy buildings, a collection that includes churches by Eliel and Eero Saarinen, a school by Richard Meier, and a library by I.M. Pei. The architectural heritage is no accident; it results from the enlightened support of the Cummins Engine Foundation, which contributes to the fees of prominent architects to ensure buildings of stature.

The San Francisco office of Skidmore, Owings & Merrill won the commission to design Columbus's primary civic building. Edward Charles Bassett, who designed it, created a triangular-shaped building with a symbolically welcoming entrance. A broad flight of steps invites visitors up into a semi-enclosed forecourt. This procession into the court—and the building—is made spatially interesting by framing the view with a pair of cantilevered brick-faced steel beams that seem to hang in space, not quite touching. Visually framed by these beams is a curved glass wall, rising the full height of the building, and containing the entrance.

The three-story building is simply clad, with Indiana limestone for the base, and brick for the upper stories. Behind the tall curved glass façade, a two-story gallery rises to a second floor balcony, and there are staircases at either end of the main floor. The upper level houses city government offices, conference rooms, and the Council Chamber. A meeting hall is located at court level of the 60,000-square-foot building, and the Police Department is located on the east side.

The life and times of the city of Columbus are depicted in various ways inside the building. There are Amish quilts, photographs, and renderings of local buildings—for which Columbus is famous—and commissioned paintings by Robert Indiana and William T. Wiley.

The Visitors Center of Columbus offers slide shows, tours, maps and other information about local buildings. For tour reservations, call (802) 372-1954. The Visitors Center is generally open from 9:00 AM to 5:00 PM Monday through Saturday. From April 1 to October 31, the center is also open on Sunday from 10:00 AM to 2:00 PM. For complete information on hours, lodging, and other activities, call 1-800-468-6564.

SEASIDE, FLORIDA, 1981 (ONGOING)

County Road 30-A
Near Panama City, Florida

Andres Duany and Elizabeth Plater-Zyberk, Master Planners

Seaside introduces a radical new vision of an American town, and the surprise is how faithfully it resembles the small cities of fifty to one hundred years past. The straight, narrow brick-paved streets are lined with neat houses built in recognizable shapes, with familiar materials, and painted in pastel colors. Front porches, clapboard walls, and tin roofs are design staples. White picket fences and rows of palm trees border the streets, which lead to the town center and to the beach. You can walk where you're going.

These simple virtues, abandoned for decades, have given way to sprawling, car-crazy suburbs with wide curving streets and complicated culs-de-sac; they all look alike. Lost in the process: a sense of place and a feeling of community, intangibles sorely missed. In an attempt to undo wrong-headed development practices, Andres Duany and his wife, Elizabeth Plater-Zyberk, peeled back the layers until they hit bedrock: the authenticity of the small-town prototype that provided America's collective memory of home.

Working with an enlightened developer, Robert Davis, Duany, and Plater-Zyberk designed Seaside's master plan for the 80-acre site with 2,300 feet of frontage along the Gulf of Mexico. The plan calls for about 450 houses, a town center with hotels, offices, shops, and a workshop/warehouse area. Such civic buildings as the post office are dispersed throughout the various neighborhoods where they act as focal points. The central role of the beach in this resort community is highlighted by the beach pavilion, a gazebo, and a small park. The main features of Seaside's plan have been incorporated into a town zoning code, which ensures continuity but also allows for individuality.

The new town of Seaside has evolved slowly, and in ten years only about half of the planned structures have been built. Along with the picturesque houses, there are prominent new architectural works: Steven Holl's retail/hotel/office complex on the central square; Walter Chatham's rooming house on the ocean; and the house of famed British classicist architect and theorist, Leon Krier, on Tupelo Circle.

Seaside is located between Panama City and Destin, on County Road 30-A between Grayton State Park and Seagrove Beach. For information, call (904) 231-4224.

YWCA Masterson Branch and Metropolitan Offices, 1981

3615 Willa
Houston, Texas

Taft Architects

Houston's Memorial Drive is the city's most pleasant parkway, winding along Buffalo Bayou west of downtown and continuing through the cool-looking forests of Memorial Park. Fortunately, instead of spoiling an otherwise pristine view, the YWCA adds something that had been missing.

Like its site, the YWCA is long and narrow. Its two main façades are distinctly different, but equally interesting. Most visitors arrive from Memorial Drive and see the back view first: a series of big, multi-colored projecting boxes and a wide open space—accurately reflecting how the sports rooms, swimming pool, offices, and courtyard are arranged on the inside. The entry façade, on the other hand, is flat and smooth, a continuous wall 350 feet long. It tells less about the 20,000-square-foot structure behind it and more about the surface decoration, a convivial graphic design of arches and gables rendered in rich terra-cotta tilework against beige stucco, a blue-gray stucco, and bright blue for lettering and accent bands. This colorful decoration also serves an important purpose by highlighting the entrances into the three separate but connected parts of the building: the office wing, the walled garden, and the recreational pavilion.

Inside there is the bracing, spartan feel of a no-nonsense gym, combined with the indulgence and friendliness of a good health club. The plan is airy and open, with big windows and tinted concrete floors. A large atrium is the heart of the recreational pavilion; its most compelling feature is a snaky open ramp that doubles back on itself, providing views of the interiors, the pool, and the park. Vivid ceramic tile accents, in the same terra-cotta and blue used on the outside, add spark to the interiors. Especially interesting is the way large overhead doors (garage doors with windows) are imaginatively deployed to create movable walls.

Visitors are welcome at the YWCA, which is open every day: Monday to Thursday, 5:45 AM to 8:45 PM; Friday until 6:00 PM; Saturday 8:30 AM to 12:30 PM; and Sunday 2:00 to 6:00 PM. One-day passes are available for a small fee to women and men who would like to use the exercise facilities. For information, call (713) 868-6075.

Atlantis on Brickell, 1982

2025 Brickell Avenue
Miami, Florida

Arquitectonica

The Atlantis on Brickell Avenue makes you think that Arquitectonica looked over the whole history of architecture and decided it was time to have some fun. In this bright, colorful, and intriguing design, the main attraction is Atlantis's astonishing sight gag: a 37-foot-square hole punched out of its mirrored walls. The audacious see-through cutout frames an exotic, bright-red spiral staircase, vivid yellow walls, and a gigantic palm tree hovering many stories in the air.

On either side of the "skycourt," the building's façades are different in design but unified by bright colors and a bold graphic look. Along Brickell Avenue, the center hole is visually balanced by a big red triangle on the roof to the right, and by four bright-yellow triangular balconies extending from the mirrored wall to the lower left. At ground level, the main entry is defined by four large red columns under a canopy; a matching set of columns reappears just inside the lobby doors.

The opposite side of the building attracts attention with a giant-scale brilliant blue-painted stucco grid superimposed over a smaller, light gray grid of balconies and railings. On this side observers also discover the fate of the "missing" hole: it appears to have landed by the tennis courts, a 37-foot yellow cube housing an exercise room and squash courts.

There are twenty floors of apartments in Atlantis, ninety apartments and six duplexes. Four of the floors open onto the surreal skycourt, with a whirlpool, a hot tub, and a spectacular view.

The lighthearted but sophisticated quality of Atlantis set a new style for Miami Beach. At the time Atlantis opened, Arquitectonica's principals—Laurinda Spear, Bernardo Fort-Brescia, and Hervin Romney—were in their thirties, and their relatively youthful success made almost as many headlines as the building. On their follow-up commissions along Brickell Avenue, Arquitectonica continued the colorful Atlantis themes.

For visitor information, call (305) 285-1269.

PORTLAND BUILDING, 1982

Fourth and Fifth Avenues, Madison and Main
Portland, Oregon

Michael Graves

The Portland Building marks a dramatic phase change in public architecture in this country, and the building that transformed Michael Graves—modern architect, artist, and Princeton professor—into *Michael Graves,* the "postmodern" celebrity with a signature style. It is also the first monument of the Post Modern age, the building that put the art back in architecture.

In eye-catching contrast to the cool and unadorned steel and glass towers of the past fifty years, the Portland Building offers classical ideas and references and yes, even ornament, rendered in an array of lusciously muted natural colors. The 15-story tower rises from a base covered in celadon-green ceramic tiles, and the entry is emphasized with enormous columns. Above this base, a cream-colored midsection is visually heightened by terra-cotta colored columns topped by giant-scale keystones. Small, widely spaced windows with terra-cotta frames in red impose a strict graphic regimen on the imaginative façades, which are decorated with blue-ribboned garlands. At the penthouse level, the building steps back to allow a balcony on all sides, with a view of Mount Hood in the distance. The three-story statue of "Portlandia," an image taken from the city seal, announces the main entry with a civic zestfulness not seen for many a year.

Graves has been called the most original architect of the immediate Post Modern period. By the late 1970s, he was breathing new life into ancient classical ideals and elements. His contemporary vision is one of visual stimulation, of color and decoration, symbolism, romance, and humor—everything the modernists had banished for so many years.

Graves's design vision is virtually total; in addition to architecture he creates tableware for Swid Powell, teapots and clocks for Alessi, corporate logos for clients such as Lenox, and furniture and fabrics for SunarHauserman. His beautiful drawings and watercolor renderings are fine art, and highly prized.

The Portland Building is open on weekdays during business hours, closed for major holidays. Guided tours are conducted on Wednesday at 9:00 AM and 1:30 PM and Thursday at 1:30 PM; reservations are required and must be made two weeks in advance by calling (503) 823-4572.

GENERAL FOODS HEADQUARTERS, 1983 (PHILIP MORRIS INTERNATIONAL/KRAFT GENERAL FOODS INTERNATIONAL)

800 Westchester Avenue
Rye Brook, New York

Kevin Roche, John Dinkeloo & Associates

Joel Garreau's book *Edge Cities* (Doubleday, 1991) charted America's vast post-war migration: city dwellers moved to the suburbs, and before long businesses began to follow people out to where they lived. The idea of building a corporate home in a natural environment seems to have inspired the design of the headquarters of General Foods in Rye Brook, New York. As if to underscore the point of a corporate residence, the building is clad in white aluminum siding. But at 560,000 square feet, it is, without a doubt, a very big "house."

Classically composed, the building features a central rotunda flanked by two symmetrical wings, and the symmetry is compounded by the building's image reflected in the man-made pond in the foreground. The main driveway bisects the pond, running right up to and through the center of the building before disappearing into the parking garage.

The central rotunda is likened to the corporate living room, and its seven stories make an exceptionally grand entrance. The rotunda lobby soars 95 feet and it shimmers from top to bottom with mirrors and mirrored finishes; even the atrium's inner dome is reflective. Despite all this glitz, the basic interior structure retains the classical, formal intent introduced outside. The most luxurious executive space is called the "tiara"—a seventh-floor gallery that rings the rotunda and overlooks the atrium.

The idea of the corporate home resurfaces in the general offices, which strive to keep a residential quality with soft colors and built-in furniture. Clerestory windows ensure that the people who work here are not deprived of natural light.

Kevin Roche and John Dinkeloo, whose firm is located in Hamden, Connecticut, have been partners since the 1960s when they worked in the offices of Eero Saarinen. Their successful headquarters building designs include the Ford Foundation, John Deere, and Union Carbide. In the late 1980s, the General Foods building was purchased by Philip Morris as headquarters for Kraft Foods International and Philip Morris International.

At this writing, tours of the building have been discontinued. For visitor information, call the Philip Morris Management Corporation at (212) 880-5000.

High Museum of Art, 1983

1280 Peachtree Street N.E.
Atlanta, Georgia

Richard Meier & Partners

The High Museum of Art is that rare building that impresses and welcomes at the same time. This is partly because Richard Meier's design offers the best-orchestrated procession of any museum since the Guggenheim.

From beginning to end, people in motion are considered part of the picture. The main approach leads you directly up a ceremonial entrance ramp that makes a twist near the door. From here you are funneled through a low, dark entry that dramatizes your arrival into the lobby: a luminous four-story skylighted atrium that seems designed to encourage mixing and mingling. From this bright and busy central fan-shaped atrium, a series of ramps that wrap the glass atrium walls will take you through the three gallery floors. Finally, exiting visitors share the long central ramp with the new arrivals.

A fascinating aspect of traveling the atrium ramp is Meier's placement of large white panels—like blank canvases—along the way. Sunlight and shadow from the atrium skylight cast constantly changing patterns on these panels, and your movement past the panels causes the patterns to change in response.

White, in dozens of shades, is the chosen color inside the museum. In the free-flowing galleries, Southern artists receive special attention. The museum is also building fine permanent collections in photography and the decorative arts.

In the year after the High Museum opened, Richard Meier received the Pritzker Prize honoring his influential contributions to modern architecture. Following the successful High Museum, Meier unveiled designs for a new J. Paul Getty Museum complex scheduled to open in Brentwood, California, in 1996.

High Museum of Art is open Tuesday through Saturday, 10:00 AM to 5:00 PM; Friday until 9:00 PM; Sunday, noon to 5:00 PM; closed Monday. For general information, call (404) 898-9540. To arrange special tours, call (404) 898-1145.

333 WACKER DRIVE, 1983

Wacker Drive, Lake and Franklin Streets
Chicago, Illinois

Kohn Pederson Fox

The starting point for 333 Wacker Drive is its one-of-a-kind triangular site, formed by a bend in the Chicago River, which intersects the city's rectilinear grid. Wacker Drive runs along the river, and the river and the street cut diagonally across the site. What is left is a neat little triangular half-block with the hypotenuse facing the riverfront.

The 35-story speculative office building that the firm of Kohn Pederson Fox designed to take advantage of this site is fan-shaped; its most arresting feature is a curved green glass curtain wall facing the river. The green glass mirrors the color of the river, and flat walls on either side frame it against the sky.

333 Wacker Drive sits across the river from the Merchandise Mart, an emphatically vertical neighbor. For their design, KPF chose to emphasize the horizontal lines. The building's curved face is horizontally banded with stainless steel bullnoses spaced six feet apart. In contrast, the sides and back of the building are flat, except for a vertical notch that rises the entire length of the building on the city side and a sawtooth configuration across the top.

The building uses geometrical optics in amazing ways. Because the site is triangular, the side walls of the building retreat sharply from the curved front face. From certain points of view, this creates the illusion that the building is breathtakingly thin—a sliver of glass projecting from the cityscape.

At the base, bands of colored granite and marble are used to create the impression of massively stacked strata. Inside, the two-story lobby is highly polished—with stainless steel ceilings that reflect marble terrazzo floors, and theatrical concentric stairs. The adjacent building at 225 West Wacker is also by Kohn Pederson Fox.

The building is open during business hours. 333 Wacker Drive is also featured on two Chicago Architecture Foundation tours (West Loop and Architecture River Cruise). For tour information, call CAF at (312) 922-TOUR.

Transco Tower, 1983

2800 Post Oak Boulevard at Westheimer
Houston, Texas

Philip Johnson & John Burgee

Transco Tower resembles a classic limestone building of the 1920s that has been sheathed in reflective glass the color of stone. But here, the tall, stepped back piers are mirrored. They face each other at the corners, so that the building takes on a faceted appearance. Visual effects can be dazzling: on a cloudy day, it is fascinating to circle this building on the nearby freeway to catch the animated reflections; in a storm, the building appears moody and electric.

A pyramid tops the 1.6 million square foot building, and the base features a huge, ceremonial arched entry faced in pink granite, although most visitors arrive by car and enter from the garage across the street through a glass-enclosed overhead walkway.

To the south of the tower is a formal park with the popular Transco Fountain, a 60-foot-high water wall also designed by Philip Johnson and John Burgee. Water cascades down both the interior and exterior sides of the arc, creating both a mesmerizing sense of vertical motion and a cooling breeze. A freestanding portal frames the water view.

The building is open during regular business hours, and there is an observation deck at the top. For visitor information, call the building owner, Gerald Hines Interests, at (713) 850-8841.

Gordon Wu Hall, 1983

Princeton University Campus
College Walk at Butler Walk
Princeton, New Jersey

Venturi, Rauch & Scott Brown

Gordon Wu Hall is slipped into a site that, like Frank Lloyd Wright's Fallingwater, did not even seem to be there until Venturi, Rauch & Scott Brown erected a building on it. The building is necessarily long and narrow, and bracketed by existing structures, prompting Robert Venturi to call it "a hyphen." This characterization is especially apt given Venturi's well-known conception of architecture as literature, a special language of signs and symbols.

The purpose of Gordon Wu Hall was to establish a new residential college entity that would include several surrounding structures. Although one of the existing dormitories is aggressively modern, the main inspiration for Gordon Wu Hall comes from the collegiate Gothic style that set the tone of Princeton's 250-year-old campus, which in turn takes its cues from Oxford and Cambridge. Venturi has pointed out that while we can no longer build classical buildings, we can represent them in our own time and our own ways.

The "modern Gothic" three-story orange brick building with limestone trim satisfyingly complements the size, colors, and rhythms of the older neighbors. It is also stimulating in its individuality—most notably for the "billboard," entry façade inset with gray granite and white marble the students describe as a cat's face with whiskers.

In contrast to the lively exterior, the interior seems suddenly subdued. But it also appears inordinately spacious because of the open views from one end to the other through the rounded bay windows. Most of the first floor is given over to a long dining room, part diner and part "great hall." A wide staircase, called the "grand bleacher," provides an indoor amphitheater as well as access to a lounge, administrative offices, and a library on the second floor.

The Philadelphia firm of Venturi, Rauch & Scott Brown is internationally known for its architecture and writings, and its aphorisms ("Main Street is almost alright") are legendary. The firm's principal designer, Robert Venturi, graduated from Princeton University and was awarded the Pritzker Prize in 1991. Following the success of Gordon Wu Hall, the firm completed two additional buildings at Princeton University: the Lewis Thomas Molecular Biology Laboratory Building (exteriors only) and the Fuller Building adjacent to the Woodrow Wilson School.

For visitor information, call (609) 258-3000.

AT&T Building, 1984

550 Madison Avenue
New York, New York

Philip Johnson and John Burgee

Philip Johnson has said that you cannot *not* know history. As if to prove the point, the design for the 36-story AT&T corporate headquarters provokes instant recall of the Chippendale highboy that seems to reside in our nation's collective memory. The architectural in-joke quickly became an icon.

The revival of historical style on such a grand scale marked an important architectural turning point—the rejection of the cold and anonymous flat glass box in favor of warmth, visual interest, and a strong identity for a prominent American corporation. It is fitting that Philip Johnson, the first American architect to champion the International Style in the 1930s, should be one of the first to bury it forty years later.

The outsized highboy is clad in pink granite, and it meets the street with a tall columned plaza and majestic 65-foot arched main entry. To the rear of the building is a retail arcade.

When the AT&T building opened, it was considered ironic that such a high-technology company resided in an "old-fashion" building. The interiors, it was always stressed, were explicitly up-to-the-minute. In 1992, another high-technology company, Sony Corporation, purchased the building from AT&T. It now houses the offices of Sony Music.

The building is open during regular business hours. For information, call (212) 833-8000.

California Aerospace Hall, 1984

California Museum of Science & Industry
700 State Drive in Exposition Park
Los Angeles, California

Frank O. Gehry

California's heroic test pilots take pride in "pushing the outside of the envelope"—breaking the barriers—and Frank Gehry's design for California Aerospace Hall achieves the architectural equivalent. It pushes museum design to new heights by displaying the "collection" on the outside for all to see.

Harmoniously disharmonious, the museum is a building in two distinct parts. The larger structure is a seven-sided hangar clad in riveted sheet metal that cantilevers out at an arresting angle. More rectangular but no less sedate, the white-stucco museum wing attracts attention with a Lockheed F104 Starfighter braced to one wall, poised to crest the building in flight.

Unlike many museums, this one opens itself to the street, secure in its ability to lure people inside where the planes and aerospace memorabilia are seductively exhibited. Planes hang suspended from the ceiling, and open walkways let you walk around and see them from all sides. Another internal advantage is the quality of the light, in part a result of Gehry's eye-catching windows that modulate the Los Angeles sun. In 1992, there will be even more to see; the museum is expanding and Gehry's building will act as a "lobby" for the new space.

Frank Gehry's practice is located in Santa Monica, and you can get quite a Gehry education by visiting his buildings in the area: his own famous residence in Santa Monica, the early Danziger Studio on Melrose, Loyola Law School, and the Chiat/Day building in Venice to name just a few. Gehry's prominence has gone international; in 1987 he was awarded the Pritzker Prize and his American Center is scheduled to open in Paris in 1992.

California Aerospace Hall is located in Exposition Park East, near the University of Southern California. It is open daily from 10:00 AM to 5:00 PM, except Thanksgiving, Christmas Day, and New Year's Day. For information about tours and exhibits, call (213) 744-7400.

Loyola Law School, 1984

1440 Olympic Boulevard
Los Angeles, California

Frank O. Gehry & Associates

All but one building on the Loyola Law School campus have been designed by Frank Gehry; he even designed the parking garage, scheduled to open in 1993. So, as the locals say, this campus is "very Gehry." There are five of the Santa Monica architect's buildings assembled here—three lecture halls, a chapel, and a mid-rise building for classrooms, administrative offices, and a bookstore—and they are make a colorful composition with their walls variously painted yellow, orange, and blue-gray. The mid-rise is the major structure, and dominates. The smaller buildings—some of them near miniature size—are arrayed in front of the main building and force the perspective. There is a sense of visual upsweep toward an acropolis—and this in close quarters, without the benefit of an actual hill. Somehow, it works.

Gehry's inventive and artistic touch is everywhere. There is a greenhouse-like temple that appears to be hatching from the top of the classroom building, and the cantilevered, lightning-bolt stairs lead the eye up to the temple through what one might take to be the cracked shell of the building. There is a logical method at work here—a method for startling the beholder. Some of the visual shock-effects come from strong lines that go where it seems they should not, or simply go nowhere. More striking effects are derived from Gehry's trademark use of "cheapskate" materials in unusual or deliberately inappropriate contexts. Still more arise from the technique of leaving parts of the understructure exposed, or constructing the building in a permanently unfinished look. The seriousness, however, is made clear: the wood may be plywood, but it is *polished* plywood.

Loyola Law School is located just off the Harbor Freeway in midtown Los Angeles, and you can see it while driving by. But because the campus is closed to the public (and closed completely in the week from Christmas to New Year's Day), you'll need to call ahead to arrange a visit at (213) 736-1000.

HERRING HALL, 1985

Rice University
Houston, Texas

Cesar Pelli & Associates

Importation of architects has given Rice University its Beaux Arts sense of style and order, as well as its new, "modern classical" buildings by high-profile practitioners: Cesar Pelli from the East Coast, England's James Stirling, and Ricardo Bofill of Spain. The reknowned New York architects Cram, Goodhue & Ferguson developed the master plan in 1910, with Mediterranean style buildings of terra-cotta-colored St. Joe's brick and limestone and red tile roofs arranged around a series of open quadrangles and lawns shaded by old oaks.

Cesar Pelli's design for Herring Hall, Rice University's graduate school of business, echoes the Rice style but introduces a new liveliness of design and decorative brickwork. He has divided the building into two long offset rectangles, each with a distinct roofline—one is pitched, the other is vaulted—and the parts are connected by a glass-enclosed central corridor and arcade. The entire exterior is imaginatively clad with brick. The soft terra-cotta of St. Joe's brick is background for horizontal stripes, including glazed burgundy brick denoting the floor slabs on the long walls. On the short side walls there is an eye-catching overall diamond pattern that has prompted students to call this "Herringbone Hall."

The three-story pitched-roof building, which houses classrooms and lecture halls, sits close to the street. Here the main entrance is marked by a tall triangle of green glass. The flat-topped atrium part of the building contains the library. This side faces an expansive lawn shaded with old oak trees; its ground-level arcade is enlivened with a vaulted ceiling and columns that are half-covered in brick and limestone, half in steel.

On the inside, Herring Hall's light and open quality is a consequence of its many large windows and the balconies and terraces that are worked into the design. The scene stealer inside is the library, a two-story vaulted space with Pelli-designed patterns on the ceiling and tile on the walls.

Pelli is a native of Argentina who holds a Master of Arts degree from the University of Illinois. In his position as Dean of the Yale School of Architecture from 1977 to 1984, he saw campus planning from the inside, which surely contributed to the success of Herring Hall.

For visitor information, call (713) 527-8101.

Humana Building, 1985

500 West Main
Louisville, Kentucky

Michael Graves

After decades of monochromania, color came back into architecture with Michael Graves's Portland Building of 1984 (see page 163), even though the building was basically boxlike. The Humana Building is different. The design is a three-dimensional extravaganza of shapes, materials, and textures. But color has not been forgotten. Graves's pretty palette appears in the materials he has selected, which include Finnish pink and Brazilian green stone; these provide a nice change from white, black, gray, and beige. Color also identifies important elements of the building, and links the structure to the natural world—browns suggest earth, blue the sky.

The Humana Building's 26 stories are treated to three different elevations, a complex division between the base, midsection, and the top, and many historically inspired motifs. Each multi-layered element plays a part in this rich mix. The six-story base appears firmly planted on the entire site, with rows of tall square columns at the perimeter creating a street-level arcade. A parapet angles out over the roof of this lower structure, with a glass triangle skylight peaking out above it.

The 525,000-square-foot tower steps back from its full-block base, occupying only about half of the surface area. The midsection, containing tenant-occupied offices, is the plainest part and the most regimental, with its rigorous rows of flat, square windows. The juggernaut top recalls ancient Egyptian and Mayan forms. On the 25th floor at the front of the building, there is an outdoor porch with a bowed balcony braced by trusswork painted deep terra-cotta.

The Humana Building's lobby is accessible weekdays from 8:30 AM to 9:00 PM, and private tours can be arranged. For appointments, call (502) 580-3610.

PA CONSULTING GROUP, 1985

**279 Princeton Road
Hightstown, New Jersey**

Richard Rogers

For sheer shock value, it is hard to top the first sight of PA Consulting Group's high-tech flagship amidst the fields of suburbia. Nine giant A-frames—tubular steel masts 60-feet high—are aligned along the building's central spine. The structural framework becomes an exposed A-frame exoskeleton tethered with cables seemingly anchored by giant washers. Within this structure, a suspended cradle holds air conditioners, heaters, and plumbing equipment, also exposed. Color coding of the mechanical elements—silver for the air handling, green for sprinklers, orange for electricals—gives the whole composition a festive air. At sunset, the building takes on an otherworldly orange glow.

The British architect Richard Rogers practically invented "high tech," along with Renzo Piano, at Paris's Pompidou Center in the 1970s. There, the wizardry of exposing and color coding structural elements drew attention to the museum and the city's position as a culture capital. At PA, the design is meant to express the advanced technological thinking of a British-based firm of management consultants and product development specialists with international reach.

In Rogers's first work in the United States, the high-tech aesthetics impose a "kit of parts" approach to the one-story 42,600-square-foot rectangle. On the inside, one does not lose sight of the superstructure that makes the exterior so intriguing: a bubble skylight runs along the building's center line, exposing the underside. A practical advantage of Rogers's design is the creation of vast areas of flexible column-free interior space.

It is surprising to learn that the intricate superstructure was not custom fabricated. All the components come right off the shelf. Even so, the industrial aesthetic of a high-tech building does not come cheaply. High costs have certainly dampened the general enthusiasm for high tech. PA is the standard bearer in this country.

Driving by will allow a complete view of the building, but because of the special nature of the work here, visits inside the building must be pre-arranged. For information, call (609) 426-4700.

Arthur M. Sackler Museum, 1985

Harvard University
Broadway at Quincy Street
Cambridge, Massachusetts

James Stirling and Michael Wilford

The internationally renowned British architect James Stirling died in 1992 at the age of 66, leaving a brilliant legacy of building in England and in Germany, but only three works in the United States—all of them on college campuses. And at all three, the biggest surprise is how little they look like Stirling's work at first glance.

The Sackler Museum, an expansion of Harvard University's Fogg Museum across the street, puts most of its architectural interest on the main façade, and inside rather than out.

If you approach the building from the northwest, you'll be greeted by a closed and somewhat forbidding system: two sides and a rounded corner striped with two-toned bands of brick, and dotted by windows placed at irregular intervals. This part of the building represents the five floors of L-shaped administrative space that wraps the three gallery levels that are the heart of the building.

The main façade is infinitely more interesting—it is almost literally a face: a wide square of glass at the brow, a long triangular window below it, and three glass doors at the base. A flanking pair of columns rising about halfway up sport ventilator grilles that look like ears. This façade is meant to work alone, or as background for a covered third-level walkway that is yet to come, which would link the Sackler Museum with the Fogg Museum (but this walkway will probably not be constructed).

All this design activity of the entry façade is prologue to the building's grand gesture just inside the front door: a steep, tall, and narrow processional staircase with a skylight at the top and bright bands of color on the walls. The stair will lead you into the double-height galleries, which occupy 11,000 square feet in the building. On the lower level is a 250-seat auditorium.

The Sackler Museum displays the university's fine permanent collections of Oriental and Islamic art, and hosts temporary exhibits as well. The museum is open Tuesday through Sunday from 10:00 AM to 5:00 PM, closed major holidays. Tours are conducted Tuesday through Friday at noon. For information, call (617) 495-9400.

State of Illinois Center, 1985

Clark, La Salle, Randolph and Lake Streets
Chicago, Illinois

Helmut Jahn

This building was intended as a new focal point for Chicago's West Loop, and it is surely that. But the attention has cut both ways. Illinois taxpayers, who paid for the construction, sometimes say this relatively short and idiosyncratic 17-story public building cost more, at $172 million, than the very much taller Sear's Tower (arguable bookkeeping, correcting for inflation). Paul Goldberger called it "architecture on amphetamines." On the other hand, it draws praise for its imaginative futuristic form, for its eye-popping full-court atrium, and for co-mingling the government's bureaucracy with retail and office coworkers.

The structure's complex design is difficult to see whole, and it looks different from every angle. But the basic idea is simple: take a block of ice and turn on a sunlamp aimed at one corner. The corner melts away, thus rounding the cube. (Retreating glaciers created Illinois terrain, putting the metaphor on the side of history.)

In real life, the main façade is a curve, stepped back in three tiers, and capped by a cylinder sheared off at a rakish angle. This complicated shape is clad with both colored and clear glass. Color is coded as a function of altitude: deep blue at the base to white at the top, with tinges of salmon. With its curved and angled walls, its variegated colors, and its many mullions, the 1.2-million-square-foot building looks like a faceted colossus.

It should come as no surprise that the interior is not "plain Jane." You walk into a great cylindrical atrium, 160 feet in diameter, rising all 17 stories—and beyond, through the roof into a bevel-topped silo (more Illinois symbolism). This atrium is a riot. Bright red strutwork covers the "skylight" and travels down the walls, which are painted in blue and salmon. Circular office floors ring the great rotunda, and the elevator banks are freestanding towers that soar to the top. Giddy looking stairways cantilever out into the atrium, making for an unforgettable spatial experience.

German-born Helmut Jahn, one of architecture's more flamboyant practitioners, designed the building with his firm, Murphy/Jahn, which is based in Chicago. He pulled out all the stops on this one, making his United Terminal at O'Hare Airport look calm by comparison.

The State of Illinois Center is quite a sight in the daytime; at night its illumination is spectacular. The building is open during regular business hours. It is also featured on the Chicago Architecture Foundation's daily Loop walking tours, "Modern and Beyond." For information, call CAF at (312) 922-TOUR.

Architecture College, 1986

University of Houston
4800 Calhoun
Houston, Texas

Philip Johnson and John Burgee

Like many Houston corporations in the 1970s and 1980s, the University of Houston selected Philip Johnson and John Burgee to crown its growth with a signature building. The signature in this case is that of Claude-Nicholas LeDoux, a French architect who lived from 1763 to 1826, and who is considered the first great architect of the Romantic Classical style.

The Architecture College is virtually an exact "quotation" of LeDoux's design for the House of Education in his ideal imaginary town of Chaux. Here the 200-year-old design is produced with modern construction methods. The formal, symmetrical composition consists of a massive cruciform base of flat, beige brick, out of which emerges a central square attic, topped by a white columned temple. Windows also rise in orderly succession: a rectangular row at ground level, superseded by a course of square windows, dominated by the band of tall arched windows, with a single occulus at the top. Each façade follows the same pattern, including the Palladian entry arch and recessed porch. On each side, too, rooflines project over the walls, creating defining lines and casting interesting shadows on the spare, flat walls.

The interior seems both more open and more ornate than the outside. The four-story, five-level central atrium court has a Victorian flavor, with its ornamented staircases, balconies, columns, and skylight. Classrooms, studios, and administrative offices, and a library and gallery are located off the central court, for the most part out of sight.

The College of Architecture is intended to mark a new gateway to the campus, and the building is visible from the I-45 South freeway. The school is open from 8:00 AM to 5:00 PM Monday through Friday. Special exhibitions are often on view in the gallery, and tours hosted by University of Houston Student Ambassadors can be booked by calling (713) 743-1000.

Los Angeles Museum of Contemporary Art, 1986

250 South Grand Avenue
Los Angeles, California

Arata Isozaki

Architecturally speaking, the Los Angeles Museum of Contemporary Art (MOCA) is an oasis of excitement in downtown Los Angeles. The first major American building by Japan's "guerrilla architect" and new wave leader, MOCA is a brilliant combination of Western geometry and Eastern tranquility. Its design is bold, but beautiful too, and the new museum was hailed as an immediate success. To Isozaki, however, the success is premature. In his view, the museum has only just begun the long, slow process of coming into its own.

As time goes by, MOCA will be increasingly surrounded by the towers of California Plaza, a commercial development of which the museum is the centerpiece. Isozaki envisioned the museum as a village among the skyscrapers, achieving by design a presence the neighboring buildings have captured by their size.

MOCA occupies a tight site, and much of the seven-level building is below grade. This layering enables Isozaki to mastermind the progression of entry: you step into the courtyard first in order to experience the building, before actually entering it.

Above ground, flanking this central court, Isozaki divides the facilities. On the north side, there are the taller buildings, dominated by the barrel-vaulted library wing with its prominent onyx windows and ticket booth cube at the door. The great pyramid skylights mark the south side. These pyramids, together with rows of saw-toothed skylights, help illuminate the upper levels of the galleries concealed below.

On the outside, the building is luxurious in its materials, colors, and details. Red Indian sandstone clads much of the building, and its seductive color is enhanced by the rough-hewn texture of the stone and offset by dark-green aluminum panels with right pink diagonal joining. Copper is used to roof the barrel-vaulted library wing and at the base of the pyramid skylights. By contrast, the inside is cool and contemplative. All-white interiors have maple floors and are minimally detailed so as not to detract from the art on view. The main gallery, a 60-foot vaulted room illuminated by the largest skylight, is among the most evocative spaces Isozaki has ever built.

MOCA is open Tuesday to Sunday from 11:00 AM to 5:00 PM, and until 8:00 PM on Thursday; closed Monday, Thanksgiving, Christmas, and New Year's Day. Tours of the exhibits are conducted Thursday through Sunday at 1:00 and 2:00 PM. For information, call (213) 621-2766.

Kate Mantilini Restaurant, 1986

9109 Wilshire Boulevard
at Doheny Drive
Beverly Hills, California

Morphosis/Thom Mayne and Michael Rotundi

This deconstructed "roadhouse for the year 2,000" began with the actual deconstruction of a 1950s-modern bank building and the subsequent insertion of an industrially elegant restaurant within the old structural framework. In the multi-layered exterior, the new walls of white ceramic tile, glass block, and plastered cement seem old, while the bank's steel cage looks new. But there is no mistaking the here-and-now nature of the overall design. Among the clues: a sundial's steel fin protruding from the roof, and the stainless steel block letters of Kate Mantilini's marquee, suffused at night in a colorful neon glow.

At the Kate Mantilini Restaurant, Morphosis has created one of the most exciting and engaging spaces in the city. The focal point of the 100-foot-long restaurant is a complicated steel sculpture—an orerry—that appears to be a continuation of the rooftop sundial that is visible through the skylight. In ancient times, astronomers used the clockwork mechanism of the orerry to portray planetary motion. The mechanisms could be earth-centered or sun-centered. The restaurant's contemporary one is self-centered. It culminates in a stylus that has "inscribed" the building's plan onto a steel plate on the floor.

The restaurant's namesake, Kate Mantilini, was a boxing promoter in the 1940s, which explains murals of fighters in the ring. The largest painting, by John Wehrle, spans the curving north wall above the counter; a smaller mural provides a backdrop for the orerry sculpture.

The architecture of Morphosis stands out from the deconstructionist competition in the sophistication of their ideas and the quality of their materials and construction. Also, as Peter Cook observes, Morphosis has the compelling ability to anchor their architecture as well as explode it.

In a town of high-concept restaurants, Kate Mantilini has become a landmark. And, since Thom Mayne and Michael Rotundi dissolved their partnership in 1991, it is one of the last collaborations of this influential pair.

Kate Mantilini is open Monday to Friday from 7:30 AM to 3:00 AM; Saturday, noon to 3:00 AM; Sunday, 10:00 AM to midnight. The phone number is (310) 278-3699.

Clos Pegase Winery, 1987

1060 Dunaweal Lane
Calistoga, California

Michael Graves

The classic shapes and muted colors of an old Tuscan farmstead have inspired Michael Graves's design for this wine-making estate located in the heart of the Napa Valley about ninety minutes north of San Francisco. A clustered village of stucco buildings with tile roofs, Clos Pegase is a 50-acre estate that includes wine-making facilities, tasting rooms that are open to the public, and owner Jan Shrem's house on the hill, which is private.

Clos Pegase is the culmination of Shrem's dream of uniting his love of wine, art, and architecture in an "epoch-making" way; this comes through in the entire design, starting with the procession of entry. The complex is approached via a long road, around the long stretch of the winery building, ending up in front of the visitors' wing. This wing will seem well composed but closed, like an old monastery or fortress. Its entry is marked by a single monumental earthen-red Tuscan column positioned dead center in the high-ceilinged entrance portico. Within a few steps, visitors see that the building turns out to be warm and welcoming. It opens to the sculpture garden straight ahead, and to the left is the Napa Valley's most beautiful tasting room, where works from the owner's private art collection are on display.

The estate's production wing, to the east of the visitors' wing, is often mistaken for the main entrance because of its architecturally monumental loading dock: a portico with four pairs of voluptuous 24-foot columns. But Clos Pegase is a working winery, and it is in the production wing that the wine-making takes place. Grapes are brought from the fields, crushed, and then fermented in enormous underground caves.

Now that Clos Pegase has been constructed, its program seems tailor-made for Michael Graves, considering the renowned Princeton-based architect's skill at evoking the classical forms of the Italian countryside and his distinct skill as an artist. But the owner chose the architect by the process of competition, under the auspices of the San Francisco Museum of Modern Art. An unusual feature of the competition was its requirement that architects collaborate with artists on their designs; Michael Graves teamed up with Edwin Schmidt, who created murals depicting the wine-making process for the outdoor rotunda, which has not yet been built.

Clos Pegase is open seven days a week for wine tastings and tours. Reservations are required and may take time to secure. September and October are harvest times, when vineyard activity reaches its peak. For reservations or information, call (707) 942-4981.

Fire Station No. 5, 1987

100 Goeller Court
Columbus, Indiana

Susanna Torre with Wank Adams Slavin Associates

Many American cities are known for their grandest public buildings—museums, libraries, and city halls—but "functional" buildings deserve their due. Columbus, Indiana, is famed for its outstanding collection of public and private buildings by world-renowned architects, and fire stations seem to be a special source of civic pride. In this town, the now-standard fire station plan of wrapping living quarters around the equipment core was devised in 1941. Susanna Torre's Fire Station No. 5 is the latest in a distinguished line that includes Robert Venturi's 1967 Fire Station No. 4.

Fire Station No. 5 responds to its small-town setting, its functional requirements, and the city's reputation for architectural sophistication. The station occupies a site that is rural on the way to being suburban, and Torre has acknowledged local vernacular styles in her design. Residential in character, the two-story building has yellow brick walls, a seamed, metal barnlike roof, and a hose tower resembling a silo.

Torre, an architect whose practice is located in New York City, organized the fire station into two basic parts: the functional "garage" and the residential "house." Public spaces occupy the ground floor, and living quarters for male and female fire fighters are on the upper floor. The two zones are linked by a circular core with stairs and a fire pole—that staple of movie and television fire fighting actually exists. The building is further divided into two wings, forming a rear courtyard, although here the walls of the building and the circular stair tower are clad in metal. More metal appears on the second-story exteriors, where the structural steel columns are clearly exposed.

Columbus calls itself the "Architectural Showplace of America." Today, in terms of the number of buildings designed by noted architects, it ranks fourth in the United States after New York City, Chicago, and Los Angeles. The Visitors Center downtown offers a fast-paced, multi-projector slide show previewing Columbus's architectural development and provides tours, maps, and other information. It is generally open from 9:00 AM to 5:00 PM Monday through Saturday, and on Sunday from 10:00 AM to 2:00 PM from April 1 to October 31. For information and reservations, call (812) 372-1954 or (800) 468-6564.

The Australian-born architects Hank Koning and Julie Eizenberg began making their reputation in Los Angeles in the early 1980s designing small houses with affordable building budgets. From this experience they developed an uncommon skill for generating new ideas in very small spaces and for using inexpensive materials with considerable style. The Hollywood Duplex represents a somewhat larger project and a more handsome budget; the site is in a very desirable area of the Hollywood Hills, with a splendid view to the east.

The space is confined by geography rather than available funds. The site is a slender triangle, and it is mostly vertical. The resulting "twin towers" design is in many ways characteristically Californian: tall rather than deep, and elbow-to-elbow with the neighbors. A particular triumph is that the two houses, angled onto the triangular site with a terraced garden and stairs between them, do not intrude on each other's space or privacy.

Each tower measures 20 feet square and four stories tall, with one room per floor: a garage on one, a studio workroom on two, a living room on three, and a bedroom on top. The kitchen and baths are in a semi-separate structure tucked behind the top floors, linked to the tower by an interior stairwell. With intelligent packing, Koning and Eizenberg have created a sense of spaciousness, and succeeded in making the beautiful natural setting an important part of the overall design.

The twin towers stand out with their cheerful colors: the concrete walls of one tower are painted mint green with yellow windows, the other is pink with white trim. The walls facing the inner courtyard are clad in sheet metal. On the inside, the houses are basically white and are detailed in a way that seems more European than American. Ceilings are exposed concrete, and the floors were meant to be polished masonite, although in one duplex unsuspecting painting contractors treated them as drop cloths and wood floors were installed instead.

The color, the openness, and the spare interiors tend to give the duplex apartments the feel of beach houses in the hills. And because of the hills and the fine, slender Italian poplars adjacent to the houses, the perch could be a ledge above Lake Como or Lake Garda in Italy.

The apartments are located in Hollywood, north of the intersection of Highland and Franklin, near the Hollywood Bowl. The houses are private residences, but the twin towers are easily seen from the street.

MENIL MUSEUM, 1987

1515 Sul Ross
Houston, Texas

Renzo Piano with Richard Fitzgerald

The Menil Museum offers an atmosphere of calm, refinement, and respect at a time when many museums seek to attract large crowds that make contemplation or even viewing of the exhibited art almost impossible.

This museum seems personal in every respect, a characteristic announced at the front door where the signatures of principal donors are carved in stone. The collection is highly personal, too, consisting of 10,000 works of antiquities, tribal arts, Surrealism, and late twentieth-century American art assembled by Dominique de Menil and her late husband, John de Menil. The museum is located in a residential neighborhood, and the building is clearly meant to fit in. Like the surrounding houses (belonging to the de Menils), the museum is gray with white trim and compatibly scaled; interior galleries are room-sized and comprehensible. The Menil Museum even indulges the human impulse to look behind the scenes: framers and conservators work in an open area on the main gallery floor.

Compared to Italian architect Renzo Piano's colorful high-tech extravaganza at the Pompidou Center Museum in Paris (with Richard Rogers), the Menil Museum is cool, spare, and very formal—a long rectangle, 402 x 142 feet, clad in gray-stained cedar siding. The museum's most arresting feature, designed by Piano with Peter Rice of Ove Arup, is the innovative system of cement light-diffusers set in a ductile iron truss. These gracefully curved "leaves" act like stationary venetian blinds above the rooftop skylights. They extend beyond the roof to shade the exterior walkways.

For most of its length, the building consists of a single story that contains the exhibition galleries, some of which are punctuated with windows and others with views of garden courts. High ceilings, white walls, and floors of black-stained pine create an interior that is almost ethereal. Administration offices occupy a mezzanine, and the second floor is given over to the "treasure house," where the collection is accessible to historians and scholars.

The Menil Museum hours are 11:00 AM to 7:00 PM Wednesday to Sunday, closed Monday, Tuesday, and major holidays. The museum shop is housed in a gray bungalow across the street from the main entrance. For museum information, call (713) 525-9400.

Berkowitz-Odgis House, 1988

Lighthouse Road
Martha's Vineyard Island, Massachusetts

Steven Holl

Steven Holl's beach house on Martha's Vineyard island captures the spirit of its austere waterfront as freshly and convincingly as Sea Ranch on the northern California coast did in the 1960s. The Berkowitz-Odgis House occupies three acres of natural shrub land on a bluff overlooking Vineyard Sound, and Holl was inspired by these rugged surroundings.

In designing the beach house, Holl was also drawn to the seafaring legends of Herman Melville's *Moby Dick*, and to the ancient customs of local Indians who built their houses by draping skins over the skeletons of beached whales. With this skeletal image in mind, Holl pushed a traditional wooden balloon frame to the outside, exposed it, and hung the three-bedroom, 1,600-square-foot house within it. The wooden "bones" of the house also allow for verandas along the south and west, and an entrance porch to the north. Wooden members are meant to harbor the natural vines of the island and soften the straight lines of the architecture.

Holl's design runs counter to the conventional wisdom that a waterfront house must first of all face the water. Here, the house is long and narrow, but it is set perpendicular to the shore. This opens up multiple side views rather than a single head-on one. Rooms follow a simple progression as they rise up the site's gentle slope: the living room, dining room (which occupies a glass-enclosed triangular bay), kitchen, two bedrooms, and the exercise room. The house culminates with a tower, with a master bedroom, sun deck, and an expansive view.

The island's building code required that the house be constructed of wood, in a natural, weathered-gray color. Part of Holl's artistry has been in transforming this requirement into one of the house's most delightful characteristics. Wood railings and balustrades, connected by brass rods, are laid out vertically, horizontally, and sometimes on the diagonal. They serve as a continuation of the structure, as well as an intriguing elaboration of it.

Berkowitz-Odgis house is a private residence with no house number, but it is located on the water side of Lighthouse Road, off Lobsterville Road. It is visible from the street.

Lucile Halsell Conservatory, 1988

San Antonio Botanical Center
555 Funston Place
San Antonio, Texas

Emilio Ambasz

An architectural fascination of Emilio Ambasz's is the combination of nature with technology, and he often solves the problem by burying his buildings. At this botanical conservatory, much of the structure is constructed below grade and faces a sunken courtyard and its water gardens. Technology appears in the series of glass pyramids and cone-shaped towers that rise out of the underground galleries. One-half acre is enclosed under glass, making this the largest conservatory in the Southwest.

In the galleries, plants grow in man-made computer-controlled approximations of their native climates (spanning the range from a Desert Pavilion to an Alpine Room). Because the building is largely subterranean, these glass projections are essentially skylights. The geometries of metal and glass visible from the surface are of course artistic statements, juxtaposing nature and technology and so forth. They are quite striking visually.

But these glass projections also trick the Texas sun, which is ferocious. An expanse of flat roof here would be the first essential component of a solar oven, and the last thing one might wish to erect over a building intended to conserve green and delicate living organisms. Ambasz's shelter for the plants has no flat surfaces on top—instead, it presents the smallest conceivable areas to the sun: thin lines and sharp points. The inclined planes of the skylights, surfaced with glass, forcibly bounce the sun away from the building.

The conservatory is Ambasz's first major built work. A native of Argentina, Ambasz works in Bologna, Italy, and in New York City, where he was curator of design at the Museum of Modern Art from 1970 to 1976. In 1989, the museum mounted a show of Ambasz's work along with that of Steven Holl—implying that they were two architects to watch.

The Lucile Halsell Conservatory is open Tuesday through Sunday from 9:00 AM to 6:00 PM, closed Monday, Christmas, and New Year's Day. Guided tours are available for groups of fifteen or more, with reservations required three weeks in advance. For information and reservations, call (512) 821-5143.

Morton H. Meyerson Symphony Center, 1989

2301 Flora
Dallas, Texas

Pei, Cobb, Freed & Partners

The Meyerson Symphony Center is a building within a building: a separately endowed concert hall situated within the symphony center structure. The striking outer building, designed by I.M. Pei, is a unique construction that appears to be a glass sphere spliced by a masonry plane. Pei has stretched a Cartesian grid over a ball in a way that makes it hard not to think of Mercator projections. But the wall is sliced and stacked to create visual discontinuities to the hemisphere. The glass-walled curve contains the Symphony Center lobby, which wraps the hall. The lobby's broad, curved staircases lead to the concert hall and generate intriguing spatial experiences as one progresses through the vast glass-walled space.

Within Pei's dynamic construction is the 1,800-seat McDermott Concert Hall, which was treated as a distinct design by Artec Consultants because of the specialized nature of the acoustics. To conserve sound quality, Artec Consultants designed the hall shoebox style: 94 feet long, 84 feet wide, and 85 feet high. To maintain seating capacity, Artec used the available vertical space with three tiers of balconies.

Three adjustable elements can be used to tune the hall: a four-piece acoustic canopy, a large reverberation chamber, and two sets of acoustic curtains. The canopy, a monumental feature that projects out over the stage and resembles the Starship Enterprise, weighs 42 tons. It can be adjusted between its lowest stop, 40 feet above the stage, and its highest stop, at 75 feet. The low setting is for chamber music, and the high setting accommodates the heroically proportioned C.B. Fisk pipe organ rising behind the stage.

The meticulous wooden wall panels are actually a veneer over concrete. The paneling conceals no subsurface voids that might deaden sound reflection. Every panel was tapped for hollow spots with a rubber mallet by the consultant, just to make sure.

The Meyerson Symphony Center is home to the Dallas Symphony Orchestra; for performance schedules, call (214) 871-4000; for tickets, call 692-0203. The building is open for events and tours only. Tours are conducted by the Meyerson Symphony Center at 1:00 PM on Monday, Wednesday, Friday, and Saturday, but performances sometimes necessitate a change in tour schedules. Groups of fifteen may arrange private tours with a notice of one month. For tour information and reservations, call (214) 670-3600.

Nelson Fine Arts Center, 1989

Arizona State University
Mill Avenue, between 10th Street and Gammage Parkway
Tempe, Arizona

Antoine Predock

A desert landscape seems especially hospitable to arresting architecture—buildings become virtually the sole scenery on the flat, open, mutely colored terrain. Although the Southwestern setting of the Nelson Fine Arts Center is actually a built-up university campus, Antoine Predock has created a scenic wonder strong enough to hold its own in the open desert.

On campus, the fine arts center is like a pueblo within the city. Its pale lavender stucco walls seem to have accrued layer upon layer, rising to a Sphinx-like "mountain" in the middle, and partially ringed by an outer arcade of vivid red brick. Labyrinthian paths and below-grade passages seem to result from ancient but purposeful crossings. The cumulative effect of this layering and seemingly indirect circulation is not haphazard at all. It is Predock's way of drawing you into an adventure where there is much to discover.

Predock's design for the 119,000-square-foot complex is in fact enormously complex—it will take you up and over, around and through. On three levels above and below grade, the center includes five major components: the university art museum, the drama wing, the dance studio and the 496-seat Gavin Playhouse, plus sculpture gardens. The central plaza is a gripping space defined by the tower bridge. (At night, projectors hidden in the bridge beam images onto a tall, facing wall that resembles a drive-in movie screen.) Performances in the dance theater are meant to spill over into the plaza outdoors.

The main public entrance on Mill Avenue leads to the art museum, and it shows Predock's mastery of managing the transition from overpowering sunlight to the cool austerity of the sunken interiors. Aiding the transition, Predock has designed a series of trellises at this entrance to introduce welcome shade and cast geometrically patterned shadows. Once inside the museum, however, you won't be able to proceed directly from the museum to the theaters; these have separate entries.

According to Predock, the Nelson Fine Arts Center is an example of "naked architecture." Its massive blank walls stand up to the strong sun, which obliterates the fine-grained detail that provides definition in other climates. Predock's subtleties work with this climate—for example, the infinite mutations of the building's lavender color in different lights and after it rains. Its interiors contain a sense of mystery, even for people who know them well.

The Nelson Fine Arts Complex is open Tuesday from 11:30 AM to 7:30 PM, Wednesday to Friday from 8:30 AM to 4:30 PM, Saturday from 10:00 AM to 5:00 PM, and Sunday from 1:00 to 5:00 PM. With two weeks notice, special architectural tours can be arranged for groups of six or more. For information and tour arrangements, call (602) 965-2787.

Wexner Center for the Visual Arts, 1989

Ohio State University
Columbus, Ohio

Peter Eisenman

If you take a map of Columbus, Ohio, and draw a bright red line from 15th Avenue to the campus football stadium, you will see how Peter Eisenman began to conceive the Wexner Center for the Visual Arts. The red line marks the convergence (or collision) of the city's grid with the campus grid, a likely starting point for an art center whose stated goal is to bring avant-garde art to town. Wexner Center's initial display of avant-garde art is obviously the building itself, America's most prominent work of Deconstructionist architecture. Like its illustrious and theoretical architect, Wexner Center speaks its own language, makes its own rules, and seeks to elicit a completely new set of responses.

Wexner Center is slotted between two existing buildings. Although most of the structure is tucked underground, its axis is clearly marked at street level by long, open, white steel framework, which Eisenman calls "scaffolding." It forms an angled outdoor street almost a block long, and a wedge of the main building intrudes into its long, gridded promenade.

Eisenman marks the center's entrance with a set of dark brick towers—the "armory"—in place of an old armory on the site that was demolished after a 1958 fire. This architectural resurrection is not entirely literal; Eisenman's towers are split and peeled away, positioned and angled in novel ways. Inside the main entrance, in the two-story lobby, the campus grid and the city grid collide in framework. Consider yourself alerted to the unconventional effects that will follow: stairs with columns, grids jammed into ceilings, grids hanging in space, windows on the floor. The lobby's grand staircase channels you down to the primary circulation spine, a long ramp off which galleries are arrayed on terraces. The lower level spaces are beautifully illuminated by windows and skylights.

Wexner Center is large—almost 110,000 square feet plus 155,530 square-foot existing buildings—and its requirements are complex: galleries, experimental theaters, classrooms, offices, an arts library, café, bookstore, and amphitheater. Before Eisenman won the design competition, his built work consisted mainly of houses. The New York architect also had a reputation as the "bad boy of architecture." His ideas work at Wexner Center, and success here has brought Eisenman several large commissions, including a new convention center in Columbus.

Gallery hours are Tuesday and Wednesday 10:00 AM to 6:00 PM; Thursday to Saturday, 10:00 AM to 8:00 PM; Sunday noon to 5:00 PM; closed Monday. Walking tours are held at 1:00 PM Tuesday, Saturday, and Sunday, starting in the upper lobby; tours are free. For information, call (614) 292-0330.

WORLD FINANCIAL CENTER AND WINTER GARDEN, 1989

Battery Park City
West Street between Chambers Street and Battery Park
New York, New York

Cesar Pelli

Battery Park City is New York City's newest neighborhood. It occupies a 92-acre strip of brand-new Manhattan real estate, which was created along the banks of the Hudson River by the systematic depositing of landfill from the World Trade Center twin 110-story towers a few blocks west of the site. The master plan by Alexander Cooper and Stanton Eckstut mixes commercial, residential, and retail development with grand public plazas and an esplanade along the river that gives New York the kind of congenial urban space you would expect to find almost anywhere but here.

The work of several important individual (and highly individualistic) architects is represented, but the most prominent buildings to date are the four World Financial Center Buildings and the Winter Garden, all of which were designed by Cesar Pelli and developed by Olympia & York Companies (U.S.A.). The statistics: 6,000,000 square feet of offices, 300,000 square feet of retail space, and 200,000 square feet of lobby and circulation space. The four octagonal office towers vary in height from 34 to 51 stories, creating a cluster of buildings housing prominent financial corporations like Merrill Lynch and Dow Jones. The Winter Garden, the centerpiece, is a magnificent glassed-in park containing shops and restaurants, and providing space for concerts and other events. For the Winter Garden's 120-foot-high vaulted roof, the glazing was put into place over a ring and stringer steel structure of heroic proportions, strongly reminiscent of a zeppelin frame. In front of the Winter Garden, there is a fine plaza created by Pelli, Siah Armanjani, Scott Burton, and M. Paul Friedbert.

The apartments in Battery Park City are masonry with stone bases, and seem inspired by the beloved 1920s apartment houses along Central Park West. The choice of material brings a continuity to the new development, a little bit of old New York for this new New York.

The office buildings of World Financial Center are open during business hours. The Winter Garden is open seven days a week: Monday through Friday from 10:00 AM to 7:00 PM and Saturday and Sunday from noon to 5:00 PM. Restaurant hours vary. For information, call (212) 945-0505.

The Dolphin Hotel and The Swan Hotel, 1990

Walt Disney World/EPCOT Center
Near Orlando, Florida

Michael Graves

Walt Disney World's companion hotels, the Dolphin and the Swan, are like larger-than-life cartoons in which a colorful carnival is in full swing. The playful atmosphere is obvious even from a distance: two gigantic dolphins are doing headstands on top of their namesake hotel, and twin swans 47-feet tall preen against the sky atop the smaller hotel. And each hotel is further "themed" by supergraphic murals—green banana leaves are painted onto the sandy background of the Dolphin Hotel, and cresting blue waves cover the surface of the Swan.

This is architecture as show business, or what Walt Disney called "entertainment architecture," and so the graphic extravaganza never stops. Tented entries, columns of banana trees and palm leaves, beach-scene wall murals, doors striped like cabanas, and carpets designed to resemble boardwalks and lily pads are just a few of the fantasy confections contributing to the tropical resort.

Michael Graves designed the two hotels as part of his master plan for Walt Disney World's new hotel and convention center located between the EPCOT World Showcase and the Disney-MGM Studio theme park. The hotels face each other across a crescent-shaped lake, with a causeway connecting the two lobbies. The larger and more ambitious of the two is the Dolphin Hotel, which is a 1.4-million-square-foot convention center. Its 27-story triangular tower is the focal point of the building, and of the whole complex. Four 9-story wings of guest rooms project from this center out over the lake. The vaulted entry is flanked by clamshell fountains splashing water down either side. The Swan, a 12-story hotel with 615,000 square feet, is divided into the main building with a gently curving roofline; two guest room wings project out toward the water. Big, colorful cabana-striped awnings tent the entry and shade the causeway that ties the hotels together.

Virtually nothing has escaped the Graves graphic touch. The restaurants feature plates ringed in oranges and tabletops painted as slices of oranges, lemons, and limes. In the guest rooms, Graves-designed furniture includes lamps with pineapple bases and furniture stenciled with waves, fruit, and flowers.

To reserve a room at either hotel, call (407) 934-7639.

Las Vegas Library/ Discovery Museum, 1990

833 Las Vegas Boulevard North
Las Vegas, Nevada

Antoine Predock

No one sees the desert quite like Antoine Predock, or uses its intense light and bleached natural colors so convincingly. His competition-winning design for the Las Vegas Library/Discovery Museum is a complex of strong shapes rendered in subtle colors that stand up to the sun and cast striking shadows. In a town where most buildings compete for attention by turning up the voltage to eye-popping wattages, Predock's work stands out as an oasis of architectural sophistication.

For the approach, Predock lays out a carefully integrated series of graphic elements—cubes, cones, towers, and strategically placed palm trees—that draws you toward the entrance. The pale, bone-colored concrete shapes play off against sandstone walls rendered in pale terra-cotta and earthy red, a subtle combination that mimics the baked-clay feel of the desert and adds just enough color to be enticing. Water, the most precious commodity in the desert, washes one of the outside walls, and continues its flow to the lobby and on to an enclosed outdoor courtyard.

As its name implies, the Library/Discovery Museum is two buildings in one. Predock locates the library in the east wing and the children's museum in the west wing, which is set off at a slight angle. On all three floors of the 110,000-square-foot complex, the wings meet in a stepped-back triangular core that juts out on the north side and houses the facility's common administrative services. On the second and third floors, the wings are spanned by a barrel-vaulted reading room for children.

The cones and towers are places of merry-making and adventure for children. The cone-shaped exterior room at the entrance turns out to be the birthday party room, shaped like a birthday party hat. Gravity experiments take place in the 112-foot tower, which doubles as a lookout post. In the galleries, windows are low to the floor, allowing children to indulge a favorite pastime, spying on the adults and children visible in other rooms.

In dealing with the desert climate from a technical standpoint, Predock has used a number of cooling effects. Some of the windows are shaded with metal grills to help screen out the sun, and some courtyards are outfitted with fabric roofs that block out half the light. Left exposed are the outdoor bleachers, remnants of the baseball field that formerly occupied the site.

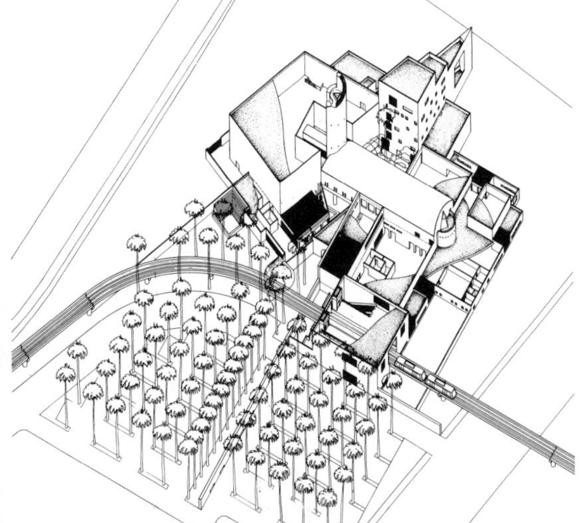

The library is open 9:00 AM to 9:00 PM Monday through Thursday; 9:00 AM to 5:00 PM Friday and Saturday; and noon to 5:00 PM on Sunday. Architectural tours can be arranged by calling the library's main number, (702) 382-3493.

MANDELL FUTURES CENTER, 1990

The Franklin Institute
Benjamin Franklin Parkway at 20th Street
Philadelphia, Pennsylvania

Robert Geddes and Michael Kihn
Geddes, Brecher, Qualls and Cunningham

Since 1933, the Franklin Institute has been famous for its "learning by doing" approach of teaching science to children as well as adults. The spunky new addition adjoins the temple-like original structure (whose depression-era plan was never completed) and adds a bright spot to the formal City Beautiful boulevard that runs alongside it.

The Mandell Futures Center could be the playground of a giant, sophisticated child whose oversized blocks include a limestone cylinder, a pyramid, and a glass cube that have tumbled to rest at a jaunty angle amid brightly painted steel beams. But as it stands, the cylinder is a huge Imax theater showing 70mm movies on a wraparound screen, the pyramid is the theater's roof, and the glass cube jutting out from the second floor is the "Science Overlook" vantage point for the outdoor Science Garden.

The designers, Robert Geddes and Michael Kihn of GBQC in Philadelphia, respected the existing structure while updating it with plentiful light and bright primary colors—a place where learning science seems like fun. The addition adds 90,000 square feet on two levels, plus underground parking. In the galleries, the Franklin Institute's proclivity for dynamic interactive displays continues, even higher tech than before. The central focus of the addition is the new museum entrance, a "Great Hall" atrium with a bright red ramp that spirals around to provide the main circulation. A lecture hall, restaurant, and bookshop were also added.

The Franklin Institute, its planetarium, and the Mandell Futures Center are open seven days a week. For information and hours, call (215) 448-1200.

Bright & Associates, 1991

901 Hampton Drive
at Washington Blvd.
Venice, California

Franklin D. Israel Design Associates

Starting with a historic shell—the famous "901" studio occupied for forty years by Charles and Ray Eames—Frank Israel has inserted a contemporary office for a corporate design firm that epitomizes southern California's contemporary architectural vivaciousness. Israel's vision is surprising, colorful, mysterious, dramatic, and sophisticated; he seems to see architecture as serious fun.

A vivid, yellow, flying-wedge canopy calls out the entry into the complex, a composite of three old, industrial structures. Inside the door, the regular, rectangular two-story exterior gives way to something completely different: a tall tower with angled walls, a skylighted roof, and high clerestory windows. This dramatic lighting illuminates mustard-yellow stucco walls with stone-gray ledge-like door frames for an overall effect that is somewhere between the medieval and the modern.

From the entrance, visitors are literally funneled through a dark tunnel to the adjacent building, arriving in an open court, also mustard-colored and modern/medieval in spirit. This court is bounded by the triangular-shaped office of the firm's president on the left and the conical wall of the conference room straight ahead. To the right, an interior arcade contains the firm's design offices. Beyond the arcade, a second set of offices is defined by curving purple walls; the sequence concludes with a mustard-yellow wall at the rear.

Inside and out, the new structure clearly resides within the old one. For example, the original 901 building's façade has been spruced up with a new sheet-metal marquee that looks contemporary but suits the industrial integrity of the older building. On the inside, the sequence of spaces within the L-shaped plan takes place under the exposed trussed roof of the old Eames warehouse.

Frank Israel is at the forefront of a generation of southern California architects influenced by the imaginative, artistic approach of fellow-California architect Frank Gehry. Israel was born in New York, holds a Master of Arts degree from Columbia University, studied at the American Academy in Rome, and worked briefly as an art director in film before opening his Los Angeles practice in 1983. You can compare Israel's work at Bright & Associates with Gehry's office building for Chiat/Day advertising, which is in the neighborhood. The offices are not open to the public.

Chiat/Day Building, 1991

340 Main Street
Venice, California

Frank O. Gehry & Associates with Claes Oldenburg and Coosje van Bruggen

Is it art or is it architecture? Frank Gehry, a self-contained collaboration of the two, has often designed buildings that confound traditional boundaries. Here the collaboration is easier to decipher. Gehry's architecture is teamed with outdoor sculpture by artists Claes Oldenburg and Coosje van Bruggen, creators of the already famous pair of giant binoculars designating the entrance to this advertising agency's West Coast headquarters. You cannot, of course, miss them.

The black binoculars, 43 feet tall, are an exaggerated focal point for a building replete with visual surprises. On the outside, the façade has two main elements that vie with the binoculars for attention. At one corner is the Tree Building, where sturdy-looking copper-clad beams—the branches—jut out from masonry columns to form a metallic forest above the windows. At the other end, the façade is cool and white; it opens up to reveal layers of walkways. Overall, strong lines forcibly veer away from the eye's foursquare expectations of where a building ought to start, stop, and go.

Creative work goes on inside the three-level, 75,000-square-foot advertising agency, and the building is designed to encourage it. The interiors are organized as a series of spacious open areas, with varied ceiling heights, all receiving natural light from the large windows and generous skylights. Gehry has specified his characteristic commonplace (he says "cheapskate") materials such as plywood and galvanized metal for the interiors and furniture he designed for the building. But here they are contrasted with richer materials such as copper sheeting, maple panels, and stone. The main entrance desk is fashioned from gnarled tree stumps, a continuation of the Tree Building theme.

The binoculars contain, at the second level, a pair of small, circular "thinking rooms." From overhead, sunlight beams down into each thinking room through a binocular eyepiece, which is also a skylight. The building is sited well and has a fine view of the Pacific Ocean.

The building is not open to the general public.

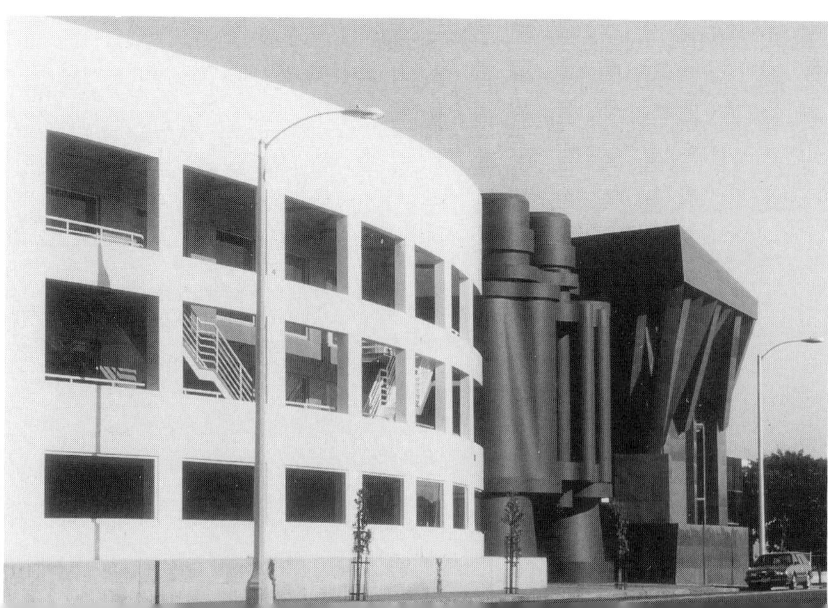

GARY GROUP OFFICES, 1991

9046 Lindblade Street
Culver City, California

Eric Owen Moss

Culver City's metamorphosis from an industrial has-been into Los Angeles's version of Soho owes much to the architecture of Eric Owen Moss. His Morganstern Warehouse of 1978 turned out to be a false start in neighborhood revivification, but it held new promise on this architecturally neglected industrial building type. Morganstern, now gone, has been followed by a progressively adventurous series of warehouse conversions for creative businesses clustered around the Culver City Studios, the one-time movie capital of America, where Orson Wells directed *Citizen Kane.*

For Gary Group, a public relations firm, Moss converted a former steel foundry into offices with exceptionally high visibility. The most prominent exterior wall is on the west side, and it presents a picture made of industrial parts. The old concrete block wall is draped with chains and studded with ladders of steel rebar in a configuration that comes off as theatrically nautical.

Around the front, the main entrance is recessed behind a new tilted wall of rust-colored block. This false front extends above the roof line and shows its support: three C-shaped metal ribs attached to three steel columns behind the façade. A shallow balcony juts out the front, and a metal staircase leads to the top of the "C." This whole construction collides with a white steel grid with a clock centered in the middle. From the parking lot, it looks like a clock tower gone berserk.

As you might expect, there is nothing conventional about the inside either. First-floor offices are grouped around an interior marble pool washed by water from residential shower heads. But the most provocative space is the conference room, with its overlay of geometric shapes, walls within walls, turning a square room into an octagonal one with tilted metal beams. Above the octagon, a round steel collar supports tilting beams that rise 25 feet through a glass and aluminum pyramid, topped by a cone-shaped skylight. The industrial-strength interiors are countered by small interior gardens planted with bamboo.

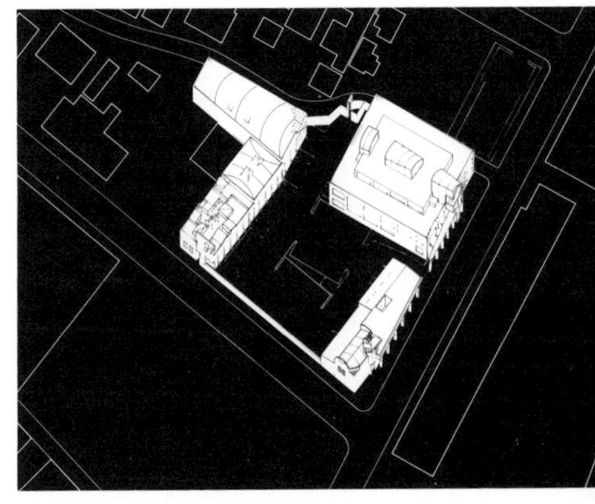

Other examples of Moss's warehouse conversions are in the neighborhood, at 8522 National Boulevard and 3958-60 Ince Boulevard. Moss's office is also nearby, at 8557 Higuera Street. The offices are not open to the public.

Seattle Art Museum, 1991

100 University Avenue at First Avenue
Seattle, Washington

Venturi, Scott Brown & Associates

The idea that a museum's building is one of its own best art works is at least as old as the Guggenheim and may have prompted the selection of Robert Venturi to bring similar architectural sophistication to Seattle. When the building opened, it was clear that Venturi had scored an architectural triumph as well as a popular success. A prime achievement is the skillful way the architectural art showcases the actual art, especially the prized Northwest Indian and African collections that had been stored away for many years.

The museum occupies a downtown corner and is set into a gentle hill, with the main entry at the bottom. The five-story building is clad with fluted gray limestone, but it is not dull. Along the street-side wall, a colorful series of arches in red sandstone, pink granite, and terra-cotta marches up the hill. This arcade—and the large windows—let you know that you are welcome here. As if to emphasize the point, the entry is an enlargement of the street-side graphic. The building also becomes its own billboard; its name is inscribed in large letters around the top.

Large windows on the front façade, and an entire floor of windows at the penthouse level, promise an interior filled with natural light and an unstuffy atmosphere. The grandest gesture appears just inside the door—a magnificent marble and travertine staircase rising up the entire street-side wall of the building with monumental Ming Dynasty figures (including camels and tigers) posted at intervals along the way. The great stair's ceiling is decorated with a series of colorful Moorish arches, and they create a complementary rhythm overhead. The large windows open the great stair to the street view and provide a natural illumination. In the exhibit galleries, Venturi continues the natural illumination with full walls of glass on the east and west.

The opening of the Seattle Art Museum found Venturi, with his wife and partner, Denise Scott Brown, at peak prominence. Their addition to the National Gallery in London was nearing completion, and Venturi received the Pritzker Prize that same year. Although Venturi and Scott Brown have long been influential theorists and proponents of a popular architecture, the accessible Seattle Art Museum has brought them popular as well as professional acclaim.

The museum is open Tuesday through Saturday from 11:00 AM to 5:00 PM and until 9:00 PM on Thursday; noon to 5:00 PM on Sunday. Closed Monday and major holidays. Museum tours are conducted daily at 2:00 PM. For information, call (206) 654-3123.

TEAM DISNEY, 1991

1375 Buena Vista Drive
Lake Buena Vista, Florida

Arata Isozaki

Animation is the art of visual surprise. In a cartoon, anything can happen. Elephants can fly. A fake tunnel, painted on a mountainside, might bring forth a train. Ducks are blue and cats turn green. Arata Isozaki's design for Walt Disney Company offices near Orlando presents an intriguing set of illusions worthy of the world's preeminent fabricator of celluloid fantasies.

Disney's most famous character, Mickey Mouse, is "immortalized" in the front gates, which are Mouseketeer ears in outline. From here, the scene shifts to a work of Isozaki's creation. The bold black-and-white plaid pattern of the two long office wings is an illusion Isozaki devised by combining dark glass and light-and-dark-colored spandrel panels. This strong black-and-white graphic emphasizes the contrast with the building's exotic centerpiece. Above the main entrance, Isozaki rivets your attention with a cluster of geometric shapes in cartoon colors. A pink and green cone-shaped tower is topped with a bright yellow disc and stylus. A 120-foot-tall tilted curve appears to be "intersected" by a deep, blue wall. It is one illusion after the next. The tower rises above a four-story reddish-brown masonry cube with a flat pink wall running though its forward corner and a bright red tilted cube on its roof.

The enormous tower turns out to be hollow, and open at the top; it is one of the world's largest sundials. The yellow stylus visible on the outside can be seen from inside the tower for what it is: a hand in the clock of the open ceiling's circle. The shadow of the stylus's spun-aluminum "ballpoint" marks solar time on red tile disks on the walls. The floor of the sundial is covered in large, smooth rocks, and the space is bridged along one side, connecting offices and a conference area. Over the door, at the base of the sundial, Mickey Mouse's ears reappear in the form of an elegantly curved steel canopy.

This building is Isozaki's first Disney building. And while Disney's high-profile "entertainment architecture" commissions have made much news, the Tokyo-based Isozaki (who also has an office in New York City) has been making his mark all over the world. No small creator of fantasies himself, Isozaki has repeatedly astonished the architectural profession—in the east and the west—with work dating back to the 1960s. One of his own celluloid fantasies appears in his design for the Museum of Contemporary Art in Los Angeles, where a curving wall is based on the shape of Marilyn Monroe.

Team Disney is open from 8:00 AM to 6:00 PM Monday through Friday and closed on weekends and holidays. Although there are no tours of the building, the sundial atrium is open to visitors. For information, call (407) 824-4500.

Islamic Cultural Center, 1992

1711 Third Avenue at 96th Street
New York, New York

Skidmore, Owings & Merrill

New York's first mosque was built by twenty Islamic United Nations countries to serve the city's entire Muslim community. Although the cooperating nations each had individual traditions, their common heritage runs deep. It is a heritage concerned with values that are humanistic, spiritual, and architectural, and the design of the mosque is meant to give contemporary expression to ancient ideals.

Given Islam's prohibition against figurative representation, the mosque is strictly geometrical. A recurrence of squares underlies the design; the mosque is basically square in shape and plan, with a dome on top. Because religious law requires an eastern orientation, the building is rotated twenty-eight degrees to Manhattan's street grid, creating a large open forecourt where worshipers gather prior to prayers.

Square granite panels, evoking endurance, make up the mosque's base. Narrow glazed channels surround these panels, admitting daylight and creating a sense of permeability. In the midsection, large glazed panels are embellished with fired ceramic surface decorations in an overlapping lattice pattern, a modern technological treatment of an ancient material. Skylights at the four corners also admit natural light. The gilded copper dome, separated from the building by a clear glass band, appears to float on a ring of light.

At the portal, geometry is again employed to evoke ancient associations. Flat, rectangular layers of cut glass are overlapped to resemble the arch, but this one is symbolic, abstracted, and modern.

Inside, the mosque is almost purely space and light. Unlike Christian churches or Jewish synagogues, there are no pews, and worshipers sit on carpets. Filling the space is an ethereal light, from the carefully placed glazing and from a circle of lights suspended by brass cords to form a halo above the congregation.

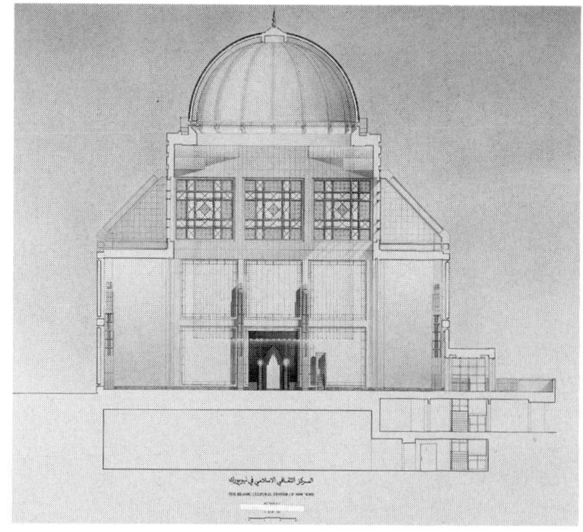

Tours can be scheduled Sunday through Friday mornings from 10:00 AM to noon, and afternoons Sunday through Thursday from 2:00 to 4:00 PM. The mosque is closed on Saturday. Religious services for the congregation only are held on Friday afternoons, when the mosque is closed to visitors. For appointments and information, call (212) 722-5234.

Shepherd School of Music, 1992

Rice University
Houston, Texas

Ricardo Bofill/Taller de Arquitectura

The Shepherd School of Music at Rice University is devoted to achieving world-class sound quality for the listener, but there is also much here that will interest its viewers. For many Americans, it will be the first opportunity to see first-hand the work of Barcelona-based architect Ricardo Bofill, who is internationally renowned for his Mediterranean classical style.

The new music school continues Bofill's tradition of curved colonnades. Facing the main campus across a vast expanse of empty green lawn, the curved, colonnaded façade seems stretched to infinity—it is 465 feet long and two stories high. Massive white concrete columns are set against pale terra-cotta brick to mimic Rice's prevailing building materials. These columns alternate with tall, narrow windows giving outside views to the teaching studios and practice rooms inside. Bofill's grand classical sweep is meant to be mirrored in a reflecting pool, which has yet to be constructed.

Two interior courtyards separate the curved façade from the more public opposite side where the main public entrance is located. Flatter and less rhythmic, this western façade reveals more clearly the building's asymmetrical massing and the outlines of its four performance halls: a 1,000 seat concert hall, a 236-seat recital hall, an opera rehearsal studio, and an organ studio, each acoustically tailored to its intended purpose.

In expanding a campus originally designed by Ralph Adams Cram in 1910, Rice University administrators have commissioned buildings by a number of internationally recognized architects, including Cesar Pelli (Herring Hall) and James Stirling and Michael Wilford (Anderson Hall). Like these architects who built at Rice University shortly before him, Bofill has fit his building into the existing brick and limestone campus tradition without losing his individuality.

Shepherd School of Music is open from 7:00 AM to 7:00 PM when school is in session. Access is limited from mid-May to mid-August, as there is no summer session. Concerts by students and faculty are held during the school year; for schedules, call (713) 527-4933. With advance notice, special tours of the building can be arranged. For visitor information, school schedules, and tour requests, call (713) 527-4837.

Harold Washington Library Center, 1992

400 South State Street
Chicago, Illinois

Hammond, Beeby & Babka, Inc.

Chicago's new library is an architectural achievement and a literary powerhouse holding 1.6 million volumes, making it one of the largest open-stack libraries in the world. The 10-story building occupies a full city block and was completed in a surprisingly short time—just five years, beginning in 1987. But to look at it, you might imagine that work on this solid, robust, classical, ornamented building had begun in the early 1900s, a time when public libraries in the Beaux Arts style were going up all over the country.

Like the classic libraries of the early twentieth century, Harold Washington Library is grand in scale and materials: granite, cast stone, deep-red brick, metal, and glass. It meets the street on all sides with a heavy base of rusticated stone, with arches framing the doors and ground-floor windows. On each side, a trio of elegant arched windows rises five stories above the base, set off by ornamental cording and garlands cast in stone. The library has a temple-like attic (extravagantly decorated by vertical helical rods) with barrel vaults laid in cruciform on the roof, glazed at the nexus.

From the outside, the library appears to be the very bastion of human knowledge, but on the inside every effort has been made to keep it accessible, easy to use, and inviting. The stacks on the library's six main levels are open, and the floors are connected by both escalators and elevators. The traditional wood paneling of classic libraries is picked up here in the escalator encasements, which are paneled in maple. Lighting, furniture, and state-of-the-art computer technology all help make the building more helpful to the public. The auditorium on the lower level is especially striking. The most exciting space in the building, however, is on the top floor: the enormous glass-enclosed Winter Garden.

The library was designed by Thomas Beeby, of Hammond, Beeby & Babka, the winner of a competition played out on public television for the whole country to see. As the competition evolved, judges considered the modern proposals. But it was the most resolutely classical design that got the vote.

The Harold Washington Library Center is open Monday to Thursday from 9:00 AM to 7:00 PM and on Friday and Saturday from 9:00 AM to 5:00 PM, closed Sunday and major holidays. For information, call (312) 747-4300. The Chicago Architecture Foundation includes the building on its Loop Walking Tour. For information, call CAF at (312) 922-TOUR.

INDEX OF ARCHITECTS

Frank Lloyd Wright

Lloyd Wright

Minoru Yamasaki & Associates

Arthur and Nina Zwebell

INDEX OF LOCATIONS

ART AND PHOTOGRAPHY CREDITS

The photographs on the pages listed below appear courtesy of the following photographers, foundations, museums, and organizations.

1 Photo by Don Kalec, courtesy of Frank Lloyd Wright Home and Studio Foundation

3 Metropolitan Museum of Art

5 Photo by Alec Tavares

6 Library of Congress, Prints and Photographs Division, HABS Collection

7 Buffalo and Erie County Historical Society

8 Library of Congress, Prints and Photographs Division

10 Library of Congress, Prints and Photographs Division

11 Fairmont Hotel

12 Frank Lloyd Wright Home and Studio Foundation

15 LaSalle Partners

16 Photo by Tavo Olmos, courtesy of Gamble House

17 © Edward S. Cunningham Photography, Owatonna, Minnesota. Courtesy of Norwest Bank

18 Library of Congress, Prints and Photographs Division, HABS Collection

20 Casey Cronin © 1990

21 © 1988 Frank Lloyd Wright Foundation

22 Grand Central Partnership

23 Woolworth Corporation

24 La Jolla Historical Society

25 Museum of History and Industry, Seattle, Washington

29 Vizcaya Museum & Gardens

31 Photo courtesy of Woodbury County; drawing courtesy of Wetherell-Ericsson Architects (retracing of original from 1916)

34 Albert Kahn Associates

35 Library of Congress, Prints and Photographs Division

40 Photo by Julius Shulman © 1982

41 Photo by Julius Shulman

42 Top: Rendering by Hardy Holzman Pfeiffer Associates, courtesy of Los Angeles Public Library
Bottom: Security Pacific Collection/Los Angeles Library

43 Photo by Julius Shulman

44 Museum of Fine Arts, Houston

45 The Chicago Tribune

46 Mann Theaters

47 Library of Congress, Prints and Photographs Division

48 Philadelphia Museum of Art

49 K.U.K.Y.

50 Arizona Biltmore Hotel

51 Beck Studio. Courtesy of I. Magnin's Landmark Store

52 Photo by Julius Shulman

53 Chicago Board of Trade

54 Cooke Properties Inc. and William A. Bassett, Jr.

55 New Jersey Institute of Technology

56 Top: Miami Design Preservation League
Bottom: K.U.K.Y.

57 Photo by Michael Schwarting, New York Institute of Technology

58 Howard J. Rubenstein Associates, Inc.

59 Cranbrook Academy of Art

62 Photo by Julie Ainsworth, courtesy of Folger Shakespeare Library

63 Photo by Jim Holm, courtesy of State of Nebraska

64 Philadelphia Savings Fund Society

65 Cincinnati Historical Society

66 Chicago Board of Trade

67 Photo by Harold Corsini, courtesy of Western Pennsylvania Conservancy

68 Photo by Ken Raveill, courtesy of Hearst San Simeon State Historical Monument

69 Photo by J. David Bohl, courtesy of the Society for the Preservation of New England Antiquities

70 Photo by Hedrich-Blessing, courtesy of Albert Kahn Associates, Architects & Engineers; Detroit, Michigan

71 Frank Lloyd Wright Foundation

72 Edward Durell Stone Associates PC

74 Kleinhans Music Hall

75 Library of Congress, Prints and Photographs Division

76 Balthazar Korab Limited, courtesy of the Columbus Visitors Center

77 © 1960 The Estate of Buckminster Fuller. Courtesy of Buckminster Fuller Institute, Los Angeles

78 Photo by Julius Shulman

79 Photo by Pedro E. Guerrero

80 MIT News Office

81 Far West Federal

82 Christ Church Lutheran

83 Photo by Julius Shulman

84 Photo by Ezra Stoller, courtesy of Philip Johnson

85 Library of Congress, Prints and Photographs Division, HABS Collection

88 Library of Congress, Prints and Photographs Division, HABS Collection

89 UN photo. 103 905 Y. Nagata/ARA. Courtesy of United Nations

90 Photo by Nick Wheeler. Original House (1951): Marcel Breuer, architect. Renovations and additions (1979 and 1981): Herbert Beckhard, architect. Courtesy of Herbert Beckhard

91 New Jersey Institute of Technology

92 Wayfarer's Chapel, Rev. Harvey A. Tafel

94 Courtesy of Yale University Art Gallery, New Haven, Conn.

95 Lawrence Tarantino AIA

96 Eduardo Catalano

97 Morris Lapidus, architect

98 Photo by Michael DiVito, courtesy of Chemical Banking Corporation

99 Photo by E.J. Deighton, courtesy of the Fred Jones Jr. Museum of Art, University of Oklahoma

101 MIT News Office

102 Illinois Institute of Technology

103 General Motors Corporation

104 Inland Steel Industries Inc.

105 Seagram Building, 1956-58. Architects: Ludwig Mies van der Rohe and Philip Johnson. Photograph by Ezra Stoller, 1958. Lent by Joseph E. Seagram & Sons, Inc.

106 © 1960 The Estate of Buckminster Fuller. Courtesy of Buckminster Fuller Institute, Los Angeles

107 Photo by Julius Shulman

109 Ezra Stoller Associates

110 Photo by Julius Shulman

112 New Jersey Institute of Technology

113 Photo by Ed Hershberger for John Graham Associates/DLR Group

114 TWA

115 United States Air Force Academy

116 Assembly Hall, University of Illinois

117 Beinecke Library. Ezra Stoller/ESTO

118 Andrés Batista

119 Photo by Roberto de Alba

120 Edward Durell Stone Associates PC

121 Photo by Hedrich-Blessing, courtesy of Bertrand Goldberg Associates Inc.

122 Photo by Rollin LaFrance, courtesy of Venturi Scott Brown and Associates Inc.

126 The Salk Institute

127 Charles W. Moore Archives

128 The Whitney Museum

130 Ezra Stoller/ESTO, courtesy of Richard Meier & Partners

131 Photo by Gail Oskin

132 Photo by Tony Soluri

133 Paul Rudolph

134 Photo by Hedrich-Blessing, courtesy of U.S. Equities Realty Inc.

135 Exterior photo by Vincent Zollner, courtesy of Mt. Angel Abbey

136 Photo by Michael Bodycomb, courtesy of Kimbell Art Museum

137 Photo by Roberto de Alba

138 Herndon Associates, courtesy of The Library, Phillips Exeter Academy

140 Port Authority of New York and New Jersey

141 Top: New Jersey Institute of Technology Bottom: Federal Reserve Bank of Minneapolis

143 Sears Roebuck and Company

144 SITE Projects, Inc.

145 Photo by Tom Bonner, courtesy of Pacific Design Center

146 The Cosanti Foundation

147 Gorchev & Gorchev, courtesy of John Hancock

148 National Air and Space Museum

149 Richard Payne, AIA, courtesy of Philip Johnson and John Burgee

150 Photo by Thomas A. Brown, courtesy of Yale Center for British Art

151 Paul Rudolph

152 Photo by Tom Marble

153 National Air and Space Museum

155 Photo by Ezra Stoller/ESTO, courtesy of Richard Meier & Partners

156 Photo by Richard Payne, courtesy of Philip Johnson and John Burgee

157 E. Fay Jones

159 Balthazar Korab Limited, courtesy of the Columbus Visitors Center

160 © Steven Brooke, courtesy of Seaside

161 Taft Architects

162 © 1982 Norman McGrath

163 Photo by Paschall/Taylor, courtesy of Michael Graves, Architect

164 Philip Morris

165 Photo by Ezra Stoller/ESTO, courtesy of Richard Meier & Partners

166 Photo by Barbara Karant, courtesy of Kohn Pederson Fox

167 Photo © Richard Payne, courtesy of Philip Johnson and John Burgee

169 Photo © Richard Payne, courtesy of Philip Johnson and John Burgee

170 California Museum of Science and Industry

171 Loyola Law School

173 Photo by Paschall/Taylor, courtesy of Michael Graves, Architect

174 PA consulting group

175 Andrés Batista

176 Murphy/Jahn

179 Top: Photo by Kurt Gunther, courtesy of Paladino & Associates Bottom: Photo by Tom Marble

180 Photo by Paschall/Taylor, courtesy of Michael Graves, Architect

181 Photo by Timothy Hursley, courtesy of Susanna Torre

182 Koning Eizenberg Architecture

183 Hickey & Robertson, Houston, courtesy the Menil Collection

184 Photo by Paul Warchol, courtesy of Steven Holl

185 San Antonio Botanical Center

186 Photo © Richard Payne, courtesy of Pei, Cobb, Freed & Partners

187 Photo by Lin Waldron, courtesy of Nelson Fine Arts Center

188 Kevin Fitzsimons/Wexner Center for the Arts

189 Photo by Wolfgang Hoyt, courtesy of Olympia & York Companies (U.S.A.)

190 Courtesy of Tishman Realty & Construction Co., Inc.

191 Antoine Predock Architect FAIA

192 Photo by Peter Olson, courtesy of Mandell Futures Center

193 Photo © M. Robert Markovich

194 Photo by Donatella Brun, courtesy of Chiat/Day

195 Drawing courtesy of Eric Owen Moss Architects Photo by Todd Conversano © 1990, courtesy of Eric Owen Moss Architects

196 Photo by Matt Wargo, courtesy of Venturi, Scott Brown and Associates Inc.

197 © The Walt Disney Company, photo by Susan E. Mitchell

198 Drawing by Gregory Ihnatowicz

200 Photo courtesy of Hammond Beeby and Babka, Inc.

The photographs on the following pages were taken by the author:

2, 4, 9, 13, 14, 19, 26, 27, 28, 30, 32, 33, 36, 37, 38, 39, 60, 61, 73, 86, 87, 93, 100, 108, 111, 123, 124, 125, 129, 139, 142, 154, 158, 168, 172, 177, 178, 199